THE VENEZUELAN ARMED FORCES
IN POLITICS, 1935–1959

THE VENEZUELAN ARMED FORCES IN POLITICS, 1935–1959

WINFIELD J. BURGGRAAFF

UNIVERSITY OF MISSOURI PRESS
COLUMBIA • 1972

ISBN 0-8262-0121-0
Copyright © 1972 by
The Curators of the University of Missouri
Library of Congress Catalog Card Number 73-185831
University of Missouri Press, Columbia, Missouri 65201
Printed and bound in the United States of America

TO MY PARENTS

ACKNOWLEDGMENTS

I am happy to have this opportunity to acknowledge my indebtedness to three scholars of Latin American affairs whose assistance in the preparation of this book was direct and valuable. Professor Edwin Lieuwen gave generously of his time and scholarly resources to assist my research, and both Professor Troy S. Floyd and Professor Martin C. Needler offered many useful suggestions for its completion. A grant from the Rockefeller Foundation made possible an eight-month visit to Venezuela in 1965, during which I completed the bulk of the research on which I based the book. Additional research, done in Caracas in the summer of 1968 and at various times in the National Archives, Washington, D.C., and the New York Public Library, filled out information I could not obtain elsewhere. I am grateful to the staffs of the following institutions for their cooperation in facilitating my research: the National Archives, the New York Public Library and the University of New Mexico Library; in Caracas the Biblioteca Nacional, the Academia de la Historia, the Ministerio de la Defensa, the Banco Central de Venezuela, the Universidad Central de Venezuela; and in San Cristóbal, Táchira, the Salón de Lectura.

It would be impossible to list here all the names of Venezuelans whose hospitality and kindness made my stays in their country most pleasant. Although I drew heavily on their knowledge of Venezuelan history and society, responsibility for the assessments and interpretations expressed in this volume rests exclusively with me.

Finally, I thank my wife, Dorothy Knoblock Burggraaff, whose patience, encouragement, and many-faceted assistance made this book possible and the effort worth while.

W. J. B.
Columbia, Missouri
December, 1971

Contents

PREFACE

Since the publication in 1960 of Edwin Lieuwen's *Arms and Politics in Latin America,* social scientists have increasingly paid attention to the political role of the military in Latin America. The studies that have appeared in the years following Lieuwen's work have provided useful generalizations and broad theories of military politics south of the Rio Grande but, in the words of Robert A. Potash, "Few have added substantially to our fund of basic information."[1] Lyle N. McAlister suggested in 1965 that the study of the military should enter a new stage in which "more intensive studies of the role of the military in a number of individual Latin-American countries" would be undertaken.[2] That stage has now been reached, and detailed works on the Mexican, Argentine, Brazilian, and Chilean armed forces, among others, have enabled us to see more clearly the local variations on the general theme of Latin American militarism.[3]

I should state precisely what I mean by "Latin American militarism," because considerable confusion has arisen over the applicability of the term *militarism* to Latin America. There now appears to be general agreement that a sharp distinction should be made between Latin American militarism and classic European-style militarism—closely associated with imperialism—that has been analyzed by Alfred Vagts and others. Indeed, June E. Hahner declines altogether to use the term *militarism* in describing the very active political role of Brazil's military establishment.[4] Another leading authority on the subject, John J. Johnson, broadly defines militarism in Latin America as "the domination of the military man over the civilian, the undue emphasis upon military demands, or

1. Robert A. Potash, *The Army and Politics in Argentina: 1928–1945,* vii.
2. Lyle N. McAlister, "Changing Concepts of the Role of the Military in Latin America," *The Annals of the American Academy of Political and Social Science,* 360 (July 1965), 95.
3. Edwin Lieuwen, *Mexican Militarism: The Political Rise and Fall of the Revolutionary Army, 1910–1940;* Potash, *The Army and Politics;* June E. Hahner, *Civilian–Military Relations in Brazil: 1889–1898;* Frederick M. Nunn, *Chilean Politics, 1920–1931: The Honorable Mission of the Armed Forces.*
4. Hahner, x–xi.

any transcendence by the armed forces of 'true military purposes.'"[5] A more precise definition of Latin militarism is that offered by McAlister: "The extrusion of the armed forces beyond their normatively defined mission of defending the state, the constitution and the laws against aggression from the outside and subversion from within. . . . Historically, [Latin militarism has involved] the overt or subvert employment of violence by the armed forces for political ends."[6] McAlister's definition is what I have in mind when I refer to Venezuelan militarism in this book.

The purpose of this study is to analyze the political role of the Venezuelan military from the death of Gen. Juan Vicente Gómez in 1935 to the presidency of Rómulo Betancourt in 1959. This analysis should contribute to a clearer understanding of the nature of military involvement in the national politics of a medium-sized Latin American nation. It should also serve as an additional case study for the comparative analysis of military politics in this hemisphere.

I should state at the outset that I have limited myself to describing and analyzing the political behavior of the Venezuelan officer corps. Mine is not a study of the military's over-all role in society, their social origins, their technical capacity, or their internal institutional squabbles over positions and promotions. Further, I have assumed that most readers are sufficiently conversant with Venezuelan politics to render detailed accounts of the fortunes of the various civilian political groups unnecessary, for such information is readily available elsewhere.

Venezuela is of special importance to the study of Latin American militarism because it is invariably cited as a notorious example of a nation whose progress has been retarded through the corrosive effects of unchecked militarism and of numerous and meaningless armed revolutions. I should like to dispel the myth that all Venezuela's ills have resulted directly from the political supremacy of its armed forces. In justice, blame for the many misfortunes the Venezuelan

5. John J. Johnson, "The Latin-American Military as a Politically Competing Group in Transitional Society," in John J. Johnson, ed., *The Role of the Military in Underdeveloped Countries*, 91.
6. Lyle N. McAlister, "The Impact of Militarism on Latin American Society," working paper at Third Inter-American Forum, sponsored by the Catholic Inter-American Cooperation Program and Saint Louis University (Davenport, Iowa, 1968), 1.

people have endured must be divided between soldiers and civilians. Indeed, it is not difficult to demonstrate that the latter, at every critical juncture, promoted and encouraged the military's involvement in politics.

Somewhat paradoxically, Venezuela has more recently been enthusiastically held up as an example of a developing country where the armed forces have acquiesced in basic social reform and, despite provocation, have not directly intervened in politics.[7] The Venezuelan military has remained in the barracks at the same time its South American counterparts were toppling civilian regimes in Argentina, Brazil, Peru, Ecuador, and Bolivia. Although the post-1959 period lies outside the scope of this study, I shall suggest why the Venezuelan armed forces, although still a powerful pressure group, have at least temporarily retreated from their traditional position as arbiter of national politics.

The sensitive and controversial nature of the subject under consideration posed certain problems in regard to sources. Most important, unpublished government papers, particularly military institutional records, were virtually inaccessible to me. Also, it was difficult to obtain interviews with military personnel, especially with officers on active duty. Despite these limitations, however, the information available to me was of sufficient abundance and reliability to convince me that this undertaking is not premature.

7. See Edwin Lieuwen, *Generals vs. Presidents: Neomilitarism in Latin America*, 86–91.

CHAPTER I

FROM CAUDILLISM TO MILITARISM

The roots of modern Venezuelan militarism extend into and derive their nourishment from the Independence period. For Venezuelans, the prime source of national pride is the predominant role their nation played in the winning of independence from Spain for northern South America. Despite its position as a backwater province throughout the centuries of colonial rule, during which it attained neither economic wealth nor political importance, it suddenly emerged as the heroic leader of the struggle against Spain. This one country had the distinction of producing both the great precursor of independence, Francisco de Miranda, and the Liberator of half a continent, Simón Bolívar.

For fifteen years Venezuela was at the thrusting point of the revolutions against Spain, and it was due in considerable measure to Bolívar's military genius and the blood of thousands of Venezuelan troops that the colonies triumphed over the metropolis. Military prowess achieved independence, and the country's long-standing military tradition memorializes this fact.

The immediate post-Independence period was a time of near anarchy and social and economic disruption. Thousands of Venezuela's best youth had fallen on battlefields stretching from the Orinoco Delta to the Peruvian Andes. Wartime devastation was nationwide. Disorder bordering on chaos was general. A republican constitution and the paraphernalia of representative government were duly manufactured but never completely effected. Furthermore, most of the peninsular aristocracy had either been killed or driven from the country. The newly dominant creole oligarchs, the *mantuanos,* were unable, because of their inexperience in the techniques of authority, to provide political solutions. Instead, many of them extracted maximum economic gains from the revolutionary upheaval. The inability or unwillingness to govern on the part of those very elements who might have guided Venezuela on the road to stable civilian government created a power vacuum that was filled by the surviving heroes of the Wars of Independence.

Foremost among these was Gen. José Antonio Páez, a *llanero* who rose from humble origins to a prominent position on Bolívar's general staff. At the conclusion of the struggle for independence, Páez was entrusted with the command of the army in Venezuela. Using that post as a power base, he succeeded in imposing his rule on the country after the demise of the Liberator in 1830. Páez' career is illustrative of at least two features of Venezuelan caudillism. One was his acceptance by and assimilation into the oligarchy, despite his lower-class beginnings; the other was the cooperation of the leaders of the economy with a strongman who promised stability and did not threaten their position. The former cowboy forged a tacit alliance with the conservative *mantuano* elite and ruled on their behalf for nearly two decades (1830–1848).

Páez and the national patriciate ruled, on balance, responsibly and well. They saw order and stability as the essential ingredients for economic recovery and advancement, and these Páez and his army set out to provide. Nevertheless, two major rebellions and a number of minor uprisings disturbed the comparative tranquility of *Paecista* rule. The revolts were typical regional movements in reaction to Páez' policy of rendering the army subservient to central authority. They were the prototypes of the localized uprisings that were to plague the country throughout the nineteenth century.

By 1840 the opposition Liberal party had formed, headed by a former Páez cabinet officer, Antonio Leocadio Guzmán, often called the republic's first civilian caudillo. He and his Liberal followers attacked the Conservatives in the press and entered candidates in national elections when permitted, but they made little headway against the entrenched *Paecistas* until unexpected help from the military brought them to power. Gen. José Tadeo Monagas, while serving as a figurehead for Páez in 1847, dismissed his Conservative ministers and replaced them with Liberals. When the Conservatives rose to the challenge, Monagas, who had built up a formidable backing among civilians and military men, defeated them and sent Páez into exile.

Monagas' success illustrates an important characteristic of Venezuelan civil–military relations throughout the nation's history. No matter what political label they bore, ultimately all political factions resorted to force to gain their objectives. This reliance on force has pervaded Venezuelan political life as it has that of most Latin American countries. Not only military figures but impatient civilian politicians have been unable to refrain from taking short cuts to power through the use of violence. As Rafael Caldera once stated, "Venezuelans are so accustomed to make the army arbiter of their political contests, that at each moment the most varied groups for the most dissimilar ends attempt to involve the army in new adventures to change our political reality."[1] The contemporary Venezuelan writer Juan Liscano adds that military intervention in politics would mean little "if it were not for the abundance of politicians and civilians, university-trained doctors, discreet advisers, esteemed publicists, who . . . incite military subversion in order to climb with it toward high government positions."[2] What has happened, then, is that Venezuelan military men have almost invariably acted after pressure from or in conjunction with civilian groups. This relationship began in the days of the caudillos, and it has continued as a political pattern, as when, more recently, the military has acted as a self-conscious corporate entity.

For twenty-odd years after the fall of General Páez, the development of Venezuela languished while the country's government did little to bring order out of political, economic, and social disorganization. Men from the Oriente—José Tadeo Monagas and his brother José Gregorio—held precarious sway over the nation's destinies for a decade. Their regimes were characterized by caudillism at its worst—repression, corruption, constant turmoil. The only permanent achievement of their rule was the 1854 emancipation law that set free Venezuela's remaining slaves.

Regional caudillism reached its zenith in the aftermath of the Federal War (1859–1863). During that conflict so many officers were raised to the rank of general by the Federalists that the pattern gave rise to the witticism that, whereas other

1. Rafael Caldera Rodríguez, in *La Religión* (Caracas), June 28, 1959, as quoted in Robert L. Gilmore, *Caudillism and Militarism in Venezuela: 1810–1910*, 13.
2. Juan Liscano, "Aspectos de la vida social y política de Venezuela," in Venezuela, Presidencia de la República, *150 años de vida republicana: 1811–1961*, I, 191.

countries had generals of brigade, Venezuela had brigades of generals. The consequence for the Venezuelan people, however, was not amusing, for this dubious practice intensified political instability and military irresponsibility.

The chaotic conditions of the 1850s and 1860s, while giving a certain impetus to social democracy, were aggravated by the concomitant decentralization. The absence of strong central authority encouraged rampant caudillism in the countryside, resulting in economic devastation and cultural stagnation. Faced with these hopeless conditions, most Venezuelans welcomed the establishment of strong national leadership. They were to have it in the person of Antonio Guzmán Blanco.

General Guzmán Blanco, son of the founder of the Liberal party, reached the heights of political power through a natural selection process. He was the best-educated, shrewdest, most widely traveled caudillo of his day. Combining these attributes with a sound head for business and a gift for generalship, he was able to maintain himself in power for eighteen years (1870–1888). Like almost all Venezuelan generals of the time, he had no formal military training. In fact, in the early stages of the Federal War, he occupied an obscure secretarial post, but his natural talent for soldiering enabled him to become, in short time, a prominent Federalist general. He then took advantage of the postwar confusion to build up sufficient civilian and military support to gain the presidency.

Under Guzmán Blanco, Venezuela prospered within a framework of order, central direction, and development that it had not experienced since the Páez days. On the other hand, the "Illustrious American" instituted an opprobrious and corrupt dictatorship, under which political opposition was harshly suppressed. Of principal concern here, however, are the methods that Guzmán Blanco employed in dealing with military opposition. His policy was to make peace with minor chiefs and crush on the battlefield the major leaders who loomed as direct threats to his control. This strategy, although effective in the short run, did not rid Venezuela of regional strongmen; they immediately reappeared when the dictator departed from the scene. Only the establishment of a strong national army and a petroleum-fueled centralized bureaucracy were to put an end to caudillism.

In the years following Guzmán Blanco's dictatorship, the

country drifted back into the instability of the 1860s. The temporary order and artificial centralization imposed on the nation by Guzmán Blanco gave way to a disturbingly rapid succession of incompetent military and civilian presidents, to rigged elections, to rebellions, and to civil strife. Gen. Joaquín Crespo, the central figure in the turmoil of the 1890s, provided occasional direction until his death, which occurred in a battle following the disputed election of 1897.

Although the results of this election produced the customary revolt by the losing faction, the eventual outcome of the 1897–1899 civil war brought unexpected changes in the nation's political life. Venezuela, in the last year of the nineteenth century, was a nation weary of perpetual revolt against central authority and of the chicanery and abuse that marked national and local government alike. With the old system, such as it was, on the verge of collapse, a new breed of men from the Andes moved into the national political scene—men who were to alter radically the traditional structure of civil–military relations in Venezuela.

From colonial times to the end of the nineteenth century, political power in Venezuela was in the control of groups that represented the Center (Caracas and surrounding area), the *Llanos,* and the northern coastal region. The only major populated region of the country that did not share power was the Andean states. Seemingly forgotten and neglected, the populous Andean states of Táchira, Mérida, and Trujillo together did not produce a president until 1898. A number of reasons account for the relative political impotence of the *Andinos.*

First, the Andean states, and in particular Táchira, had developed separately from the rest of the country. This separateness was the result of geographical isolation, difficulties in communications and transportation that impeded interchange with the rest of the country, racial composition (the heavily Indian Andes lacked the Negro strain more common to the lowland and coastal areas), and socioeconomic differences.

Second, partly as a result of geographical isolation from other Venezuelan states, Táchira State—the state most crucial to this discussion of the political power of the armed forces—was linked more closely to the culture and economy of the neighboring country of Colombia than to Venezuelan affairs. Tachirans held more in common with their Colombian neighbors than with the *Caraqueños* and coastal Venezuelans because of the dominance of a commonly shared Indian ancestry, ties that formed during the colonial period when western Venezuela was ruled administratively from Bogotá, familial bonds (there was much intermarriage between Tachirans and Colombians), close commercial relations, and a common ground of political beliefs. The majority of Tachirans and eastern Colombians were Liberals, and Liberals of one country would frequently aid Liberals of the other country in the civil conflicts against opposition Conservatives.[3]

Third, the Tachirans had in effect neglected politics at the national level in order to pursue agriculture and business. The nineteenth century was Táchira's Golden Age. In those years the area underwent the greatest economic boom in Venezuelan history until surpassed by the post-World War I oil boom. Táchira's prosperity was based primarily on coffee exportation. Tachiran coffee, first cultivated in the temperate valleys of the Venezuelan Andes about 1800, was by the end of the century Venezuela's leading export. Coffee-induced prosperity led to a vigorous social and economic development that contrasted sharply with the economic and social stagnation in malaria-infested, caudillo-ridden lowland Venezuela. Coffee was exploited, not by a few great *hacendados* in control of masses of servile peons, but mainly by many proprietors of small and middle-sized holdings. This greater degree of social democracy and the more equitable distribution of land and wealth resulted in, among other things, a sense of superiority and a consequent separateness on the part of the Tachirans. Indeed, contemporary observers pointed out that the inhabitants of Táchira were better-fed, better-housed, better-educated, and therefore better workers and soldiers than most Venezuelans outside the Andes.[4]

But in the last decades of the century, Tachirans realized that, while they had economic power, they lacked political

3. Domingo Alberto Rangel, *Los andinos en el poder: balance de una hegemonía, 1899–1945,* 43–44.

4. See, for example, Emilio Constantino Guerrero, *El Táchira físico, político e ilustrado,* 68–70, 73–74; José Gregorio Villafañe, *Apuntes estadísticos del Táchira,* 43–44, 75; Rangel, *Los andinos,* 34, 57.

power. To consolidate their economic gains and to continue
to develop the local economy at a sufficient rate demanded
either a national government willing to support the interests
of the area or seizure of power by Tachirans. The first option
was virtually impossible because of the government's neglect
of, if not outright hostility to, the Andeans, and the failure of
the central authorities to follow a rational economic program.[5] Tachirans increasingly felt that their welfare
depended on their own initiative. They had a burgeoning
economy and abundant manpower, but not enough rewarding
jobs to satisfy the growing population, especially the educated middle-class males. They needed a movement that
would produce a national leader who could fight for and
articulate their regional objectives. They got both in the
1890s: the movement was the Liberal Restoration; its leader
was Cipriano Castro.

Castro was born in 1858 of middle-class parents in a small
Táchira town. Many young Tachirans went to Colombia for
secondary schooling, and Castro attended the seminary at
Pamplona, where he came into contact with leaders of the
Colombian Liberal party. Apparently inspired by the Colombian brand of liberalism, he returned home after completing
his *bachillerato* to write journalistic essays devoted to the
issues of the day. The coherent Liberal program that he
expressed found a ready audience among young Tachirans
who were chafing under provincial stagnation and eager for
basic changes in the prevailing political system. These frustrated youths provided a receptive audience for Castro's
increasingly revolutionary propaganda.[6]

During the 1890s Castro gained experience in national and
local politics as a sometime Liberal deputy to the National
Congress and as a local chieftain. When political reversals
forced him into exile in Colombia in 1898, he began to as-
semble a rebel force, which was to fight under the banner of
the Revolution of the Liberal Restoration.

General Castro's revolutionary army, in contrast to previous rebel bands, was young, largely urban-based, and semi-
educated. Aside from the *Jefe* and his principal lieutenant,
Gen. Juan Vicente Gómez, the officers and troops ranged in

5. Villafañe, *Apuntes estadísticos,* 31; Gilmore, *Caudillism,* 119;
and Rangel, *Los andinos,* 35–37.
6. Rangel, *Los andinos,* 61–68.

age from fifteen to about thirty. For the first time a Venezuelan revolutionary army was composed mainly of men from the cities and towns, not from the countryside, and the level of education was several notches above that of earlier *campesino* armies.[7] Some men had just completed their secondary education;[8] others were young teachers, tradesmen, and clerks. In the future the national army was to maintain these urban roots, and the superior educational level of Castro's Andean force would be perpetuated through the academic training of officers initiated by Castro and Gómez.

In the spring of 1899, when conditions in the country were ideally suited for a successful rebellion, General Castro crossed the Colombian border into Táchira. To the cry of "To the Capitol, or Death," the revolutionaries of the Liberal Restoration forced the government to surrender in five months.[9] In October, 1899, the victorious Castro entered Caracas and set about organizing an administration that, he declared, was to be guided by "New Men, New Ideals, New Methods."

Cipriano Castro in power was not the same Castro who had preached the revival of democratic liberalism. Beneath his veneer of idealism he was insincere and contradictory. A product of rough-and-tumble caudillo politics, he instituted none of the reforms he had promised. His financial mismanagement became notorious; the country sank further into debt, to the extent that pressure from European creditors to collect on Venezuelan debts led to foreign intervention.

In terms of national political development Castro made only one contribution, but it was important: the establishment, on a permanent basis, of central authority in such strength that all regional challenges to the national government were repulsed. He accomplished this centralization through two principal methods: the defeat of rival caudillos

7. Rangel, *Los andinos,* 67.
8. For example, future General in Chief and President Eleazar López Contreras, who joined the revolutionary army at the age of seventeen, months after receiving his diploma from the Colegio del Sagrado Corazón de Jesús in La Grita, Táchira.
9. For a participant's account, see Eleazar López Contreras, *Páginas para la historia militar de Venezuela,* 3–34. For contemporary accounts by foes of Castro, see Antonio Paredes, *Cómo llegó Cipriano Castro al poder,* and Ignacio Andrade, *¿Por qué triunfó la Revolución Restauradora?*

on the battlefield and the organization of a strong national army.

Castro recognized, as had Guzmán Blanco earlier, the need for strong central direction, but unlike the "Illustrious American," he was aware that it could not be implemented until Venezuelan-style feudalism ended. Destruction of the regional caudillos was essential to the development of both a strong central government and a powerful national army. In 1901 a coalition of caudillo armies led by Gen. Manuel Antonio Matos, a banker, and backed by foreign capital, launched the so-called Liberating Revolution, which has been described as "the most powerful revolution organized since the birth of the Republic."[10] The revolution's objective was to drive from power the Andean upstart who represented a grave threat to the perpetuation of the "system" and was, to the revolutionaries, an intruder in their private domain of Venezuelan politics.

Although the size and experience of the army of the Liberating Revolution exceeded those of General Castro's tough Andean army, the Castro forces withstood its challenge. The main revolutionary force was crushed in the battle of La Victoria (1902), "the greatest armed action ever fought on Venezuelan soil."[11] This victory brought with it a major alteration in Venezuela's political dynamics. Freed from further threats to his authority from traditional quarters, Castro was able to consolidate central control. His enemies were scattered and demoralized. Having suffered a severe loss in prestige, they found it difficult to obtain additional financial support from abroad or to recruit troops for a resumption of hostilities. From that point on, no caudillo was able to come to power by way of a regional revolt. The victory at La Victoria assured the triumph of a new centralized and autocratic order that, although repressive, offered a more modern and effective solution to national problems than had the feudalism of the previous century.

The centralized authority could not, of course, be sustained without the means to enforce it. The first objective of the Andean rulers was to build a strong national army that would be responsible to the national caudillo. The need for such a force resides in Venezuelan military history.

10. Pablo Emilio Fernández, *Gómez el Rehabilitador*, 124.
11. Fernández, *Gómez*, 140.

The struggle for independence from Spain had brought into being a formidable military machine. At war's end Bolívar's army was large and disciplined and might have formed the basis of a powerful national army. The disintegration of Gran Colombia in the late 1820s, however, initiated a process of military disorganization that reached alarming proportions later in the century.[12] General Páez interrupted the process briefly. During his regime a military school was created under the directon of two scientists, Juan Manuel Cajigal and Col. Agustín Codazzi, who managed to maintain some degree of cohesion in the field of military education in particular and in the military institution in general.

Army discipline regressed, however, during the Federal War (1859–1863) and the subsequent period of Liberal rule as a result, partly, of the federal caudillos' practice of awarding commissions and high ranks in order to gain supporters. The number of military commissions outstanding, in relationship to the total male population and the number of active troops, rose to absurd proportions.[13] Men who were completely ignorant of the rudiments of military science boasted ranks of general or colonel. Excessive decentralization under the Liberals brought in its wake an exaggerated personalism that submerged whatever national army that theoretically existed into a mass of rival partisan armies, composed of temporarily armed civilians. The national army was little more than the force mustered by the current national caudillo, who benefited from the constitutional prerogative to conscript troops.[14]

Such was the situation that Cipriano Castro faced when he stormed to power in 1899. The absence of a powerful federal army had been to his advantage as a rebel, but once in pow-

12. Santiago Ochoa Briceño, "Evolución del ejército venezolano," *Sumario de Occidente*, 1 (September 1945), 113.

13. To illustrate, in the years between 1859 and 1864, over 100 men were commissioned generals in chief (Gilmore, *Caudillism*, 65). The decision of a military tribunal in 1872, as recorded in Venezuela, Presidencia de la República, *Documentos que hicieron historia: siglo y medio de vida republicana, 1810–1961*, II, 46–52, was signed by twenty-three generals in chief. Finally, the census of 1873 indicated that in one state alone, Carabobo, out of an adult male population of 22,952, there were 3,450 commissioned officers, including 449 generals and 627 colonels (Guillermo Morón, *A History of Venezuela*, 151).

14. Ochoa Briceño, "Evolución," 116.

er, it was a distinct handicap. For example, at the outbreak of the Liberating Revolution the regular army (Castro's) numbered little more than 4,000, while military rolls listed no fewer than 11,365 active and inactive officers.[15] Almost none of these officers had any military training other than the school of combat. Castro's victory at La Victoria, however, helped to rid the country of the remnants of past regimes. The rebel army melted away completely in 1903, following one last flicker that was snuffed out by General Gómez.

Once internal order had been established, President Castro set about organizing a permanent military institution. A logical nucleus of the new army were his Andean supporters from the campaigns of 1899 and 1901–1903. His makeshift army—the rebels of 1899—had fused rapidly into an effective fighting force, and was now augmented by the fresh recruits Castro gained during the Liberating Revolution. His call for volunteers from the Andes had been greeted enthusiastically, as thousands of his compatriots flocked to a cause that they identified with the welfare of their region.[16]

The dictator, using loyal coregionalists as a base for his organization, wasted no time in consolidating his military position. He immediately ordered the creation of a general staff to provide central direction. Soon in operation, this central body established a chain of command that ran from the General Staff to the commandants of each state and local contingent. The initial responsibility of each commandant was to bring the local chieftains to terms. Under the new command, the latter faced three alternatives: lay down their arms and join the government; risk a fight with the better-equipped and expanding national army; or retreat into the interior to carry on guerrilla activities.[17] Since neither fighting nor running could succeed against the burgeoning army, most *guerrilleros* entered either the ranks of the military or the civil bureaucracy.

The confiscation of weapons complemented the policy of dismemberment of guerrilla bands. The forced surrender of arms by private paramilitary bodies at the same time that the government was building an ever more powerful arsenal of weapons helped to stifle armed opposition to the dictator.

15. John J. Johnson, *The Military and Society in Latin America*, 72.

16. Rangel, *Los andinos*, 126–27.

17. Rangel, *Los andinos*, 165.

Subsequently, soldiers could gain power only by subverting or dominating the national army itself. Caudillism was giving way to militarism.[18]

Castro's military policy was built upon by Gen. Juan Vicente Gómez, who seized power from the ailing President in 1908, after the latter had sailed to Europe for medical treatment. Gómez, like Castro, viewed the new national army as his main pillar of support; the military institution therefore expanded under his regime. Military education on a systematic basis began with the opening of the Academia Militar de Venezuela in Caracas. Although established by a decree of Castro as early as 1903, it did not begin functioning until 1910 under General Gómez. While not equal to prevailing European standards, the school imparted the rudiments of military science and created a nucleus of professionally— or at least semiprofessionally—trained officers.[19]

Like many Latin American states in the late nineteenth and early twentieth centuries, Venezuela called in foreign missions to organize, train, and advise its army. Initially, Gómez depended on a Prussian-trained Chilean mission, which began operations in 1913. The Chileans set up a modern general staff structure and provided administrators and instructors for the infant military school. After World War I European missions were introduced. These included Belgian aviators, who came to assist in the Aviation School (established in 1921), and a small-scale German mission. The French, however, formed the most important contingent of foreign advisers and also served as the principal suppliers of

18. Robert L. Gilmore states correctly that "caudillism was the preeminent trait of the political system of Venezuela from 1814 to 1935," whereas "militarism has been . . . a recent problem for Venezuela" (*Caudillism,* 3). He defines caudillism as "a political process in which violence is an essential element. It is anarchic, self-generating, instinctively aspirant to the vanished role of the monarchy" (*ibid.*). Militarism, on the other hand, involves the departure of the armed forces from their legitimate constitutionally sanctioned functions in order "to participate in or to influence other nonmilitary agencies and functions of the state, including its leadership" (*ibid.*). This definition is essentially the same as McAlister's, mentioned in the Preface. For an extended treatment of caudillism as a general Latin American phenomenon, see Johnson, *Military and Society,* 36–61.

19. See Martín García Villasmil, *Escuelas para formación de oficiales del ejército: origen y evolución de la Escuela Militar.*

equipment for the Army, Air Corps, and Navy.[20]

Important strides in weapon development by the industrial powers in the two decades prior to and during World War I made available to nonindustrial nations good-quality repeating rifles, machine guns, and other high-power weapons. The Venezuelan government, its financial resources now swelled by growing petroleum revenues, took advantage of the availability of sophisticated weaponry. The new military matériel strengthened the national army and its authority and further weakened the far poorer regional armies.

Gómez' program of road construction also fostered the government's supremacy. Although not undertaken exclusively with a military purpose in mind, the building of highways facilitated the rapid transport of troops when they were needed to stamp out local rebellions.

The dictator followed a military policy that was successful but self-contradictory, a result of his dichotomous objectives. On the one hand, he realized that minimal professional standards were necessary for the development of an efficient army. He thus consented to the introduction of foreign missions, to structural organization, to establishment of military educational facilities, and to other innovations. On the other hand, he encouraged these progressive measures for reasons that were not consonant with the professionalizing of an army. He wanted a powerful army, not to defend his country against foreign aggression, but to crush domestic opposition. By using the Army to advance his own political interests, he perverted the process of military professionalization, which is "the formation of a technically trained . . . officer corps comprised of paid career men dedicated solely to professional matters."[21] Despite its new function as a force within a centralized government, the emerging Venezuelan Army became the personal instrument of the most personalistic dictator in the country's history. It was bound neither to the Constitution nor to the impersonal support of a national government, but to Juan Vicente Gómez, Supreme Caudillo.

20. U.S., Department of State, Decimal Files, 831.20/5, McGoodwin to Secretary of State, Caracas, July 5, 1921. Hereafter cited as DFDS. Unless otherwise noted, all DFDS dispatches cited were sent from Caracas.

21. Marvin Goldwert, "The Rise of Modern Militarism in Argentina," *Hispanic American Historical Review,* 48 (May 1968), 190.

His insistence that the Army serve as a personal guard was a vestige of prior caudillo practice, and his treatment of the Army as his praetorian guard prevented the shaping of the fledgling organization into a highly professionalized institution.

Gómez' lack of professionalism was exhibited in a number of ways. First, the new army had a strong regional complexion. Beginning in 1899 Castro placed *Andinos* in high military posts throughout the country. Now Gómez put even more kinsmen, friends, and fellow Tachirans in positions of command than had his former chief. Nepotism through presidential appointments increased when economic difficulties befell Táchira in the early twentieth century; young Tachirans entered the military school and services for economic security.[22] The result was an officer corps that was 75 to 90 per cent *Andino,* and the vast majority of those *Andinos* were Tachirans.[23] By continuing regional favoritism in the later Gómez period, the *Andinos* assured themselves of uninterrupted command of the armed forces. The development of a truly national army, in the sense of being representative of the entire population, was indefinitely postponed.

Another perversion of professionalism was the use of military personnel in nonmilitary capacities. For one example, army officers who lacked legitimate functions in the military monopolized most state presidencies. For another, during World War I Gómez, convinced that Venezuela needed to step up its agricultural output, ordered troops to work on his extensive haciendas.[24] The men, compelled to do menial farm chores, worked under the supervision of Academy-trained junior officers who had absorbed a strong sense of professionalism. The servile nonmilitary functions to which they were assigned jarred their ideal image of the professional soldier and further exposed the limitations of Gómez' military modernization program. Worse, the practice of using

22. Rangel, *Los andinos,* 166–67, and Charles C. Griffin, "Regionalism's Role in Venezuelan Politics," *Inter-American Quarterly,* 3 (October 1941), 32.

23. See, for example, Johnson, *Military and Society,* 107–9, and Rangel, *Los andinos,* 165. Guillermo Morón estimates 65 per cent of all officers were natives of Táchira (*A History of Venezuela,* 194). Based also on interviews in May of 1965.

24. Eleazar López Contreras, *Proceso político-social: 1928–1936,* 17.

the military for nonmilitary functions continued after the wartime emergency ended.

The system of promotions also failed to meet professional standards. It was common for favored officers (usually Táchira henchmen of Gómez) to receive as many as two promotions a year. Particularly in the 1899–1914 period, anyone who exhibited valor on the battlefield could become a general without the slightest acquaintance with the rudimentary principles of military science.[25] In contrast, promotions for graduates of the Military Academy came very slowly. These graduates saw illiterate, incompetent men entrenched in the General Staff and in command posts, while they languished in obscure positions. The discontent that arose from the favoritism shown to caudillo cronies of the dictator played a role in military insurrections not only in the Gómez regime but in subsequent governments.

Although the main underpinning of Gómez' regime was the Army, he relied heavily on civilian advisers. In this respect he was following the policy of his former *Jefe,* for, once in power, the unpredictable Cipriano Castro had forgotten his slogan, "New Men, New Ideals, New Methods." His army boasted new men—the *Andinos*—but in the upper echelons of the civil bureaucracy the same old faces reappeared. Castro's first Cabinet, for example, did not include a single Tachiran. Instead, it was filled with cronies of earlier presidents—even of Guzmán Blanco.

To Castro the veteran politicians and civil servants served a vital need; they knew national politics, whereas the *Andinos* who marched on Caracas in 1899 could point to little or no political experience—certainly, none on the national level. His provincial forces were ill equipped to deal with questions of diplomacy, national finance, and other sophisticated affairs of state. As a result, the new president was from the beginning dependent on carry-overs from previous regimes, corrupt and untrustworthy as many of them were. So it was that in the economic realm, the Caracas oligarchy maintained its privileged position and its grip on the highest positions in the government.[26]

25. Roque Leal, "La pava persigue a los generales," *Venezuela Gráfica* (October 3, 1958), 6.

26. Interview, Caracas, in March of 1965. Castro's successor continued to favor *Caraqueños* with important posts. A study of the regional origins of Cabinet members during the Gómez regime

The same pattern prevailed under Juan Vicente Gómez. The latter, a self-educated, primitive rancher, quite early succeeded in winning over the most influential civilian elements. The internal stability and sound financial management his government provided gave the business sector the opportunity to expand without the countless interruptions it had endured previously. Later in his regime many landowners and industrialists came to resent Gómez' increasingly monopolistic stranglehold over numerous profitable industries and his confiscation of the best agricultural land in the country.[27] But by the time of their disaffection Gómez, with the aid of growing oil revenues, had built up an extremely effective dictatorial machine that made the loss of civilian support of little consequence.

Much has been made of the *hegemonía andina* under the first two Tachiran presidents. That term should be qualified. Tachirans and other *Andinos* dominated the military institution, to be sure, as well as the state presidencies and lower bureaucratic berths, but in other areas *Andinos* exercised only limited influence and power. Under both Castro and Gómez the traditional non-Andean economic elite continued to prosper, and under Gómez, the dictator, his large clan, and a few close Tachiran supporters became wealthy through a variety of investments and through graft. But most Tachirans received little benefit from their leaders in the capital. Neither Gómez nor his government invested in his native region. Even when the price of coffee plummeted, threatening Táchira with economic disaster, he did not come to the aid of his own state.[28] To deepen their disadvantage, Táchira was at this time being misgoverned by the sadistic and thoroughly ruthless cousin of the dictator, Eustoquio Gómez. In sum, the only significant material contribution the *Andino* caudillos made to their people was the Trans-Andean Highway,

---

reveals that approximately 30 per cent were from Caracas, and 65 per cent were non-*Andinos*. Of the twenty-four *Andinos* in Gómez' cabinets, nineteen were from Táchira, four from Trujillo, and one from Mérida.

27. O'Reilly to British Foreign Office, November 19, 1930, copy enclosed in DFDS, 831.00/1466, Trammell to Secretary of State, November 25, 1930. See also DFDS, 831.00/1498, Wilson to Secretary of State, November 25, 1931.

28. Rangel, *Los andinos,* 263–64.

which Gómez built to link San Cristóbal, in Táchira, with Caracas.

Although the crafty dictator maintained absolute and uninterrupted control of Venezuela for twenty-seven years, this is not to say that he never faced serious opposition. On the contrary, hardly a year passed in which Gómez was not confronted with a rebellion. It has been estimated that he overcame more than twenty-five conspiratorial movements, including at least a dozen invasions.[29] The majority of the insurrections were led by bitter caudillo rivals (such as Cipriano Castro, the bitterest of all), disgruntled generals, and well-meaning but ineffective idealists. They not only had little they could offer the country in terms of a realistic alternative to the prevailing regime, but their success might have reversed the positive aspects of Venezuela's economic development achieved under the rule of the dictator.

Of all these rebellions, the only opposition movement relevant to this study was the civil–military uprising of April 7, 1928. Unlike the typical caudillo rebellion, it was distinguished by the youth of its participants, its espousal of modern political ideology, and the alliance of civilian and military groups to bring about reform.

The civilian participants were mostly students and recent graduates of the Central University in Caracas, members of what has come to be known as the "Generation of '28." This group included two future presidents—Rómulo Betancourt and Raúl Leoni—and other students who were later to become prominent in the nation's political and intellectual life. At the university, the headquarters of the "Generation of '28," discussion groups formed to debate the issues of the day. Since tight censorship was imposed on all reading matter, the students suffered from a gross lack of information on current issues and hence could shape only vague and ill-conceived solutions to national problems. But they surely felt the influence of such external events as the Mexican Revolution, World War I, and the Russian Revolution. Although differing on many specifics, most of the group were democratic leftists who supported the principles of constitutional democracy, fundamental socioeconomic reform, a more nationalistic economic policy, and a more equitable distribution of the

---

29. Pedro Luis Blanco Peñalver, *López Contreras ante la historia,* 23.

nation's growing wealth.[30] Their more immediate need was a wider range of economic and professional opportunities for themselves, opportunities that were severely restricted by the extremely conservative and myopic policies of the Gómez regime.

In 1927 these students formed the Federación de Estudiantes de Venezuela (FEV)—the Venezuelan Student Federation—which functioned without hindrance from the authorities until it developed plans for a "student week" in February, 1928. On the surface the event appeared to be a Venezuelan version of an American college homecoming, including the crowning of a student queen. But underneath ran a strong current of political unrest. The long-whispered ideas of the students found open expression at three points: a fiery speech by a future political party leader, Jóvito Villalba; the reading of a nationalistic poem by a young writer, Pío Tamayo; and an incendiary closing address by Rómulo Betancourt.[31] The demonstrations and public agitation surrounding these events forced the government to react. The three speakers, FEV head Raúl Leoni, and other leaders were jailed. Nevertheless, students continued their open defiance of the regime; they called a nationwide student strike, and the *Caraqueños* went on a solidarity strike in their support. Public pressure, in fact, became so great (probably because so many of the implicated students came from influential families) that the government relented and released the student activists.

These activists, encouraged by the uncharacteristically light punishment and by the demonstration of public support, envisioned the toppling of the dictatorship and the establishment of a democratic regime. They now realized that, to overthrow the imposing Gómez regime, they needed careful planning and military support. They thus turned to sympathetic elements in the armed forces.

The "sympathetic elements" were principally cadets in the Military Academy and Academy-educated junior officers. Discontent was rife among the Academy group for many reasons. Illiterate old caudillos, untouched by professional-

---

30. Rómulo Betancourt, *Venezuela: política y petróleo,* 87–88. See also Edwin Lieuwen, *Venezuela,* 50.

31. John D. Martz, "Venezuela's 'Generation of '28': The Genesis of Political Democracy," *Journal of Inter-American Studies,* 6 (January 1964), 18.

ism, still held the choicest posts while young professionals received assignments that were totally incommensurate with their abilities. Their superior training infused into them a desire to reform the military institution thoroughly—beginning at the top.

Other direct causes for unrest were the low salary scale for junior officers and the extremely slow rate of promotions. It was possible for an Academy graduate to remain a lieutenant until near retirement age.[32] Another grievance was Gómez' policy of using officers in unprofessional capacities, such as supervising farm chores.[33] Hence, junior officers were sympathetic to the university students' entreaties to join the conspiracy. The cadets at the Academy were receptive to subversive overtures because of the influence exerted on them by restless young officers, their friendships with university students, and the abuses they claimed to suffer at the school.[34] They too responded to the revolutionary call.

Both the uniformed and civilian malcontents expressed democratic and nationalistic ideals. The military conspirators saw an uprising as a means to move up in rank and even to control of the Army, while the students saw it as an opportunity to free their countrymen from despotism, seize political power, and impose their solutions to national problems. After much negotiation the two groups arrived at a carefully conceived plan.

Their strategy was to take the two principal Caracas barracks, Miraflores and San Carlos, the latter of which was the city's main deposit of arms and ammunition. Rebels would then distribute arms to the public. They would also blow up the bridges between Caracas and Maracay (Gómez' unofficial capital to the west of Caracas)—to prevent reinforcements from entering Caracas—block all entrances to the capital, seize all communications installations, and block off key officials from the area of combat.[35] By the end of March numerous civilians were involved as well as almost the entire

---

32. Rangel, *Los andinos,* 170.

33. Thomas Rourke, *Gómez: Tyrant of the Andes,* 229.

34. Martz, "Generation of '28," 19, and Francisco Betancourt Sosa, *Pueblo en rebeldía: relato histórico de la sublevación militar del 7 de abril de 1928,* 60.

35. Betancourt Sosa, *Pueblo en rebeldía,* 61–62, and interview in May of 1965.

corps of cadets. The coordinator was Capt. Rafael Alvarado Franco, who was assisted by three lieutenants. Civilian leaders included Rómulo Betancourt and Jóvito Villalba.

The insurrection was tentatively scheduled for April 8, but two days earlier the conspirators learned that their plot had been discovered. They hurriedly set their plans in operation the afternoon of April 6, and the armed revolt broke out early the following day.[36] The insurrectionists managed to capture Miraflores barracks and hold it briefly, but they had less success at San Carlos, outside which a civilian delegation waited to pour in, seize the arms, and supply them to the people. The military and civilian contingents designated to capture that barracks were prevented from doing so by their own mistakes and by the effective countermeasures employed by the government.

The commander of the Caracas garrison, Gen. Eleazar López Contreras, having been informed on April 6 of an imminent military uprising, alerted the barracks commanders, took other precautions, and then decided to undertake a quiet investigation in an effort to reduce the scope of the inevitable dictatorial revenge. But he was interrupted by word that the Miraflores barracks had already been taken and that San Carlos was at the point of rebellion. López Contreras audaciously moved on the focal point of the rebellion, San Carlos, without troops to cover him, gained entrance, and caught the rebels by surprise. He then took charge of the government's defense and in a short time forced the rebels to surrender.[37]

The iron hand of *Gomecista* justice fell, but it was tempered by López Contreras' adroit handling of the affair. He first attempted a discreet inquiry to weed out the ringleaders and spare the majority from the brutal punishment that could be expected. Next, during the outbreak, he took swift command, refused to call in reinforcements, and saved the regime without resorting to wholesale slaughter of civilians and young soldiers. In the immediate aftermath of the insurrection, López Contreras prevented indiscriminate shooting and torturing of prisoners; apparently the only par-

36. Betancourt Sosa, *Pueblo en rebeldía,* 63–64, and López Contreras, *Páginas,* 155.
37. López Contreras, *Páginas,* 155–57. See also Betancourt Sosa, *Pueblo en rebeldía,* 70.

ticipant tortured was Captain Alvarado.[38] In an effort to maintain some personal influence over the prisoners' fate, López Contreras attempted to bring them under military justice, but he was ordered to turn them over to the less sympathetic governor of the Federal District.[39]

The implicated students were imprisoned, exiled, or impressed into road gangs, and the Central University was closed. In addition, General Gómez temporarily shut down the Military Academy. When it reopened three years later, Gómez had shifted its site to Maracay, where he could keep a wary eye on the cadets. General López Contreras was another victim of the affair. He came under suspicion for his reluctance to take maximum suppressive measures and was transferred to the Andes garrison, a military Siberia, as an admonishment. Gómez, however, became reassured of his loyalty shortly thereafter and brought him back to Caracas, where, in due time, he was appointed Minister of War.[40]

The 1928 uprising was the opening battle in a war between the forces that had been governing Venezuela since the beginning of the century and the members of a younger generation, principally middle-class intellectuals and military professionals, who represented a fresh political outlook. The young students and professionals in exile formed cells in which they studied new currents in economic and social thought, wrote manifestoes, and awaited the day when they could return home to reconstruct their country along new lines.

* * * * *

At the death of General Gómez in 1935 the power of the regional strongmen had evaporated. Castro and Gómez had

38. A controversial sidelight to the 1928 revolt was the conduct of General López Contreras toward his son, Eleazar López Wollmer, one of the implicated cadets at the Military Academy. The boy was arrested and imprisoned, but his father in no way sought to obtain preferential treatment for him. According to Betancourt Sosa (*Pueblo en rebeldía,* "Notes"), young López would have died in prison if he had not managed to get transferred to a hospital through the aid of friends. As it was, he died shortly thereafter, partially due, it is claimed, to his loss of health while in prison.

39. López Contreras, *Páginas,* 157–60, and Betancourt Sosa, *Pueblo en rebeldía,* 72–74.

40. López Contreras, *Páginas,* 160, and DFDS, 831.00, Engert to Secretary of State, July 8, 1929.

destroyed the old system, such as it was, and had replaced it with autocratic centralization. Each in his terms of office had reinforced central authority by the deliberate building of a strong national army. By the end of the Gómez era, the Army was generally recognized as the sole road to power. Invasions on horseback and localized rebellions were passé. Power, it was clear, was in the hands that controlled the armed forces. For a revolt to succeed it required the support of one or more factions in the military. The Army, being the only truly national institution, therefore became the road to power for politically ambitious officers as well as an increasingly attractive object for seduction by civilian politicians.

It is important to understand that the Army did not take over the state under Gómez. Venezuelan militarism differed significantly from the European variety, in which society became oriented toward and controlled by a professional military caste. By contemporary European standards the 8,000-man Venezuelan Army would have appeared to be a small, inefficient, and uninfluential military establishment. In essence the Venezuelan Army was not master, but servant, of the state. It was the instrument of power for one man, Gómez, the only important "military politician." Under him the Army served as a tool of the traditional elite and foreign business interests by preserving order, quelling opposition, breaking strikes, and maintaining in general a propitious climate for private enterprise to flourish.

Finally, the abuse of power, ultraconservatism, distortion of the economy, flagrant peculation, rise in living costs, and lack of economic opportunities under the Andean governments of Castro and Gómez produced profound discontent in the younger generations: in the civilian sphere, among the "Generation of '28"; in the military sector, among the corresponding generation of junior officers and Military Academy cadets. Although the military institution had reached a degree of technical competence under Gómez never before achieved, remaining inequities, incompetence, and differing levels of professionalization created serious tensions between what really amounted to two armies: the old-style warriors and the Academy-trained personnel. The new generation, despite the failure of its revolt in 1928, revealed to the nation the widening rift between the modernizing elements in society and the *Gomecistas.*

CHAPTER II

A DECADE OF TRANSITION

Juan Vicente Gómez died on December 17, 1935. Within hours of his death the Cabinet met and selected the Minister of War, Gen. Eleazar López Contreras, to finish out the presidential term. At the conclusion of that term, López was elected constitutional President by Congress for a seven-year period. Although López had benefited by the provisions of the old constitution, he urged the adoption of a new constitution, by which, among other changes, the presidential term, beginning with his own, was reduced to five years. In May 1941 López peaceably relinquished his office to another Andean general, Isaías Medina Angarita. López' successor did not complete his term; he fell victim to pressures and forces that had been building up since Cipriano Castro took power in 1899. The 1935–1945 decade, which began with an unusually smooth transfer of power, ended in violence and revolution.

Important changes in the political role of the military had taken place during the López Contreras–Medina years. To understand them, it is necessary to examine the succession crisis of 1935; the popular reaction against thirty-six years of Andean dictatorship and the government response to it; the changing character of the Army and the effect of professionalization on officer attitudes; and the rise of new forces that advocated the restructuring of Venezuelan government and society.

Eleazar López Contreras, the son of Col. (later general) Manuel María López and Catalina Contreras, was born in 1883 in the small Táchira town of Queniquea. After completing his primary schooling locally, he attended the highly regarded Colegio del Sagrado Corazón de Jesús in La Grita, where he received the degree of Bachelor of Philosophy and Letters in 1898.[1] He planned to continue his studies at the medical faculty of the University of Mérida, beginning in the fall of 1899. During much of the intervening year he traveled

1. Eleazar López Contreras, *Páginas para la historia militar de Venezuela*, xvi–xix.

about the towns of Táchira, and was caught up in the fervor of Cipriano Castro's revolutionary movement. By chance, López was in Castro's home town on May 23, 1899, the day the rebel crossed into Táchira to begin his campaign. The boy, abandoning his plans for further education, volunteered to join the movement of Liberal Restoration and was accepted into the makeshift army.[2]

During the next fifteen years López Contreras served the national government in a variety of civilian and military posts. His last civilian assignment ended in 1914, when President Gómez appointed Colonel López Contreras to the command of a battalion; nine years later he became a brigadier general, with command of the Caracas Brigade. After a brief tour of duty in the Andes, he returned to Caracas, and from 1931 to Gómez' death he filled the number-two position in the regime, Minister of War and Navy.

General López Contreras built an excellent reputation in army ranks and, except in a few instances, enjoyed the full confidence and support of the dictator. Besides being a combat-hardened veteran of the last successful caudillo uprising, he had the advantage of a formal education that was superior to that of most of his fellow officers. It was he, more forcefully than any other man in the Gómez regime, who gave real impetus to the professionalization of the officer corps. His most fruitful opportunity to reform and update the military institution came when he was made Minister of War.

When he took over that post the military organization was in chaos. Commissions and promotions were granted capriciously; civilians with no military experience whatever filled strategic staff and field positions.[3] The dictator, obsessed with his ambition to retain absolute control of the military, continued to commission men solely to increase loyalty to him in the officer corps. The new Minister of War was immediately faced with problems of loose discipline, insubordination, low morale, and a reactionary officialdom. Resentment among the handful of Academy-trained officers was mounting. López Contreras, aware of these obstacles, strove to raise the moral and technical level of the services and to

2. López Contreras, *Páginas,* xxi–xxii.
3. Eleazar López Contreras, *Proceso político-social: 1928–1936,* 16.

instill an *esprit de corps* in his fellow officers.[4]

López Contreras experienced at least some success in attempting to professionalize the Army, in part because he himself had no formal military training. He was proud of being a veteran of the 1899 revolution, and of having served his country on the battlefield.[5] These qualifications endeared him to many of the old *Castristas* and *Gomecistas* in the military hierarchy, who resented the new breed of Academy-trained officers. In the other camp, he won the admiration of the younger officers through his efforts to expand their opportunities for advanced study and through his efficient, honest, and austere conduct in office. At the same time, his apparent lack of political ambition, frail physique, and studious habits earned him the trust and friendship of General Gómez, who felt that a soldier who wrote books in his spare time could not be a serious rival for power.[6] López Contreras won the respect of the civilians, in particular the *Caraqueños,* through his dignified bearing, his education and culture (in marked contrast to many *Andino* officers), and his moderation in dealing with the public disturbances of 1928. His record and reputation did not escape the cognizance of the diplomatic community. Successive United States ministers, for example, were impressed with his leadership ability and political potential.[7] From the 1920s on, then, he was a rising figure in the military hierarchy and, consequently, in national affairs.

Gómez, as mentioned in the preceding chapter, became temporarily suspicious of López Contreras' loyalty after the 1928 uprising. Consequently, later that year the General, a victim of intrigues by his rivals, was relegated to the comparative oblivion of the Andes. There he was approached by conspiratorial elements who sought a high-ranking officer to lead their movement. He discouraged rebellion, maintaining that Gómez was stronger than ever and warning the plotters

4. López Contreras, *Proceso.* See also Isaías Medina Angarita, *Cuatro años de democracia,* 142.

5. López Contreras, *Proceso,* 59. He was wounded in the last major battle of the 1899 civil war.

6. Pedro Luis Blanco Peñalver, *López Contreras ante la historia,* 33–34; also DFDS, 831.00/1498, Wilson to Secretary of State, November 25, 1931.

7. DFDS, 831.00, Engert to Secretary of State, July 8, 1929, and 831.00/1519, Summerlin to Secretary of State, August 24, 1934.

that such movements would meet with disaster. For himself, General López Contreras avowed loyalty to the regime and expressed his aversion to winning power through civil war and the sacrifice of his compatriots.[8]

López Contreras' banishment to the Andes was short-lived; he was soon back in Caracas as Minister of War. The critical importance of his position became apparent during the early 1930s, when those closest to Gómez realized that the aged President's health was failing steadily. Despite entreaties to name a successor, Gómez refused to do so. Consequently, numerous political figures began plotting to seize power in expectation of his demise.

These intrigues accelerated to a frantic pace by 1934. Leading candidates to replace the senile dictator included his cousin Eustoquio, reputedly "the most hated man in Venezuela,"[9] a number of generals serving as state presidents, and a handful of high civilian officials. Among the latter were Pedro Manuel Arcaya, Venezuelan Minister to Washington; Rafael Requena, the dictator's private secretary; and Pedro Rafael Tinoco, the Minister of Interior Relations.[10] Tinoco probably had the best chance for succeeding to the presidency as well as the strongest ambitions among the civilian contenders, but it was highly improbable that any civilian could take over the presidency, given the stage of Venezuela's political development in the mid-1930s.[11]

The most logical successor was, of course, the Minister of War. Because of his command of the armed forces, his importance as a key member of the Cabinet, his popularity in both civilian and military circles, and his shrewd political instincts, López Contreras was in a dominant position to win any power struggle. As early as 1931 a list of possible candidates, compiled by the United States minister in Caracas, placed López Contreras eighth in line for the presidency. By discounting members of the Gómez clan, he moved López up to third position on the list. Then, after discussing rapidly

8. López Contreras, *Páginas,* 174.
9. DFDS, 831.00/1550, Nicholson to Secretary of State, December 23, 1935.
10. DFDS, 831.00/1519, Summerlin to Secretary of State, August 24, 1934.
11. Interview, May, 1965. Rafael Requena was described by U.S. Minister Summerlin as "next to [Gómez], the most influential man in Venezuela"; DFDS, 831.00/1513, Summerlin to Secretary of State, October 16, 1933.

changing developments, the minister concluded that López Contreras should head the list. He appeared to be the only high-ranking Tachiran in the Army who commanded the respect of the *Caraqueños,* and in the event of a crisis, he was the best-qualified person in the country to maintain order without indulging in a Gómez-style bloodbath.[12] Three years later the United States minister wrote that López Contreras "is adored by the army and is a most popular figure in Caracas as he also has the confidence of the strong Andino faction. . . . No group can be assured of any success without the cooperation and support of General López Contreras."[13]

Although he gave no outward indication, the dictator himself probably favored his Minister of War as successor. He knew better than anyone that the next president, to be at all effective, would have to come from the Army. At the same time he was opposed to the assumption of power by anyone in his own family, fearing it would lead to fratricidal struggle. General López Contreras, he was confident, would favor the Gómez clan and permit it to retain its vast financial and property holdings.[14]

The succession crisis intensified throughout 1935. The military officialdom seethed with factionalism and personal rivalries. Most ambitious of all was General Eustoquio Gómez. On the other hand, a sizable contingent of officers actively espoused the candidacy of General López Contreras. In discussions with them, however, he cautioned them about the dangers of military disunity and advised them to forget politics and to devote themselves to their proper military functions.[15] In his writings López Contreras leaves the impression that he was entirely devoid of political ambition, ready to serve anyone whom Gómez or the Cabinet appointed. In truth, one may reasonably conclude that, despite a lack of evidence he was discreetly and effectively working to consolidate his position as successor to the presidency.

By early December it was apparent that General Gómez was near death. The same day that López Contreras saw Gó-

12. DFDS, 831.00/1472, Summerlin to Secretary of State, May 4, 1931.

13. DFDS, 831.00/1519, Summerlin to Secretary of State, August 24, 1934.

14. Rodolfo Luzardo, *Notas historico-económicas: 1928–1963,* 37. See also López Contreras, *Proceso,* 9.

15. López Contreras, *Páginas,* 235–36.

mez alive for the last time, December 12, he received word that the faction supporting Eustoquio Gómez was preparing to seize power. Eustoquio's henchmen were keeping a close watch on all movements to and from Gómez' estate in Maracay, and arms were reported to have been distributed to workers on the Gómez haciendas. López was informed that a member of the dictator's family was planning to murder him upon the death of Gómez.[16]

The situation was indeed grave. It was obvious that a coup was imminent and that Eustoquio, in his desperate efforts to close the door on the other aspirants to power, would resort to violence. In order to prevent such a disaster and, also, to assure his succession, López took the initiative to negotiate a peaceful settlement with the *Gomecistas*. He met with Eustoquio and proposed that all parties abide by the wishes of the President while he still lived and by the decision of the Cabinet after his death.[17] Since the Minister of War was the most obvious choice in both circumstances, the proposal received a cold response from the dictator's cousin.[18] Within twenty-four hours López learned that Eustoquio had attempted to subvert the battalion stationed in Maracay and had sent instructions to the presidents of several states (who had military as well as civil powers), directing them to obey him, not the Ministry of War.[19]

On December 16, the day before Gómez' death, López Contreras decided to take whatever measures were necessary to crush the impending coup. When he issued arrest warrants for some of the plotters, Eustoquio went immediately to the Ministry of War and demanded just cause for the arrests. López Contreras replied that he was the head of the armed forces and that he was determined to maintain order against any insubordination. His responsibility required him to do so while Gómez still lived, and, once again, he told Eustoquio that he would carry out the directives of the Cabinet afterward. To these statements Eustoquio had no response, and he hurried out.[20]

16. López Contreras, *Proceso,* 26, and *Páginas,* 239.
17. According to the constitution in force, in the event that the President failed to designate a successor officially, the responsibility fell to the Cabinet.
18. López Contreras, *Páginas,* 236–37.
19. López Contreras, *Proceso,* 26–27.
20. López Contreras, *Páginas,* 240.

The last time the two rivals met was on the morning of December 18, at the bier of the deceased caudillo.[21] The Cabinet had already met in the early hours of that day to elect General López Contreras provisional President. With a proper and constitutional election to the highest office, the backing of the Cabinet, and the support of most military factions, he was in an impregnable position. Although the details of his methods are not clear, he had succeeded in restricting Eustoquio's movement to a few Army units in Maracay and other scattered locations while retaining the support of a majority of field commanders. On December 21 Eustoquio was mortally wounded in an apparent attempt to seize the palace of the Federal District governor and died shortly thereafter.[22]

The emergence of General López Contreras as the victor in the contest for national power was partly the result of his popularity among key civilians, his political finesse, his firmness against insubordination, and a divided opposition. The most important factor in his triumph was his ability to secure the loyalty of his officers through his role as bridge between generations and reconciler of factional differences.

Once the succession crisis had been resolved, the new president had to face the difficult problem of maintaining order while trying to effect a smooth transition from the *Gomecista* tyranny toward more democratic political forms. The demands confronting him were these: on the one hand were arrayed the aroused masses who had been silenced for three decades and now were reacting violently against the long years of despotic control. They went on a destructive rampage, looting and burning the homes of the Gómez clan and of the regime's chief collaborators. Their initial impulse was vengeance, but soon they became inflamed by the propaganda spread by the returning exiles. A number of radical political organizations, formed almost overnight, projected as their main goals the establishment of complete freedom of expression, universal suffrage, dissolution of Congress, and stern measures against everyone associated with the Gómez regime. These organizations held frequent public gatherings, which often ended in violent outbursts and public disorder.

On the other hand, López faced the intransigence of the

21. López Contreras, *Páginas*, 240.
22. *La Esfera*, December 22, 1935.

hard-core *Gomecistas,* especially members of the dictator's sprawling family, who saw no reason for any fundamental changes in the prevailing system. Many were ensconced in high posts in the bureaucracy and Army and had no desire to vacate their lucrative sinecures. They were furious with the new president for not clamping down on the mobs and the radical leaders, and they blamed him for the destruction of their property by the insurrectionists.[23]

How did Brigadier General López Contreras, an Army man who had emerged from the same environment as Castro and Gómez and a pillar of the Gómez dictatorship, respond to the demands that faced him on the right and on the left? Viewed in the perspective of history, his regime bridged the gap between the stultifying dictatorship of Juan Vicente Gómez and the liberal regime of Isaías Medina Angarita, his immediate successor. At times President López Contreras was tough and implacable; at others he was tolerant and permissive. He committed himself to dismantling the machinery of the Gómez tyranny, but as a realist he was aware of the risks inherent in trying to establish a wide-open democratic regime immediately on the heels of the longest and most oppressive dictatorship in Venezuelan history. He succeeded, with his gradualism, in rationalizing and humanizing Venezuelan government and, to a degree, in separating the military from the civil government.

In the first years of the new regime political opposition centered in three negative impulses: anti-*Gomecismo,* anti-*Andinismo,* and anti-*Lopecismo.* The popular reaction against the survivors of the old regime took many forms, including personal violence and the destruction of property. López Contreras, claiming that he could not guarantee their safety, urged the remaining members of Gómez' personal and official families to leave the country. As time went on, the President slowly replaced *Gomecistas* in the government with men not identified with the previous regime and, hence, more acceptable to liberal elements. Moreover, his government instituted judicial proceedings to reclaim much of the wealth the Gómez clan had taken from the public treasury.

---

23. See Santiago Gerardo Suárez, *El régimen de López Contreras,* 12–13, and Juan Liscano, "Aspectos de la vida social y política de Venezuela," in Venezuela, Presidencia de la República, *150 años de vida republicana: 1811–1861,* I, 201.

The anti-*Gomecismo* outbursts were highly personal, the anti-*Andinismo* protests were more general. Who could forget that *Andinos* had gripped the government bureaucracy in a stranglehold and had dominated the officer ranks of the Army and national police for almost forty years?[24] An article that appeared in a Caracas newspaper in early 1936 and that attacked *Andino* dominance should serve to illustrate the violence of anti-*Andinismo* feeling. The author declared that, although *Andinos* entered the government under Cipriano Castro, it was really under Gómez that they began to monopolize positions on every level of national affairs. The political ideology of this band of "rustic illiterates," according to the author, was expressed in their invariable question about a prospective job: "How much will it get me?" He admitted that Táchira had been exploited as ruthlessly as any other part of the country, but he added that the Tachirans avenged themselves by oppressing the people in the rest of the country. The author of the article blamed the *Andinos* for every injustice suffered by the nation during the entire span of the Gómez dictatorship.[25] Undoubtedly this blatant expression of hostility toward the *Andinos* was echoed by many citizens in other sections of the country.[26] Such attacks were modified, however, by more explicit and balanced appraisals of Andean rule.

For other observers, the tyrannical administration of Eustoquio Gómez in Táchira, with its expropriations, tortures, and violence, offered sufficient proof that Táchira suffered along with the rest of the country. In addition, these authors remarked that the *Andinos* were far from being the only element who enjoyed the usufruct of power. On the contrary, men of influence from the coast, the Llanos, and the Oriente collaborated with the Andean strongman, and, in fact, reaped the greatest rewards. They argued strongly against singling out *Andinos* for total blame.[27]

24. See DFDS, 831.00/1547, Nicholson to Secretary of State, December 21, 1935, and 831.00/1557, Nicholson to Secretary of State, December 30, 1935.

25. Vicente Fuentes, "La ficción del regionalismo y su lógica solución en el país," *El Universal* (Caracas), February 12, 1936.

26. DFDS, 831.00/1547, Nicholson to Secretary of State, December 21, 1935, and 831.00/1557, Nicholson to Secretary of State, December 30, 1935.

27. E. Urdaneta Aubert, "Los prejuicios regionalistas," *La Esfera,* February 3, 1936; Rafael Antonio Ruiz Rueda, "El pueblo

López Contreras responded to the anti-Andean sentiment by removing some of the more notorious Tachirans from public service. In fact, he was sharply criticized by fellow *Andinos* for putting a halt to the so-called *"hegemonía andina."*[28] He also spoke and behaved like a sincere democrat during the early days of his administration, and some Venezuelans felt this beginning was a sign of a democratic millennium to come. A few hours after his election by the Cabinet, he ordered the release of all political prisoners and allowed the repatriation of all exiles. When he returned to the capital after Gómez' burial in Maracay, he was met with a jubilant reception by the *Caraqueños.*[29] His first pronouncements, although stressing order, encouraged those who hoped for an abrupt shift to democratic forms.[30] The new president quickly gave his approval to the formation of political parties, and soon a confusing array of them appeared on the scene.

Immediately after Gómez' death, the old Venezuelan Student Federation (FEV) was reactivated under the dynamic leadership of Jóvito Villalba. Although not strictly a political party, it was militant in its stand on ridding Venezuela of all vestiges of *Gomecismo* and moving the nation toward modern democracy, characterized by complete freedom of expression and a more nationalistic economic policy.[31] The list of political organizations included the Unión Nacional Republicana (UNR)—National Republican Union, the Organización Venezolana (ORVE)—Venezuelan Organization, the Partido Republicano Progresista (PRP) —Progressive Republican party, and the Maracaibo-centered Bloque Nacional Democrático (BND)—National Democratic Bloc. The first of these was a rather moderate group that drew its membership from liberal, middle-class elements and from some agrarian interests. Several UNR leaders were elected to Congress.[32]

---

que sufrió más," *La Esfera,* April 12, 1936; and "No odiamos a los andinos," *El Heraldo* (Barquisimeto), March 16, 1936, reprinted in *El Universal,* March 19, 1936.

28. López Contreras, *Proceso,* 41–42.

29. *El Heraldo* (Caracas), December 19, 1935.

30. See *La Esfera,* January 2, 1936.

31. Manuel Vicente Magallanes, *Partidos políticos venezolanos,* 75.

32. Magallanes, *Partidos,* 80.

ORVE was not so much a political party as a popular front that sought to bring into its fold almost all elements opposed to the recently ended dictatorship. It cut across class lines and appealed to wide segments of the population.[33] Among its founders were Rómulo Betancourt, Raúl Leoni, Gonzalo Barrios, and Luis Beltrán Prieto Figueroa, all to become prominent political figures, and two outstanding intellectuals, Mariano Picón-Salas and Andrés Eloy Blanco. Its leadership was composed mainly of members of the "Generation of '28" and the younger university generation of 1936–1937. Many of its leaders were later to re-emerge in the Acción Democrática party during the Medina administration.[34]

The PRP included diverse elements, but the dominant influence was Communist. It was violently anti-*Gomecista* and anti-imperialistic, and its greatest appeal was to the urban proletariat.[35] It soon was declared illegal. The BND was active in the state of Zulia where its principal organizer, Valmore Rodríguez, a future Acción Democrática leader, sought to extend its influence nationally. Its objectives were similar to those of ORVE.[36]

Several attempts were made to unite the leftist opposition. Early in 1936 UNR, PRP, and ORVE formed a short-lived coalition front, which was followed in October by the union of ORVE, PRP, BND, and other groups into the Partido Democrático Nacional (PDN)—the National Democratic party. The PDN, with Jóvito Villalba as Secretary General and Rómulo Betancourt and Raúl Leoni as other leaders, took a militant stand against the López Contreras administration and, as a result, was soon operating in secret. Carefully organized into small cells, party members tried to infiltrate professional and other organizations. At the time of the 1941 election, the PDN reorganized under the name, Acción Democrática.[37]

A number of other national and regional political organizations came into being at that time, but the groups men-

33. Magallanes, *Partidos,* 83–84.
34. John D. Martz, "Venezuela's 'Generation of '28': The Genesis of Political Democracy," *Journal of Inter-American Studies,* 6 (January 1964), 26.
35. Magallanes, *Partidos,* 87. See also DFDS, 831.00/1613, Nicholson to Secretary of State, April 7, 1936.
36. Magallanes, *Partidos,* 89.
37. Magallanes, *Partidos,* 124–26.

tioned above had the greatest impact on the general public. As one would expect, the young politicians, presented with their first opportunity to conduct political activity openly, did not take the most adroit advantage of their circumstance. Being totally inexperienced, hot-headed, and impatient, they committed a number of blunders in strategy and indulged in demagogic excesses that invited prompt and repressive government reaction.[38]

The resolutions of two crises illustrate López Contreras' approach to the political problems he faced during the first years of his administration. In the first weeks after Gómez' death, leftist organizations provoked a number of noisy demonstrations and public rallies, while sporadic attacks on the property of *Gomecistas* continued. On January 5, in an attempt to restore order and establish his authority, López ordered the suspension of constitutional guarantees.[39] This action was countered by a large rally in one of the main plazas of Caracas, where opposition leaders exhorted the crowd to defy the executive decree.[40] Agitation continued throughout the next weeks. On February 12 the governor of the Federal District, Gen. Félix Galavís, imposed tight censorship on all means of communications—an order directed mainly against the opposition newspapers. To enforce the decree, he set up a censorship office. At a protest demonstration two days later, Governor Galavís apparently ordered his troops to fire on the crowd gathered in front of his headquarters. When the firing had ceased, eight persons were dead and a large number wounded.[41] The mob then rioted destructively. López undertook stern measures to bring the disturbance under control, but there was no wholesale revenge, "a la Gómez," in the aftermath. Instead, López conducted an investigation into the massacre, relieved Galavís of his post, arrested him, and appointed a new governor who was more acceptable to the popular forces. Later, when conditions had quieted, he lifted the censorship decree and restored constitutional liberties.

A week after the massacre on February 14 in Caracas, President López Contreras addressed the nation and pro-

38. See Martz, "Generation of '28," 27, and Liscano, "Aspectos," 201–2.
39. *El Universal,* January 6, 1936.
40. Suárez, *López Contreras,* 31.
41. *La Esfera,* February 16, 1936.

claimed what came to be known as the Program of February. This program, the first plan of government to be proclaimed by any Venezuelan president,[42] expressed a genuine understanding of many of the nation's most urgent needs. It included provision for labor organization and legislation, health and agricultural reforms, and the modernization of the instruments of government.[43] Administrative acts implementing the Program of February were cautious during the López regime, but successive governments were to broaden, intensify, and accelerate efforts along its original lines. From the political standpoint, López' policy declaration, which was partially inspired by radical pressures, stole some of the thunder from the leftist groups and won him valuable support in moderate circles.[44]

Nevertheless, radical opposition to López Contreras continued unabated through the remaining months of 1936. In June labor organizers called a four-day general strike, which López ended by executive decree. Then, in mid-December the hastily organized petroleum workers called a strike that involved more than 20,000 oil company employees. On January 23, declaring that the strike would have a grave effect on the national economy, López ordered the strikers back to work with only a token raise.[45] Afterward, the President showed his displeasure with the strike organizers by removing from office a handful of opposition candidates who had triumphed in the congressional election of January 28. About the same time, the legal authorization to function as a political party was revoked from ORVE, PRP, FEV, and two labor groups.[46] His action eliminated virtually all the effective opposition to the new regime. Remaining was a handful of narrowly based, moderate parties with little influence among the masses.

Meanwhile, agents of the Secret Service of Investigation had been preparing evidence against opposition leaders, which was compiled in what came to be known as the *Libro*

---

42. Mariano Picón-Salas, commenting on the presidential address in *El Universal*, February 22, 1936, declared: "For the first time in the political history of Venezuela, we have a program of government."

43. *Gaceta Oficial* (Caracas), February 21, 1936.

44. Suárez, *López Contreras*, 60.

45. *Gaceta Oficial*, January 22, 1937, and Edwin Lieuwen, *Petroleum in Venezuela: A History*, 81–82.

46. *El Universal*, February 5, 1937.

Rojo. It presented an impressive array of letters and documents purporting to link most of the radical leaders to Communist doctrine. Although some distortions existed, much of the evidence was authentic. The government used the controversial *Libro Rojo* against various individuals as proof of their association with Communist ideology and involvement in subversive activity. President López, acting on that evidence and still unready to accept the kind of strident, militant opposition the radical leadership represented, decided to rid himself of the most troublesome of his antagonists. Using the broad powers granted him by Clause 6 of Article 32 of the 1936 Constitution, he expelled forty-seven opposition leaders from the country, for a period of one year, on the grounds that they were "affiliated with Communist doctrine."[47] Among the alleged Communists ordered into exile early in 1937 were Rómulo Betancourt, Gonzalo Barrios, Raúl Leoni, Valmore Rodríguez, Jóvito Villalba, and Gustavo Machado. Machado and a handful of the forty-seven were indeed Communists at that time and remained in the Marxist camp, but most of the young men were acting from a potpourri of liberal-democratic, socialist, and Marxist ideas. Some were emphatically anti-Communist. Not only was López Contreras inaccurate in labeling all of them Communists, he also made a tactical error by banishing them from the country. The one-year exile made martyrs of them and allowed them to score a propaganda victory, in which his regime was likened to the despotic rule of his predecessor. To the leaders of the left, the "democratic honeymoon" was over.[48]

In fairness to López Contreras, however, with the constitutional powers he had at hand, he could have expelled from Venezuelan soil or incarcerated the forty-seven indefinitely. Instead, he limited the term of exile and made arrangements for the group to embark on a French passenger ship, on which they were given first- and second-class accommodations. Moreover, each exile was given 1,000 *bolívares* if single and 2,000 if married, for expenses during the first weeks abroad.[49]

President López Contreras was unprepared and unwilling to permit a completely unfettered opposition to operate. Also,

47. *Gaceta Oficial*, March 13, 1937.
48. Rómulo Betancourt, *Venezuela: política y petróleo*, 113.
49. *El Heraldo*, March 27, 1937.

pressures on him from the military and business sectors were intense. According to those groups, he was treating Communists and subversives with kid gloves; what was needed was the iron fist that Gómez had applied so effectively. Diplomatic dispatches, for example, testify to the intransigence of foreign businessmen, particularly oil company officials.[50] Under such pressure from the right, López Contreras realized that he had to move cautiously, and to effect a gradual transition he had to silence the proponents of revolutionary change. Nevertheless, his relatively mild reaction to leftist activity indicates that changes in governmental methods had indeed occurred since the harsh Gómez days.

From the spring of 1937 to the end of his constitutional term, López Contreras governed without any effective organized opposition, although the PDN continued to operate under cover. The only officially recognized political group was the President's own government party. Drawing its inspiration from the political philosophy of Simón Bolívar, it took the name of Agrupaciones Cívicas Bolivarianas (ACB) —Bolivarian Civic Groups. Various economic and other interest groups that had been supporting the regime coalesced into the ACB, which, as an essentially elitist organization, failed to attract mass support.

Although General López relied heavily on the support he received from civilian centrists and rightists, more crucial to his political survival was the continued backing of the Army. The Venezuelan Army in the late 1930s was still the arbiter of national politics. The President realized that to accomplish anything worth while he needed its support. At the same time, however, he tried to modify its structure in order for it to be a military institution that would concern itself only with its proper constitutional functions, not with politics.

On his assumption of the presidency, López Contreras was in a better position than anyone else in the country to further the professionalization of the military institution without provoking a massive reaction in the uniformed hierarchy.[51] No longer restrained by the more primitive notions of Gómez and his henchmen, he was able to speed up the process

50. DFDS, 831.00/1579, Nicholson to Secretary of State, February 8, 1936; 831.00/1628, Nicholson to Secretary of State, June 22, 1936; 831.00/1669, Nicholson to Secretary of State, April 20, 1937.
51. Suárez, *López Contreras,* 70.

of modernization that he had initiated as Minister of War. Between 1936 and 1941 he reorganized the Military Academy for more efficient professional training; separated the Military and Naval academies into two autonomous entities; introduced a United States Naval mission at the start of World War II (which began operating under the Medina administration); purchased modern war equipment in greater quantities than in any previous period; initiated social welfare measures for officers, which included a mutual aid fund.[52]

Another significant development was the creation of a fourth branch of the service, the National Guard. Initially it fell under the jurisdiction of the Ministry of Interior Relations, but later it was transferred to the Ministry of War. The assigned functions of the National Guard were numerous and varied: the guarding of highways, railways, and border entrances; control over illicit international trade; maintenance of public order in conjunction with the police forces; and certain responsibilities in the field of public health and social assistance. The Guard began on a modest scale, from which it declined in size and importance in the 1940s, but later it was put on a par with the other services and, at least in outlying areas, gained an admirable reputation among the people.[53]

Advanced training in foreign military institutions was stepped up markedly under the López Contreras regime. For instance, in 1938 Venezuelan cadets were studying in Italy, Chile, Argentina, Peru, Ecuador, and the United States.[54] Although greatly enlarged subsequently, the study program received its first major impetus in the years between 1936 and 1941.

Despite the increased attention paid to technical improvement and superior training facilities, the proportion of the national budget devoted to the armed forces did not increase appreciably. Some civilians were critical of the amounts spent on the Army; they felt the money should have been devoted to attacking Venezuela's basic economic and social

52. Medina Angarita, *Cuatro años*, 142. For a more complete account, see López Contreras, *Páginas*, 309–22.

53. Alberto Aguirre Rojas, *La Guardia Nacional de Venezuela*, 20–24, 34–36.

54. Venezuela, Ministerio de Guerra y Marina, *Memoria del Ministerio de Guerra y Marina: 1939*, xvii.

problems. But Minister of War Medina Angarita defended the military spending of the regime with the argument that Venezuela was spending no more than 16 per cent of the total budget on the military, while other nations set aside much higher percentages for the sustenance of their armed establishments.[55] In fact, in some of those years the percentage allotted to the Venezuelan Ministry of War was closer to 12 or 13 per cent.[56] This amount was not considered excessive by military authorities, who warned of the danger to Venezuela's oil industry posed by the Axis Powers. A comparison of the priorities of the military and civilian regimes shows that the civilian governments of the 1958–1963 period devoted almost 10 per cent of their budgets to the armed forces while collecting revenues many times those of the López administration.[57]

In the sensitive area of political affairs, the Army generally played a restricted role. During the succession crisis of 1935, most officers had ignored inducements to join one political faction or another, and had remained loyal to their commander. In recognition of the officer corps's stability in a chaotic time, Colonel Medina, in his first report as Minister of War, commended the Army in its role during the change in regimes and in the disturbances that followed.[58] Indeed, a serious civil conflict might have erupted; many Army commanders who were relics from the early Gómez era had absorbed no professional training or spirit whatever. López Contreras deserves credit for keeping the armed forces united, even though that unity was probably due to their personal attachment to him. Nevertheless, the nonintervention of most

55. Venezuela, Ministerio de Guerra, *Memoria: 1937,* x.

56. *Inter-American Statistical Yearbook* (1942), 943. Whereas at the height of the Gómez dictatorship (1920), it was almost 20%; see Venezuela, Ministerio de Guerra, *Memoria: 1921.* A sampling of other American republics reveals that Argentina in 1938 devoted 19% of its total national budget to defense, Bolivia (1939) 30%, Chile (1938) 26%, Colombia (1939) 16%, Cuba (1939) 22%, Ecuador (1938) 14%, Mexico (1938) 17%, Peru (1938) 22%, and the United States (1938) 20%; *Inter-American Statistical Yearbook* (1940), 570–71.

57. In the five-year period 1958–1963, the percentage of the national budget allocated to the Ministry of Defense was, in order, 9.5, 8.8, 7.9, 9.3, and 10.3; Foreign Area Studies Division, Special Operations Research Office, The American University, *U.S. Army Area Handbook for Venezuela,* 543.

58. Venezuela, Ministerio de Guerra, *Memoria: 1936,* vii.

of the officers in the succession conflict gave rise to hopes that the military was forming new attitudes toward politics.

Once the new regime was installed, López Contreras and his Minister of War continually reiterated their determination to depersonalize the Army. To be truly professional, they explained, the Army had to serve the government out of duty and responsibility, not because of any personal attachment to the individual occupying the highest office; the Army was to stand aside from partisan politics and remain indifferent to the entreaties of interested parties who sought armed assistance for their particular causes.[59]

To what extent was this lofty ideal translated into action? Generally speaking, the Army left political activity to its commander in chief and his civilian collaborators. Furthermore, it did not overtly resist the trend toward civilianizing the regime.[60] López himself set an example by exchanging his elaborate general's uniform for a business suit, which he wore to all but military functions and ceremonial occasions. That seemingly insignificant but deliberate act was considered a symbol of the demilitarization of Venezuelan government. López was trying to show that he was constitutional president through election by Congress and not by virtue of his command of the instrument of force.[61]

López Contreras also began the delicate task of easing military men out of civilian posts. Although forced to move with caution, by the end of his term he had made substantial progress. Of his initial appointments of state presidents, governors of the two federal territories, and governor of the Federal District, nineteen of twenty-three were military officers. At the close of his term only four were military men.[62] Appointments to less important but more numerous offices followed this same pattern.

López' policies were not unchallenged. Resistance soon came from intransigent elements in the Army who felt that the new president was moving too fast, too soon in the transition to democratic, civilian-oriented government. For example, a secret meeting of officers was held in Valencia in

59. Medina Angarita, *Cuatro años,* 142–43.

60. See Rafael Caldera Rodríguez, "Ejército apolítico," *El Universal,* March 14, 1936.

61. Arturo Uslar Pietri, *Materiales par la construcción de Venezuela,* 60.

62. Blanco Peñalver, *López Contreras,* 120–25.

August, 1936, which resulted in a document known as the "Valencia Memorandum." It amounted to an ultimatum, warning the President that he could expect serious trouble from his officer colleagues unless he took a stronger stand against the leftist opposition.[63] Although it is difficult to document, López' mass expulsion of leftists the following year could well have been his response to this military memorandum.

On the other extreme, the United States chargé d'affaires in Caracas reported in early 1937 that he had heard that "Communist elements" had been in touch with Army officers—presumably junior officers—in an attempt to subvert them and that a number of garrisons were on the verge of revolt. But when he brought the matter to the attention of the Venezuelan Foreign Minister, he was informed that those civilian overtures had "in every instance been met with flat rejection and prompt reporting to superior officers."[64] Whatever the case, such attempts to encourage a military uprising failed.

Nevertheless, it is likely that contact with aggressive civilian groups added fuel to the fires of discontent that inflamed the young officers. There are several reasons for believing so. First, for both political and personal reasons, General López Contreras had left many ill-trained, semiliterate *Gomecista* caudillos in important commands. While he had encouraged advanced training and professional standards in the educational institutions and lower ranks, he had left the higher echelons largely in control of incompetents. True, there were some professionally oriented officers in the high command, including Minister of War Medina, but he and a handful of others were exceptions to the general rule. This imbalance in education and professional attitudes brought about an intensification of the generational conflict within the officer corps. The younger officers resented the President's stopping at half measures in the professionalization process.

Second, the same long-standing grievances remained unassuaged: low pay, slow advancement up the career ladder, and assignment to obscure posts and outlying garrisons. In regard to officer salaries, for example, General Medina

63. DFDS, 831.00/1659, Villard to Secretary of State, February 16, 1937.
64. *Ibid.*

urged that junior officers' salaries be raised, since they had not kept pace with the rising cost of living, but little was done to correct this inequity.[65]

Third, although not a major source of conflict within the barracks, the percentage of *Andinos* in the officer corps was almost the same at the end of López Contreras' term as at the beginning. It rankled many non-Andeans, both inside and outside the military, who felt that the Army should be more representative of the entire nation.[66]

Finally, junior officers became infused with an *esprit de corps* during the 1936–1941 period. They now tended to think and act in unison, as members of a noble profession and a prestigious institution, rather than following blindly General Fulano or Colonel Zutano. This new spirit was based not only on common resentment of the military establishment, but also on a sense of pride in superior training and ability. Corporate pride, however, led to an unexpected, but critical, new development. Whereas in the past military caudillos most often rebelled individually, with little planning or coordination, the younger officers—majors, captains, lieutenants —would in the future engage in insurgent activity as a group.[67] Although López Contreras forestalled any overt manifestation of insurgency among the junior officers, such a movement was to prove the downfall of General Medina when he succeeded to the presidency.

In an effort to demonstrate that he did not have continuist inclinations, López Contreras reduced the presidential term to five years, with no immediate re-election. Consequently, as the year 1941 approached, the presidential succession became a matter of immediate concern for the President. The leftist opposition urged the election of the president and Congress by the direct vote of the people. López and the conservative Congress refused, however, to change the system of indirect elections by which the Congress elected the president, and the state legislatures elected the congressmen. As 1941 drew near, López made no effort to change the electoral process, in the belief that the masses were not yet ready to participate in the direct election of the chief executive. Since the government had a substantial majority in Congress,

65. Venezuela, Ministerio de Guerra, *Memoria: 1937*, xi.
66. Luzardo, *Notas*, 108.
67. Suárez, *López Contreras*, 74–75. Based also on an interview, Caracas, May, 1965.

the person López Contreras nominated as his successor was certain to be elected.

The man he eventually chose, Minister of War Medina, was not the only candidate he considered. In a series of conferences that he arranged to hear suggestions, the names of high military officials such as Antonio Chalbaud Cardona and Juan de Dios Celis Paredes—both generals—were put forward. Among the civilian candidates mentioned were at least four present or former Cabinet members.[68] After long consultations, from the number of men suggested the President decided on Medina. Undoubtedly there was strong pressure from the armed forces for López Contreras to pick a military man—an *Andino* besides—but this notion is difficult to document. Rodolfo Luzardo claims that the choice of Medina was urged on López by, among others, a group of high-ranking Táchira Army officers, led by the powerful old *Gomecista*, Gen. León Jurado.[69] No matter how the decision was reached, from early March, 1941, Medina was presented as the "official" candidate, and the government rallied support for him throughout the country.

As the time of the election (April 28) drew near, López Contreras, well aware that his candidate was assured of victory, permitted a token opposition movement to campaign relatively unhampered. The candidate of the liberals was Rómulo Gallegos, Venezuela's leading novelist, who had served briefly as Minister of Education in the early days of the López Contreras administration. More the artist than the politician, Gallegos felt uncomfortable in the political arena, but he consented to run in order to spread the opposition's message throughout the country. The two key issues raised by Gallegos and his backers were the need for direct suffrage and the systematic refusal of the government to legalize the parties of the opposition.[70]

Many civilians were dissatisfied with the choice of another general to be the nation's leader, and they reacted against what they called *continuismo militar*.[71] This complaint was countered by the regime's defenders, who replied that Me-

68. Blanco Peñalver, *López Contreras*, 52–53.
69. Luzardo, *Notas*, 92.
70. "La izquierda democrática nacional habla sobre el momento político," *El Universal*, April 25, 1941.
71. DFDS, 831.00/1755, Corrigan to Secretary of State, April 18, 1941.

dina would continue in the "civilista" tradition of General López; Medina, they said, was a man with strong convictions of
civilian supremacy. Others with a more sociological bent
claimed that Venezuela still lacked the generalized civilian-
oriented culture necessary to enter an exclusively civilian
stage of political development.[72] On the other hand, stated
one writer, the best example of "civilismo" in recent years
had been General López Contreras himself, a professional
soldier. He contrasted the President's principled leadership
with "that egocentric and divisive civilism" of the leaders on
the left and with the "bourgeois and conservative civilism" of
the spokesmen for the right.[73] In a declaration published
about the same time, a group of thirteen well-known intellectuals publicly attested to their confidence that Medina would
respect civilian institutions because the armed forces and
General López Contreras—the key backers of Medina—had
been the "most self-denying forgers" of the civilian pattern
of government then evolving.[74]

A further charge the supporters of Medina had to counter
was that of *continuismo andino.* Nothing they said could
alter the fact that one more *Andino* general—the fourth in
succession—was virtually assured of election to the presidency. In making his final decision, López probably decided
that Venezuela still needed a military man who had the
support of the armed forces but who also espoused constitutional and democratic principles. That he was in effect preserving the *Andino* monopoly of the presidential office for
another five years did not seriously disturb him or his successor.

Medina was, to be accurate, half-*Andino;* his mother was
from Táchira, but his father was a native of the coastal state
of Falcón. Furthermore, he had spent little time in Táchira
and in temperament was more like a *Caraqueño* than a
Tachiran. His supporters tried to downgrade the regionalist
question with their attitude that it was a dead issue and that

72. Santiago Hernández Yepes, "El General Medina, candidato
lógico," *El Centinela* (San Cristóbal), April 1, 1941. See also Rafael
Pinzón, "Militares de academia," *El Universal,* April 7, 1941, and
Horacio Blanco Fombona, "El primer problema del futuro presidente," *El Universal,* April 23, 1941.

73. J. Penzini Hernández, "Demagogia y caudillismo," *El Universal,* April 2, 1941.

74. *El Universal,* April 8, 1941.

it should be ignored in the campaign. Most Venezuelans now felt, declared one confident writer in support of Medina, that "Venezuela does not end where the Andes begin."[75]

On April 19, the last day of his regular term of office (he was named provisional President for the period between April 19 and Medina's inauguration on May 5), President López Contreras presented his closing message to Congress. After reviewing the accomplishments of his regime, he remarked that the time was almost ripe for "the culmination of democratic practices." He expressed confidence that the day was not far distant when a broader democracy could be established, including the direct popular election of the president.[76] Later that day he held a reception in his residence, which was attended by the two presidential candidates. In a gesture of good will and equalitarianism that impressed all but the cynics, he embraced both Medina and Gallegos, accompanying the *abrazo* with a "Viva Venezuela" for each.[77]

The results of the election were, of course, predictable except for the precise distribution of votes. Medina was the winner with 120 votes; Gallegos was a distant second with 13.[78]

The constitutional President for the 1941–1946 term was born in San Cristóbal, July 6, 1897, the son of Gen. José Rosendo Medina and Alejandrina Angarita. He took his primary schooling first in Táchira and later in Caracas. At the age of fourteen he entered the recently opened Military Academy in Caracas, from which he graduated in 1914. He filled a variety of military posts, including instructorships at the Academy. By the early 1930s Medina had advanced to high posts in the General Staff and the Ministry of Defense, and he was appointed chief of staff soon after López Contreras became acting president. A few months later he was appointed Minister of War, a post he held throughout the López Contreras regime. He was promoted to the rank of brigadier general in 1940. In March, 1941, he resigned as Minister

75. Heriberto Ramírez, "Candidaturas o en la lonja de la política," *El Universal,* April 16, 1941.

76. *El Universal,* April 20, 1941.

77. Andrés Eloy Blanco, "La trompada de 'La Quebradita'," *El Universal,* April 26, 1941.

78. *El Universal,* April 29, 1941.

of War upon accepting the presidential candidacy.[79]

Isaías Medina Angarita was one of the most atypical presidents in Venezuelan history. He was an intelligent, cultured, and humane individual, possessed of a captivating charm and an ingratiating personality. Unfortunately, he lacked the seriousness of purpose and the firmness in handling political and state affairs that the times required. Although a better administrator than his predecessor and surrounded by capable subordinates, he did not have the fighting instincts of López Contreras; surprisingly, he paid scant attention to political and security problems—an unusual weakness among Venezuelan rulers. That weakness, combined with an excessive fondness for alcohol, contributed to his downfall.[80]

General Medina was a sincere believer in the free expression of political opinion. In fact, many present-day Venezuelans consider the Medina regime the most democratic in the republic's history. During his entire foreshortened regime, there was not a single political prisoner nor a single exile, a statement no other Venezuelan administration, before or since, has been able to make. Immediately after his inauguration he restored most opposition parties to full legality, and by the end of his term all political organizations, including the Communist party of Venezuela, were operating freely. Neither was there any form of censorship. Virulent attacks on both the person of the President and the regime in general, which intensified toward the close of his term, drew no reprisals whatever.

Medina also gave added impulse to administrative modernization and social reform. He did this at a difficult time. The world was at war, and Venezuela felt sharply the economic effects of the conflict. Because of a transportation

79. *El Universal,* April 29, 1941.

80. In a personal interview in Caracas, March 29, 1965, General López Contreras told the author that he considered Medina to have been an excellent president, over all. He also agreed with those who said that Medina's regime was more democratic and progressive than his own. But he claimed that it was his administration—a self-admitted transitional government—that had paved the way for his successor's more liberal regime. According to the former President, Isaías Medina's major weakness was his lack of political toughness. He took political and security affairs too lightly and was unable or unwilling to come down with an iron hand when necessary. On the contrary, he felt that he had lasted out his own difficult term because he knew when to be severe with his adversaries.

squeeze and economic disadjustments abroad, all commodities from food to construction materials were in short supply. Worse, government revenues fell off substantially because of a severe cut in petroleum exports.[81] Nevertheless, the Medina administration accomplished much in the four and one-half years of its duration. Among its achievements were: the introduction of reforms in the fields of education, industry, and finance; modernization of labor legislation; passage of an obligatory social security act; institution of tax reforms, including Venezuela's first progressive income tax; expediting of public works programs, notably a major reconstruction project in the downtown Caracas area of El Silencio. In September, 1945, the Congress passed the Agrarian Reform Law that, since it was passed only a month before the October coup, was never implemented.[82] Most important of all was the Petroleum Reform Law of 1943. Under López Contreras, timid attempts at reform had been advanced, but when Medina came to the presidency, the companies were still enjoying the benefits of antiquated laws that dated from the earliest period of large-scale exploitation. The Medina law updated and rationalized the existing maze of legislation and introduced reforms designed to bring the government's share of the profits up to approximately 50 per cent.[83] Although the latter objective was not attained under Medina, due to a lack of aggressive implementation, the measure still forms the basis of all petroleum legislation and policy today.

President Medina's military policy followed the same general lines set down by López Contreras. In his effort to instill in the officer ranks a professional aloofness toward politics, he repeatedly told military personnel that the Army had only two proper functions—the defense of the nation's sovereignty and the maintenance of public order.[84] In all civil matters it was to maintain a posture of complete political neutrality.

81. Uslar Pietri, *Materiales*, 41.

82. Left-wing politician and economist Domingo Alberto Rangel claims the Medina law was more progressive than the one passed by the Acción Democrática government three years later. There is little other support for this position, however. See his *Los andinos en el poder*, 321.

83. For a detailed discussion of the 1943 Petroleum Reform, see Lieuwen, *Petroleum in Venezuela*, 95–97.

84. Medina Angarita, *Cuatro años*, 143.

Under Medina there was continued progress in military education. The Naval Academy in Maiquetía was completed, and plans were laid for a new and better location for the expanding Military Academy. More officers than at any previous time went abroad for advanced training in specialized fields. The officers received a number of fringe benefits, including pension and social assistance funds, and they were now able to borrow money at low interest and on favorable terms. The junior officers' salaries rose slightly, although living costs during the war years kept pace with them. A more important step was the setting, for the first time, of a maximum retirement age, designed to prevent an accumulation of superannuated officers in the senior ranks while lending impetus to a faster promotion rate.[85] Finally, to the powerful Ministry of War post, President Medina successively appointed two capable career officers, Col. Carlos Meyer and Gen. Manuel Morán, neither of whom was an *Andino*.[86]

Despite substantial progress in both the civilian and military spheres, pressures that Medina was unable to control were building up in both sectors. Six months before his presidential term was to end, it was abruptly terminated by a coalition of civilian and military forces that turned Venezuela from its gradual evolutionary course toward bourgeois democracy. Social revolution became the rallying cry of the new national leaders, but it led in the process to the most familiar of all Venezuelan political solutions—military dictatorship.

85. Medina Angarita, *Cuatro años,* 145–47.
86. Medina Angarita, *Cuatro años,* 151.

CHAPTER III

THE OCTOBER 18 REBELLION

On the evening of July 6, 1945, while President Isaías Medina Angarita watched a Gary Cooper–Ingrid Bergman movie at a local theater, restless young civilians and Army officers gathered elsewhere in Caracas to plot his overthrow.[1] The civilians were leaders of a populist political party, Acción Democrática (AD). The young officers were members of a conspiratorial junior officer lodge, the Unión Patriótica Militar (UPM)—the Patriotic Military Union,[2] and it was they who proposed revolution to AD at the clandestine rendezvous. The political crisis had deepened during the Medina regime, a three-cornered struggle for the presidential succession had developed, and reform-minded officers and civilians came together to form a successful conspiratorial alliance through a unifying process. The rebellion of October 18 was a natural—almost inevitable—result of the dissatisfactions of the reformists.

The struggle between the uniformed bureaucrats and the Academy group came to a head during Medina's term of office. The President's achievements toward professionalizing the Army had succeeded only in widening the gap between the generations. The new President's official acts fell far short of the junior officers' expectations. He made little effort to remove the most incompetent and corrupt members of the military hierarchy, and the reforms he introduced were not drastic enough to satisfy the frustrated young lieutenants and captains.[3] They were still serving in what they regarded

---

1. Alfredo Tarre Murzi, "El golpe del 18 de octubre," *El Nacional* (Caracas), October 18, 1965. This chapter appeared in altered form as an article, "The Military Origins of Venezuela's 1945 Revolution," in *Caribbean Studies,* 11 (October 1971), 35–54.

2. Some sources use an alternate form: Unión Militar Patriótica (UMP).

3. Ana Mercedes Pérez, *La verdad inédita: historia de la revolución de octubre,* 44–45, 122, 169. This book consists largely of interviews with the UPM leaders.

as the *burocracia armada* that López Contreras had inherited from Gómez years previously.[4]

It should be noted at the outset, however, that military disaffection was not confined to the young officers. Many senior Army officers were also pulling away from the President because of his deviation from López Contreras' more conservative policies. Although alike in regional and professional background, López Contreras and Medina had little else in common. Some accounts state that the split between them erupted only after Medina became President,[5] but temperamentally and philosophically the two generals had always been dissimilar.[6] Since he was not López Contreras' automatic choice as successor, Medina, after assuming the presidency, drew away from his predecessor and rarely sought his advice.

Their unexpressed opposition broke out into the open as the negotiations to decide on Medina's successor for the 1946–1951 term commenced. López Contreras most likely desired the "official" nomination, while Medina preferred to select someone more loyal to him and more in agreement with his own political philosophy. The former President, on his part, became more and more disillusioned with "the policies of the regime."[7] By June of 1945 López Contreras was so distraught over the liberal direction in which the Medina administration was heading that he threatened to break all ties with his successor and publish a manifesto highly critical of the President. The latter in turn had become provoked with López Contreras' political activities, but through the good offices of a mutual friend, they reluctantly met to resolve their differences and discuss the candidacy question. However, they were unable to reach a satisfactory agreement, and no further talks were held.[8]

Medina privately insisted that López Contreras not be the official candidate because, in his opinion, the General's return to power would have been disastrous for both of them. The former President would appear to have an insatiable appetite for power, while Medina would be cast in the role of

4. Domingo Alberto Rangel, *La revolución de las fantasías,* 51.

5. Rodolfo Luzardo, *Notas histórico-económicas: 1928–1963,* 89–90.

6. Interview, May, 1965.

7. Julio Diez, *Historia y política,* 11.

8. Diez, *Historia,* 11–13.

López Contreras' tool for return to the presidency. It was common knowledge that the two generals had gone their separate ways politically for several years. Such a maneuver, Medina argued, would expose them as "the two biggest actors in Venezuelan history."[9] Meanwhile, López Contreras, suspecting that he had no chance of winning Medina's endorsement, became more receptive to overtures by the conservatives. The forces of the right organized themselves into a front called Agrupaciones Pro-Candidatura Presidencial de López Contreras—Group for the Presidential Candidacy of López Contreras. Their mouthpiece, the Caracas morning daily newspaper *Ahora,* denounced Medina and his administration in bitter terms, at times referring to the President as a "fascist" and to his regime as "totalitarian."

The conservative reaction to Medina in the civilian sector had its counterpart in the military institution. Conservative officers were in sharp disagreement with Medina's progressive policies and his flirtation with the local Communist party.[10] From their point of view he was neglecting a Venezuelan chief executive's traditional base of support and, indeed, power—the Army—and this they strongly resented.

From the President's viewpoint, however, his loss of support from the traditionalist López Contreras faction necessitated broadening his own political base. He thus created a new party, the Partido Democrático Venezolano (PDV) —Venezuelan Democratic Party, and formed an alliance with the Communists.[11] His growing reliance on civilian support was further demonstrated when he selected as his principal political adviser Arturo Uslar Pietri, whose liberal ideas, friendships with leftists, and antimilitary and anti-*Andino* posture were not calculated to win friends in the barracks.[12] One can reasonably conclude that junior officers,

9. Diez, *Historia,* 13.
10. DFDS, 831.00/1864, Corrigan to Secretary of State, August 20, 1943; 831.00/6-2644, Corrigan to Secretary of State, June 26, 1944; 831.00/10-1844, Corrigan to Secretary of State, October 18, 1944.
11. DFDS, 831.00/1864, Corrigan to Secretary of State, August 20, 1943.
12. Laureano Vallenilla Lanz, *hijo, Escrito de memoria,* 198, and *New York Times,* May 6, 1943. See also DFDS, 831.00/1768, Corrigan to Secretary of State, June 11, 1941; 831.00/11-444, Corrigan to Secretary of State, November 4, 1944; 831.00/12-1544, Corrigan to Secretary of State, December 18, 1944.

desperate for more attention to be given to modernizing the military institution and to their own career problems, looked askance, like their conservative seniors, at Medina's civilian maneuvering. The irony for Medina, of course, is that while he thought the greatest threat to his administration was from the old Army, the attack came from the new.

One of the few members of the 1945 generation to have written about the movement, former National Guard Commandant Oscar Tamayo Suárez, states that General Medina was unable to keep the development of the armed forces in step with the over-all development of the country. The armed forces "cannot remain static while the country advances." Tamayo adds that the "President had practically severed his connection with the Armed Forces. . . . He attempted to relegate the Armed Institution to the function of a simple praetorian guard."[13] This, naturally, was not in line with the junior officers' more grandiose image of the role of the Army in a world at war. Tamayo asserts further that General Medina, by neglecting his military colleagues, forgot the history of his country, in which the military had always served a "directive function."[14] The officer corps refused to have their institution relegated to a secondary status.

Furthermore, the perennial problems of low pay and slow promotion rate, instead of being alleviated under Medina, were exacerbated. Second lieutenants received less pay than the average skilled laborer.[15] The situation, according to the disgruntled young officers, became intolerable when senior officers were exposed in the misuse of public funds and large-scale graft. Their flamboyant style of living contrasted sharply with the modest, sometimes penurious, living standard of the junior officers.

Venezuela's young officers chose the road of revolution not only because of their grievances with a system they regarded as anachronistic, but also because of a complex set of external influences. The young men who went abroad for advanced training returned home filled with zeal to change their country's existing order. For example, the high stan-

13. Oscar Tamayo Suárez, *De frente a la realidad venezolana,* 38.

14. Tamayo Suárez, *De frente,* 38.

15. Speech by Rómulo Betancourt, October 30, 1945, in *El Universal,* October 31, 1945, and Tarre Murzi, "El golpe del 18 de octubre," *El Nacional,* October 18, 1965.

dards of military training offered in the United States seem to have made a telling impact on them. The visitors were impressed by the powerful war machine that the United States had developed so rapidly. Moreover, it is possible that some Venezuelans were inspired by the democratic system with which they had been in contact and hoped to install a similar system of universal suffrage and direct elections in their own country.[16]

A more direct influence on the public thinking of Venezuelan junior officers came from Peru. At the outbreak of World War II, the Italian military mission to Venezuela was withdrawn; a Peruvian mission replaced it. Under Peruvian supervision, the Army underwent a program of reorganization. New battalions were created, and some of the organizers of the 1945 movement were attached to those crack new units.[17] At about the same time, the government instituted a program to send outstanding graduates of the Caracas Military School to Peru for advanced instruction. A number of these men took command and staff courses at the Superior War College of Chorrillos, one of the more prestigious military academies in Latin America. Among its Venezuelan graduates were Marcos Pérez Jiménez and Martín Márquez Añez, two of the principal organizers of the 1945 *coup d'état.*

After its disastrous defeat in the War of the Pacific, Peru had begun a long, painful rebuilding program in the military sector that, by the early 1940s, had achieved a high degree of success. When Venezuelan officers witnessed what the Peruvians had accomplished in building a technically proficient and professionally oriented military institution (at least by Latin American standards), they were motivated to equal or surpass them.[18] With the sophisticated training in military administration and general staff organization they had received at Chorrillos, these bright young officers judged themselves equipped to assume direction of the task.

Pointing to the subsequent careers of Pérez Jiménez and his associates, however, some antimilitarists have implied

16. Interview, Caracas, May, 1965: U.S.-style democracy possibly had an influence on some North American-trained Venezuelan officers, but the influence should not be exaggerated.

17. Interview, Caracas, July, 1965. See Pérez, *La verdad,* 196, and Vallenilla Lanz, *Escrito,* 229.

18. Interview, Caracas, May, 1965.

that their sojourn in Peru marked the resurgence of militaristic and authoritarian tendencies within the Venezuelan Army. Venezuelan officers who studied in the Peruvian military schools contemporaneously with Pérez Jiménez have denied the charge and have characterized their ambitions as strictly professional. Márquez Añez, for example, went through the same study program with Pérez Jiménez and yet, years later, was a political prisoner for having the audacity to criticize the dictator for the corrupt and repressive nature of his regime.[19]

Partly because of the timing of their coup, the military conspirators of 1945 have also been linked with *Peronismo.* But the 1945 group stresses that, aside from perhaps indirectly borrowing the idea for the *logia militar,* Argentine ideological influence was slight at the time of the October 18 movement. Many Venezuelan officers later came to regard the Peronist experiment as ludicrous, especially after it appeared that Eva Duarte de Perón, a woman, was becoming as powerful as Colonel Perón.[20]

World War II undoubtedly had its effect on the thinking of the junior officers. After reading daily reports from the war zones and coming into contact with participants, the *juventud militar* was eager to flex its muscles and put theory into practice. This is not to say that the craving for combat experience was of primary importance among the motivating factors for the revolution. Rather, it may have given the conspirators one additional reason to move in strength against the government.

The immediate origins of the UPM can be traced to mid-1942, when a sizable contingent of young officers in the Caracas garrison began quietly to communicate their grievances and aspirations. Shortly afterward, they were joined by Francisco Gutiérrez and Márquez Añez, both lieutenants, and Pérez Jiménez, a captain, the latter two of whom had just returned from Peru. Their arrival from Chorrillos gave strong impetus to the incipient movement. A superb organizer, Pérez Jiménez quickly rose to prominence in the conspiratorial group. About the same time, the popular Capt. Mario Ricardo Vargas joined the cabal, along with his brother,

---

19. Based on interviews, Caracas, in May of 1965.
20. Interviews, May, 1965.

Maj. Julio César, who had also been at Chorrillos.[21] Others were added continuously; by the end of 1944 there were conspiratorial cells in most Caracas barracks, the strategic Maracay garrison, the aviation branch of the Army, and the Military School.

The junior officers' secret lodge, the Unión Patriótica Militar (UPM)—the Patriotic Military Union, was founded in mid-1945, only months before the *coup d'état*. According to Captain Vargas, in the early days of 1945 he, along with Captain Pérez Jiménez and Lieutenants Edito J. Ramírez and Márquez Añez, met to set up the organizational machinery for the movement.[22] At the same time another small group of captains and lieutenants was devoting itself to the same objective independently.[23] It was simply a matter of joining forces and settling on an effective form of union.

In planning the group, the UPM members were most directly influenced by the type of military lodge that had been influential within the Argentine military establishment since the 1920s. The secret lodge concept had filtered from the Platine region into the Andean area, including Peru. Because it was to Peru that Venezuelan officers went for advanced training in the early 1940s, it was from there that the *logia militar* idea was brought into Venezuela.[24]

It is also possible that the volume of memoirs of the Chilean general, Carlos Sáez Morales, *Recuerdos de un soldado: el ejército y la política* (1933), which describes the Chilean military movements of 1924–1925, was influential in the organizing of the Venezuelan secret lodge. Ana Mercedes Pérez quotes Capt. Carlos Morales (no relation to Sáez Morales) as telling her, "It is a great book which gave wings to our enthusiasm! Upon reading it and observing the country's situation we asked ourselves: 'How is it possible that we do not do something similar?' "[25] Morales recalled that the official oath and the structural division into cells were derived from Sáez Morales' memoirs. It should be added, however,

21. Pérez, *La verdad*, 35.

22. Pérez, *La verdad*, 197. Substantially the same version appears in "La revolución de octubre en Caracas," *Revista de las Fuerzas Armadas* (Caracas; October, 1946), but the date given is late 1944.

23. Pérez, *La verdad*, 124.

24. Interview, Caracas, March, 1965.

25. Pérez, *La verdad*, 33.

that this is the only mention of this book as a catalyst for the Venezuelan junior officers' conspiracy.

The UPM was run by the Central Committee, operating from Caracas. It was composed of Majors Pérez Jiménez (recently promoted), Julio César Vargas, Capt. Mario Vargas, and Lieutenants Francisco Gutiérrez and Horacio López Conde.[26] In September the UPM gained the adherence of Maj. Carlos Delgado Chalbaud, a brilliant French-trained officer, who was academic director of the Military School. The Central Committee organized a subcommittee in the Maracay military compound and formed similar groups in other Army installations and in the Navy. All had liaison agents who reported to the Central Committee in Caracas. By mid-October committees had been formed in all major installations throughout the country.[27]

The Constitutive Act and statements by its leaders yield a general idea of the UPM's public objectives. Theirs was to be a movement of political and military renovation; the prevailing institutions and methods of government needed to be completely overhauled. Their movement would terminate forever incompetence, peculation, and bad faith within the government and would replace them with ability, honesty, and justice as the ruling norms of the future. They sought to establish a democratic government based on the universal and direct vote of the Venezuelan citizenry and constitutional reform produced through the expression of the national will. They would support all political and administrative measures that contributed to national progress. They made clear that they were defending neither personal nor class interests but, on the contrary, had only the nation's interests at heart. The leaders did not design the movement to bring the armed forces to power but conceived it as a mere instrument to bring into being a new government comprised of patriotic, able, and honest men who were backed by popular opinion.

Military reforms were to occur simultaneously with political regeneration. The creation of a truly professional army was part of the plan and, to make certain the new army developed properly, it was to have material, moral, technical, and economic resources adequate for its professional objec-

26. Pérez, *La verdad,* 124.
27. See Pérez, *La verdad,* 190.

tives.[28] This lofty *pronunciamiento* should be read, of course, in the knowledge of the junior officers' personal grievances, economic tribulations, susceptibility to outside currents of opinion, the Army's traditional political activism, and the subsequent behavior of its leaders, particularly Marcos Pérez Jiménez.

Once organized, the UPM needed to decide a basic question: Should the group move against the government independently of others or, as their forerunners had done in 1928, enter into an alliance with civilians? Since the purpose of the UPM ran directly counter to a unilateral military take-over, and since the members thought it imperative to enlist popular support, they decided quickly that they would attempt to bring civilians into the movement. But with which elements in the civilian sector should they make contact? Of the four major political factions—Agrupaciones Pro-Candidatura de López Contreras; Partido Democrático Venezolano; Acción Democrática; and Partido Comunista de Venezuela (PCV) —the Communist Party of Venezuela—the first two were automatically ruled out because they represented the very elements the UPM was opposing—*Lopecismo* and *Medinismo*. The Communists were also rejected quickly for obvious ideological incompatibility and for their support of the administration. AD, by a process of elimination, was the only party with which the UPM could conceivably work.[29]

AD, an offshoot of the old PDN, had been organized officially in the early days of the Medina administration, and by 1945 the party's secretary-general, Rómulo Betancourt, was already recognized as one of the shrewdest and most aggressive politicians in the country. He and other party ideologists developed a loosely organized political philosophy that combined elements of democratic liberalism, *Aprismo,* and Marxism.[30] Within a few years AD had spread throughout Venezuela, its principal strength drawn from the previously uninvolved peasantry, organized labor in the cities and oil fields, and urban professionals.

The UPM leaders thus attempted to forge a conspiratorial

28. This summary is based mainly on the Constitutive Act of the UPM (Pérez, *La verdad,* 194), and the five points presented by Pérez Jiménez at the initial meeting with AD leaders (*ibid.,* 137–38).

29. Pérez, *La verdad,* 195–96.

30. See John D. Martz, *Acción Democrática: Evolution of a Modern Political Party in Venezuela,* 120–25.

alliance with AD. One of the lodge's founders, aviation Lt. Horacio López Conde, was a relative of a Caracas physician, Dr. Edmundo Fernández, who was a friend of Rómulo Betancourt. López Conde was to ask Fernández to arrange an interview with the AD leader. Fernández, an AD-leaning independent, agreed to speak to Betancourt.[31]

According to Fernández' account, his friend was momentarily stunned by the news of a well-advanced military conspiracy and was extremely skeptical about bringing AD into it. Betancourt told him that "at the bottom of all military movements some fascist intention was hidden and that his Party . . . would be used as an easy instrument to hide the antidemocratic ideas of a Government controlled by bayonets."[32] Fernández persuaded him to attend an exploratory meeting, although the party secretary insisted that such action should in no way obligate him or his party. The AD executive committee also agreed to the meeting with the same reservation. Betancourt and Raúl Leoni were to represent the party.[33]

Five officers attended the July 6, 1945, meeting as liaison agents for the UPM: Major Pérez Jiménez, Captain Morales, and Lieutenants López Conde, Márquez Añez, and Gutiérrez. The senior officer present, Pérez Jiménez, acted as spokesman for the military faction. After propounding the grievances of his group, he told the AD agents that the rebellious officers did not seek political power but would serve as the necessary instrument to bring about the new order, which would be characterized by civilian, constitutional rule and the adherence of the officer corps to strictly military functions. Pérez Jiménez made clear that the UPM was committed to putting into effect its plans to overthrow the Medina regime, and he invited AD to join in their efforts.[34] Secretary-General Betancourt was not authorized to make a final decision then, but he is reported to have said: "I have seen that you are sincere; I will speak with the National Executive Committee of my Party. I congratulate you; I never thought I would find men in the Army who nourished those ideals."[35]

31. Pérez, *La verdad*, 88.
32. *Ibid.*
33. Rómulo Betancourt, *Venezuela: política y petroleo*, 223–24.
34. His five points are set forth in Pérez, *La verdad*, 37–38, and Tamayo Suárez, *De frente*, 42.
35. Pérez, *La verdad*, 38.

A member of the AD national executive committee, Gonzalo Barrios, also reported that Betancourt and Leoni returned with a very favorable impression of the military representatives. In fact, he stated, "[This meeting] revealed to us to what degree the Nation was possessed with a great moral reserve among the young professionals in the Armed Forces."[36]

In party councils following the secret meeting, AD chiefs debated whether to join the cabal. The party professed strong opposition to political meddling by the military, and its leaders were reluctant to lend their support to such a movement. Barrios, for example, suggested that "a cycle of adventurism and of low ambitions might be unleashed and terminate . . . in a military dictatorship."[37] Nevertheless, AD leaders were impressed by the apparent idealism, sincerity, and democratic inclinations of the young officers and agreed to continue negotiations with them. They were reasonably confident that, once power had been achieved, the military would retreat to the barracks and devote themselves to their proper military responsibilities.[38]

More important, probably, the series of clandestine meetings impressed upon AD representatives UPM's intention to go through with the revolt "with or without" the collaboration of the party.[39] They knew that over a hundred officers were implicated, among them some of the best-educated and most capable in the armed forces.[40] The executive committee thus agreed, in the event of a political impasse, to throw in their lot with the UPM.

While negotiations between AD and UPM progressed, search for a peaceful solution to the political crisis had by no means been abandoned. The question of who was to succeed General Medina became the most hotly debated political question of 1945. Discussion centered on a select group of military and civilian figures: General López Contreras and another nonactive general, Juan de Dios Celis Paredes, a former Minister of War and Federal District governor, who was currently Minister of Communications; among the civilians, Secretary of the Presidency Arturo Uslar Pietri, a weal-

36. Pérez, *La verdad*, 77.
37. *Ibid.*
38. Betancourt, *Venezuela*, 225–26, and Pérez, *La verdad*, 76–77.
39. Betancourt, *Venezuela*, 226.
40. *Ibid.*

thy young writer and former Cabinet officer; Rómulo Gallegos, the token liberal front candidate in 1941; and Caracciolo
Parra Pérez, a noted historian and public servant.[41]

The most prominent potential candidate, the personal
choice of President Medina, was Ambassador to the United
States Diógenes Escalante. A Tachiran by birth, Escalante
was respected throughout the country as a liberal statesman.
Possibly as early as December 1944 Medina had approached
Escalante about his receptivity to becoming the "official"
nominee, but the diplomat requested several months' delay to
mull over his decision.[42] Medina agreed, but as the *Lopecistas* stepped up their campaign on behalf of the former President, Medina pressed Escalante into making an early decision in order to have time to maneuver, in the event his reply
was negative. Citing his health as reason, the Ambassador
declined the nomination, and Medina, discouraged, resumed
his talks with friends and subordinates. The same names
cropped up again and again: López Contreras, Celis Paredes,
Uslar Pietri, Parra Pérez. One new name, however, appeared
on the list: Angel Biaggini, a relatively obscure Táchira
attorney currently serving as Minister of Agriculture.[43]

Minister of Labor Julio Diez, upon learning that Biaggini
was under serious consideration, told Medina that it was
time he undertook three measures that would win him the
gratitude of the Venezuelan people; one was to put forward a
civilian candidate. It was time, said Diez, that the government be civilianized at the highest level. This counsel raised
no obstacle against Biaggini's eligibility, of course, but Diez'
second recommendation did: to select a non-*Andino* as president. Diez, a non-*Andino* himself, denied that he was
expressing regional prejudice; on the contrary, he was trying
to counteract the rise of anti-*Andinismo*. Diez also suggested
that Medina's proposed electoral reform should include provision for direct election of the president for the next term.
According to the Minister of Labor, Medina agreed with this
suggestion; he had, he said, discussed the reform with Tachiran army officers.[44]

Meanwhile, Medina and officials high in the administra-

41. Federico Landaeta, *Nueve lustros y cuatro generales:
1899–1944*, 79–87, and Diez, *Historia*, 9.
42. Diez, *Historia*, 8.
43. Diez, *Historia*, 9.
44. Diez, *Historia*, 10–11.

tion urged Escalante to reconsider his decision against nomination, realizing that he was the one man among those under consideration who was respected by Acción Democrática. The Ambassador reluctantly agreed to accept the PDV candidacy.[45] The administration was confident that he would become a national unity candidate, backed by right, center, and left, and the country could thus avoid what promised to be an extraordinarily bitter election campaign. AD was favorably disposed to Escalante's candidacy and to the idea of a united front, if the party could be assured that the unity candidate would sponsor broad electoral reform. With that purpose in mind, two AD leaders, Rómulo Betancourt and Raúl Leoni, hurried to Washington to consult with the Ambassador. They returned with the conviction that Escalante's liberalism and advocacy of electoral reform were sincere.[46] After relaying their Washington conversations to other AD officials, the party agreed to back Escalante. In early August the Ambassador returned to Caracas to begin his campaign, but shortly thereafter he suffered a severe nervous collapse, which removed him permanently from public life.

Escalante's sudden withdrawal threw the presidential race into confusion. Hope for a united front vanished. Medina dejectedly resumed his consultations and, according to the President, his tabulation revealed Angel Biaggini to be the preference of his advisers.[47] Medina made his decision, and the PDV wasted little time in postulating the Tachiran lawyer as its official candidate. The party announced its candidate to the public on September 11.

There has been much speculation about Medina's reasons for choosing the little-known Biaggini as his successor. Some theorists suggest that Medina was psychologically incapable of accepting a non-*Andino* as president after a half-century of Andean rule. A more credible theory is that Medina was afraid that the powerful clique of Tachiran senior officers would look with extreme disfavor on the candidacy of a non-*Andino* and, hence, would react against Medina personally, perhaps to the extreme of military intervention.[48] The loss of

45. Diez, *Historia,* 13.
46. Betancourt, *Venezuela,* 227–29.
47. Isaías Medina Angarita, *Cuatro años de democracia,* 45, and Diez, *Historia,* 14.
48. Luzardo, *Notas,* 113.

the Army's support would have been fatal to his political future, and the youthful President probably had visions of returning to power in 1951. By selecting a nonmilitary *Andino,* Medina virtually assured himself of control over the armed forces during the next term. Moreover, an undynamic person like Biaggini in the presidency would have permitted Medina to remain dominant in shaping national policy. Finally—although this theory was immediately ridiculed by the regime's enemies—it may have been possible that Medina and PDV leaders felt Biaggini had certain statesmanlike qualities that would blossom forth when he became president.[49]

Whatever Medina's reasoning, the Biaggini candidacy met violent objections outside official circles. The *Lopecistas* refused to support him, and from September to the eve of the *coup d'état* the supporters of General López Contreras and Medina waged a verbal war in the press. The war intensified when Biaggini became the PDV's nominee on September 30 by winning 252 of the 259 votes cast in the party convention, the remaining votes going to López Contreras and Uslar Pietri.[50] The next day, *Ahora* termed the PDV convention a mere façade to cover up a decision made solely by Medina weeks before the convention.[51] *El Centinela* of San Cristóbal, Táchira, which backed López Contreras, declared that Biaggini's candidacy "defrauded the popular will" and was imposed by an "oligarchic clique" surrounding the President.[52] As the campaign progressed, words became sharper and their tone more ominous.

What further stirred the wrath of the conservatives in López Contreras' camp was Medina's acceptance of the Communists' support in the last stage of the campaign. The PCV had offered its support to the Administration, and, in return, on October 10 the party became a legal organization for the first time in its history. The *Lopecistas* immediately attacked the Medina-Communist alliance, with the assertion that the Communists had been totally insignificant as a political force in Venezuela until Medina became President.[53] In truth, the Communists had by this time lost control of labor to AD, and Medina was working with the PCV only for

49. See Medina Angarita, *Cuatro años,* 46.
50. *El Nacional,* October 1, 1945.
51. *Ahora* (Caracas), October 1, 1945.
52. *El Centinela,* October 3, 1945.
53. *Ahora,* October 17, 1945.

short-term strategic political reasons; ideologically, the PCV and the moderate PDV were far apart.

The *Pedevistas* launched an equally sharp counterattack against the elements that were coalescing behind López Contreras. They accused him of serving as front for all the reactionary interests in the country, including the oil companies and foreign capital. One newspaper article, for example, attacked the former President for failing to rise against the "ferocious dictatorship" of Juan Vicente Gómez when he was in the best position of anyone in Venezuela to do so. Once Gómez was out of the way, the article continued, López Contreras was clearly intent on maintaining the Gómez system, and changed his tactics only slightly when he realized it was impossible to reimpose the Gómez methods.[54]

Minister of Labor Diez, a firm *Medinista* but an admirer of López, lamented the widening rift between the two factions. He felt that in the early Medina period the forces backing the two rival generals had been fairly united and in a strong position to resist the challenge from the left posed by AD. The ultimate effect of the conservative–moderate split was to benefit AD.[55] The partisans of López Contreras created an atmosphere so hostile to the Medina regime that it, in effect, prepared the public psychologically for revolution. López Contreras admitted that he had been offered armed support to overthrow the regime, but he had refused it on constitutional grounds.[56] Nonetheless, the charge that General López Contreras was preparing to return to power through armed revolt was taken up by AD and other opposition groups.[57] When the revolution erupted on October 18, most *Caraqueños* assumed that the tough old ex-President was at its head. Diez denied that López Contreras was responsible for the revolt, and there is little to indicate that he had formulated specific plans for a coup.[58] Nevertheless,

54. *El Tiempo* (Caracas), September 14, 1945.

55. Diez, *Historia,* 14–15.

56. Diez, *Historia,* 11.

57. Some justification for this charge was seen in statements by Gen. López Contreras on October 14, in which he pointedly remarked that he still had his general-in-chief's uniform in his house; he had not put it away (Betancourt, *Venezuela,* 233).

58. Interview, Caracas, July, 1965. Diez (*Historia*), served in the López Contreras administration, was Minister of Labor and Communications under Medina, and was governor of the Federal District under the 1958 Junta. He also served as deputy and senator

the intensity of the campaign, the lack of experience in free and open electioneering, and López Contreras' well-recognized ambition to regain power lent credibility to the charge. In all probability the intent of the *Lopecista* propaganda was to inject a revolutionary current into the charged atmosphere, in hope of setting off an explosion in the barracks.

AD, through its newspaper *El País* and public rallies, kept up a sharp attack on both the *Lopecistas* and the PDV-PCV front. The issue the party harped on the most was the selection of Biaggini as successor in the presidency. AD spokesmen claimed that they had been willing to work with Escalante as a unity candidate, but in Angel Biaggini's nomination they saw an "inadmissible candidacy" that was imposed on the Venezuelan people by a coterie of close advisers to Medina.[59] To Domingo Alberto Rangel, Biaggini's candidacy was a futile attempt to extend the Andean hegemony. He assailed what he termed Medina's clique of Andean henchmen who "aspire to govern the country with a tribal criterion." He confidently asserted that the *Andinos,* who had gained nothing from four decades of provincial hegemony, were disillusioned with both Tachiran candidates and were flocking to AD.[60]

Party president Rómulo Gallegos made one last-ditch effort to persuade Medina to institute direct election for the office of president. Medina again rejected the proposal, in the face of a veiled threat that failure to adopt it could lead to dire consequences. For AD, "no other road remained than that of direct action."[61]

With both partners to the conspiracy committed to armed rebellion, the only question remaining was that of timing. Rómulo Betancourt urged the military to wait until the war in the Pacific ended, fearing possible adverse international repercussions.[62] But the *coup d'état* had to take place before the first of the year, since promotions and personnel transfers were made on that date. Enough men would have pledged their support before then, for, by mid-November, the UPM

---

from Falcón State to the National Congress. In 1965 he was named president of the National Economic Council.

59. *El País* (Caracas), October 2, 1945.

60. "Las dos candidaturas y los Andes," *El País,* October 4, 1945.

61. Pérez, *La verdad,* 79.

62. Pérez, *La verdad,* 102.

leaders expected to have some 300 junior officers sworn to the conspiracy.[63] After heated discussion, the conspirators agreed to take action at the end of November, barring accidental discovery of the plot. In that event, the coup would commence "at the first arrest."[64]

During September and early October the two groups held joint meetings, and each faction also met frequently in separate sessions. Meanwhile, the UPM central committee and the liaison officers from key installations met regularly to work out details. They also labored assiduously until the very day of the coup to secure adherents.[65] But several days before October 18 the conspirators began to suspect that the plot had been discovered. On October 16 their suspicions were confirmed by a report that a relative of the President had managed to obtain a list of names of the UPM leaders.[66] That evening they called an emergency meeting, with Betancourt in attendance, at which they agreed to move at the end of the week. On the following afternoon the President received a message advising him to be on the alert for action from a widespread conspiracy that extended to the ranks of the presidential guard. The note listed the names of eight of the ringleaders, and Medina was disturbed to see among them some of the best young officers in the Army.[67]

President Medina reluctantly launched an investigation, still naively holding to the belief that no serious plot could be afoot, certainly not among the junior officers. This unwillingness to take immediate action was characteristic of Medina, for he had always displayed a strangely casual attitude toward possible insurgency. He tended to ignore the rumors of subversive activity and, in any event, he was preoccupied with the challenge from the *Lopecistas*. His confidence in his officers had not been shaken by an abortive revolt of troop detachments in November, 1944, for a subsequent investiga-

---

63. Pérez, *La verdad,* 39–40.

64. Indeed, the UPM's watchword was: "The movement begins at the first arrest."

65. Pérez, *La verdad,* 124, and interview, Caracas, July, 1965. Some officers, like Lt. Jaime A Fonseca, declined to join the UPM. Fonseca, one of the few progovernment junior officers of the Caracas garrison, was approached by fellow officers at an outing the weekend before the coup. He was later cashiered.

66. Pérez, *La verdad,* 49.

67. Medina Angarita, *Cuatro años,* 165, and Diez, *Historia,* 6.

tion revealed that not a single officer had been implicated.[68] In mid-1945 the President learned that a young officer of the Caracas garrison had been overheard commenting that the junior officers would choose the next president. Medina directed the young man's commanding officer to keep him under surveillance, but instead of quietly observing his actions, the commander brought the officer to Medina to assure the President of his loyalty. The commander and other high officers praised the young man for his patriotism and professional ability. Medina was reassured that any fears of a rebellion within the junior officer corps were groundless.[69] Then, a few days before October 18, an official of the Administration told Medina that some officers had been discovered sharply criticizing the government. When he asked for specific names, the official was unable to supply them, and the President brushed off the incident as typical youthful voicing of grievances against superiors.[70]

Medina was apparently convinced that his military policy should have kept the officer corps content. Later, while in exile, he prepared a defense of his military policy, the main points of which are of interest here. He wrote, first, that as both Minister of War and President he had endeavored to depersonalize and professionalize the Army. Never had any officer been asked to violate his principles or to act against the legitimate constitutional functions assigned to the armed forces.[71] He went on to summarize the reforms made during his administration, singling out the new military law and the enforced retirement age for officers as two important innovations.

Medina was shrewd enough to have realized for some time that the system of promotions was always high on the grievance list of junior officers. He had been aware of the charge that he had refused to dislodge the ill-trained officers in the higher ranks, which prevented the rapid promotion of more competent junior officers. To defend himself, he had put personnel problems in the framework of the times. The modern Venezuelan Army had developed slowly and tortuously under Castro and Gómez, taking on only a few features of a professional army. The Military Academy had

68. Medina Angarita, *Cuatro años,* 161–62.
69. Medina Angarita, *Cuatro años,* 164.
70. Medina Angarita, *Cuatro años,* 164–65.
71. Medina Angarita, *Cuatro años,* 153.

been functioning since 1910, but was still quite small, even in 1945; consequently, professionally trained officers were still a small minority. Many minor strongmen and political bosses had become part of the officer corps with little or no training, but they had been legally commissioned, they held seniority, and therefore they could not be summarily dismissed or frozen at a certain level in deference to Academy graduates. To do so would have been unwise from a practical standpoint also. The Military Academy graduated only enough officers each year to replace those who retired or died. If all the non-Academy senior officers were to be cashiered, the officer ranks would be greatly depleted, to the detriment of the institution and national security.[72] In his written defense of his military policy, Medina argued that the young officers would eventually have moved into command positions, but by a normal evolutionary process. He accused the rebellious junior officers of an abnormal anxiety to reach the top; he likened their impatience to attain positions of power in the military to AD's hunger for power in the civilian sector.[73]

Medina also knew that the junior officers' dissatisfaction with their salaries went hand in hand with their grievances about promotions. Although admitting that salaries had not increased greatly, he claimed that they had risen enough to improve the standard of living of the men. He wrote that he had, in fact, intended to request a substantial pay increase for military personnel in his last message to Congress. The reason for his delay was primarily political. If he had used his executive powers to put through a pay hike, his action would have given rise to the suspicion that he was buying support in the Army—a bribe to assure support for his "continuist intentions," as his critics put it. Therefore, he postponed the request, in the hope that the political crisis would soon subside.[74]

72. Medina Angarita, *Cuatro años,* 148–50.
73. Medina Angarita, *Cuatro años,* 162–63.
74. Medina Angarita, *Cuarto años,* 167. According to reports that came to the attention of the U.S. Embassy in May, 1945, the government intended to increase salaries for officers of the rank of captain and below by graduated amounts from six bolivares per diem downward. The presumed motivation for these salary increases was to minimize dissatisfaction with living conditions by young officers confronted with rising costs (DFDS, 831.00/5-2645, Flack to Secretary of State, May 26, 1945).

For a military president, Medina appeared remarkably sensitive to the allegation, emanating from opposition elements, that he followed a policy of favoritism to the military institution. Indeed, he was so concerned about accusations of being too closely identified with or dependent on the military that he pursued a contrary course, which gave rise to one of the UPM's principal complaints, his neglect of the armed forces.

The truth lies somewhere between Medina's apologia and the UPM's propaganda. Medina, one of the first graduates of the infant Military Academy, had a much more limited concept of military modernization than the generation of 1945. Although his intentions were good and his administration took substantial steps in the direction of professionalization, the Venezuelan armed forces were inadequately trained, commanded, equipped, and remunerated. Whether or not these administratively determined lacks justified military intervention, hundreds of casualties, and the bitterness and hatreds that still surround the events of October 18, is a question that divides Venezuelans even now.

On the morning of October 18, the President launched a discreet investigation to avoid embarrassing or implicating innocent officers and to quiet rumors of a scandal involving the armed forces, which at that juncture would have been politically damaging. His aides interrogated officers in the principal Caracas units and also alerted the commander of the Maracay compound to a possible conspiracy. In the course of the investigation, two of the highest ranking members of the UPM central committee, Majors Pérez Jiménez and Julio César Vargas, were interrogated and detained. When news of their arrest reached UPM coordinators at the Military School, the organization sprang into action.[75]

The revolt commenced at the Military School, where virtually the entire officer staff had joined in the conspiracy. The UPM quickly took control of the school and arrested its director. The successful rebels there soon learned that the barracks of the presidential guard and the presidential palace itself had both been captured without the firing of a shot.[76]

Meanwhile, President Medina, initially unaware of the gravity of the situation, toured military installations that

75. Pérez, *La verdad,* 63–64.
76. Pérez, *La verdad,* 63–66, 198–99.

were still loyal to the government. Late that afternoon he was encouraged by reports that, after a furious battle, one of the principal barracks had been recaptured from the insurgents.[77] Medina set up headquarters in the barracks of the loyal cavalry, where he convoked an impromptu meeting of the Cabinet. The principal function of the meeting was to issue an executive decree suspending constitutional guarantees.[78]

The President hoped to restrict the fighting to Caracas, where he controlled several key units, but the UPM took the fight to the interior, centering on the Maracay compound where rebels quickly seized the barracks of the armored battalion and the Aviation School. The artillery battalion held out in the face of heavy firing, but it too was forced to capitulate late in the evening of the eighteenth. News of the fall of Maracay came as a crushing blow to the President, who had accurately predicted that success or failure there could well mean total victory or defeat. With the crack armored battalion, the aviation branch, and the Army's central supply depot in the hands of the insurgents, he felt it useless to continue resistance to the revolt.[79] One witness, a close friend of the President, stated that, from the instant Medina learned of Maracay's surrender, he appeared to accept the inevitability of defeat.[80]

General Medina, however, delayed his decision to surrender until the next morning, possibly hoping for some miraculous reversal of fortune. The miracle never materialized. The military aviation forces, now in control of junior officers, bombarded Caracas with propaganda leaflets early on the morning of October 19.[81] Shortly thereafter, planes flew low

77. Medina Angarita, *Cuatro años*, 173.
78. Medina Angarita, *Cuatro años*, 172, and *El País*, October 18, 1945.
79. Medina Angarita, *Cuatro años*, 174.
80. Diez, *Historia*, 5.
81. The leaflets carried messages such as "Down with López Contreras, Medina, and Biaggini," to make clear to the public that the movement was not a right-wing coup engineered by Gen. López Contreras (Pérez, *La verdad*, 230). Nevertheless, the U.S. Embassy reported that a PCV handbill was circulated on October 19 and 20, that urged the people to overthrow "insurrectioners captained by López Contreras." (U.S., Department of State, *Foreign Relations of the United States: Diplomatic Papers, 1945, IX, The American Republics*, 1403–4.)

over the capital, this time dropping not leaflets, but bombs and grenades aimed at the centers of resistance. Medina's headquarters, meanwhile, was being subjected to a mortar bombardment. In mid-morning, stating that his only alternative was to plunge Venezuela into civil war, President Medina surrendered and ordered loyal officers at other locations to do likewise. He next ordered his aides to release Majors Pérez Jiménez and Vargas and other arrested members of the UPM; Pérez Jiménez himself escorted the President to the Military School, where he was detained with General López Contreras and other prominent citizens.[82]

Sporadic fighting continued in Caracas, Maracay, and at isolated locations in the interior. The biggest potential threat came from San Cristóbal, Táchira, where the commander of the strong Andes garrison, Gen. David Henríquez, initially offered resistance. However, when he became convinced that the rest of the country was in the insurgents' hands, he ceased action and submitted peacefully.[83] By October 22 the movement had triumphed throughout Venezuela.[84] The price of victory, in terms of casualties, was high: estimates range from 100 killed and 300 wounded to 2,500 total casualties.[85]

By prearrangement, leaders of the UPM and AD were to form a new government as soon as conditions allowed. By the evening of October 19, the insurgents considered the situation well enough in hand to permit them to organize a provisional government. They met in Miraflores Palace amid the whine of bullets, in a room dimly lit by gasoline lanterns.[86]

According to most accounts, the composition of the Revolutionary Junta had already been settled; there were to be four *Adecos,* one independent, and two military members. It

82. Luzardo, *Notas,* 119, and Pérez, *La verdad,* 252–55.

83. *El Universal,* October 23, 1945.

84. Detailed descriptions of the action as it unfolded October 18–21 may be found in *El Universal* and *El Nacional,* October 22–31, 1945; *El Nacional,* October 18, 1965; *Revista de las Fuerzas Armadas* (October 1946), 169–72; Pérez, *La verdad, passim;* Diez, *Historia,* 2–7; Luzardo, *Notas,* 117–19; Medina Angarita, *Cuatro años,* 167–76; Vallenilla Lanz, *Escrito,* 221–28.

85. The first figure is Revolutionary Junta secretary Leonardo Ruiz Pineda's estimate (*New York Times,* October 22, 1945); the other is in Lieuwen, *Venezuela,* 70. I would estimate that there were at least 500 casualties. See *El Universal,* October 22 and 23, 1945, and the *New York Times,* October 21 and 24, 1945.

86. Betancourt, *Venezuela,* 235.

was the selection of the two uniformed representatives that produced the sharpest controversy. All the UPM leaders were ambitious to be appointed, but Maj. Carlos Delgado Chalbaud, who had joined the conspiracy only weeks before, and who had few close friends in the officer corps, displayed the greatest skill at taking advantage of an opportune moment. Aware that AD wanted Capt. Mario Vargas on the Junta, he also knew that Vargas' brother, Julio César, had backing among the *Adecos*. As Betancourt recalls it, Delgado made a statement to the effect that the military movement had largely been the work of captains and lieutenants; few majors had been involved. Feeling that the great majority of the rebellious officers should have representation on the governing council, he suggested Captain Vargas, who he knew would be approved unanimously. Delgado added that Maj. Julio Vargas should by all rights represent the majors, but since it would not be ethical to have two brothers on the Junta, he would be the other member. Needless to say, this coup within a coup was bitterly resented by Major Vargas, but the result stood and Delgado Chalbaud became the ranking officer on the Revolutionary Junta.[87] That body was completed with Rómulo Betancourt, Raúl Leoni, Gonzalo Barrios, and Luis Beltrán Prieto Figueroa representing AD, and Edmundo Fernández as the lone independent. Betancourt, by previous agreement, assumed the post of Junta president.

*　　*　　*　　*　　*

Most of the reasons for the success of the October 18 rebellion can be summarized briefly: It was conceived and executed by a well-organized and tightly controlled clandestine military organization; it was carried out by the best-trained, most ambitious elements in the armed forces, young men who knew far more about military operations than most of their seniors; the capture of the armored battalion and military aviation at an early stage in the conflict gave the rebels a firepower and a psychological advantage that were impossible to overcome; and the UPM had as its civilian accomplice

87. Betancourt, *Venezuela,* 237–38, and interview, July 31, 1965. Gonzalo Barrios, in his brief account of the meeting (Pérez, *La verdad,* 82), avoids mention of the incident.

a disciplined, tightly-knit political party, led by the ablest politicians in the country.

Nevertheless, these positive factors do not entirely account for the rebels' victory. The government forces labored under the handicap of weak and inept leadership from General Medina, who revealed two serious professional failings that were results of his being a product of the *Gomecista* peace; unlike his Andean predecessors, he had no fighting experience nor any inclinations to fight. Further, he lacked the advanced degree of technical preparation that the younger generation of officers possessed. His leadership of the defense of the regime revealed that he was incapable of commanding effectively in a military encounter. When the occasion arose in which he had to direct a complex military operation, he presumably realized his inability to do so, and for that reason, among others, he yielded.[88]

In addition, a case can be made for a psychological failure of will as a contributory factor in Medina's desultory leadership. The President had suffered a series of illnesses in the months immediately preceding his fall. He was also drinking heavily and leading an active social life. His behavior might be interpreted as escape from the burdens of office and the critical decisions he was called upon to make throughout 1945. The incident that points most tellingly to emotional trouble occurred on the day the rebellion broke out. In the early afternoon, when the Military School was in open revolt and the fighting was spreading to other installations and when he knew that a serious subversive movement was afoot, President Medina fell into a state of lethargy so profound that his aide had to shake him to awaken him.[89] This was, to say the least, unusual behavior for a general in the midst of a military crisis.

Additional accounts of his behavior during October 18 and 19 indicate that the President was subdued, indecisive, almost lethargic and that he never really came to grips with the situation. Officers and friends continually volunteered to carry out missions and stage a counteroffensive, but Medina put them off by telling them to await developments.[90] Thus, the

88. Based in part on interviews in March and May, 1965.
89. Interview, May, 1965.
90. Diez, *Historia*, 5–6, and Pérez, *La verdad*, 250–55. See also Antonio Arellano Moreno, *Mirador de historia política de Venezuela*, 251.

probability that the Chief Executive was experiencing some mental crisis must be looked upon as at least a contributing factor in the success of the rebels.[91]

What were the essential characteristics of the 1945 movement? First, the "Generation of '45," unlike the famous "Generation of '28," was more military than civilian in orientation.[92] Despite the complicity of AD, the coup was directed by the military. The seeds of what was to grow into the October 18 *golpe de estado* had germinated within the junior officer ranks. AD had only vague revolutionary notions until it was brought into the conspiracy by invitation of the young officers. During the four days of fighting, AD's role was strictly marginal, confined to guard duty and propagandizing the bewildered populace into accepting the results of the coup.

The 1945 generation was also marked by a perfecting mentality. In contrast to the civilian-oriented 1928 generation, which fought against the harsh despotism of a reactionary tyrant, the 1945 movement was a renovating effort. Those involved were fighting a basically democratic, flexible ruler and a regime that in almost every respect was superior to the stultifying Gómez dictatorship. Essentially, what the revolutionaries wanted to achieve was the perfecting of the prevailing system, the elimination of certain glaring inequities (such as indirect election of president), and the refinement of the government and military machinery that had already been partially modernized in the 1936–1945 decade. Finally, and again in contrast to the student generation of 1928, the 1945 clique was disciplined and methodical in its preparations to take power. The previous movement had tended to be more doctrinaire, demagogic, and disorganized. The revolutionary mystique of the "Generation of '28" was replaced in the "Grupo de Octubre" by a basically pragmatic outlook.

91. A common explanation by the President's detractors is that Medina was inebriated during most of this crucial period, a matter I was unable to substantiate and for which I find little basis.

92. On this point there is agreement between, for example, Julio Diez (Diez, *Historia,* 17), a Cabinet member and personal friend of Medina, and one interviewee, an independent who fought with the UPM and AD in the October 18 revolution and whose personal collection of books on military affairs was of assistance to the conspirators.

The 1945 revolt brought about at least three important changes in Venezuela's political order that were to affect civil–military relations. First, it brought to an abrupt halt the slow evolutionary development toward democracy and modernity begun by General-Presidents López Contreras and Medina. After 1945, while modernization surged ahead, the course of politics was to be irregular, subject to sudden and, at times, violent alterations. The events of October 18, 1945, led to some equally memorable dates: The November 24, 1948, military counterrevolution; the December 2, 1952, nullification of national elections and arbitrary assumption of power by Colonel Pérez Jiménez; and the January 23, 1958, civil–military movement that forced General Pérez Jiménez to flee the country.

Second, since October, 1945, Venezuela has been governed by new men with new ideas. Medina's surrender brought to an end forty-six years of *continuismo andino*. True, the military generation of '45—the officers of the UPM—were predominantly Andeans,[93] but the new generation had little in common with the generations represented by Gómez, López Contreras, and Medina. The ideas and events that influenced these new men were totally different from the parochial influences that shaped the careers of the early *Andino* caudillos. And in the civilian sector, 1945 commemorates the modernization and institutionalization of national politics. Henceforth, multiclass, programmatic political parties and organized interest groups would interact on the political stage, replacing the traditional struggles based on personal loyalties and regional rivalries.

Finally, the October revolt reversed the trend toward the depoliticalization of the military institution that was initiated by Presidents López Contreras and Medina. It was at this point that neither the UPM nor AD had a clear understanding of the limits of military professionalization in the Latin

---

93. Marcos Pérez Jiménez and his brother Juan, the Vargas brothers, Miguel Nucete Paoli, Martín Carrillo Méndez, and scores of others were from the Andes. Carlos Delgado Chalbaud was Tachiran on his father's side. Twelve years later (1957), of the twenty-five most important civil and military offices in Venezuela, fourteen were held by Andeans (Philip B. Taylor, Jr., *The Venezuelan Golpe de Estado of 1958: The Fall of Marcos Pérez Jiménez*, 37–38).

American context.[94] The 1945 *golpe* did not remove the Army from politics. On the contrary, for the next dozen years the Army, as a self-conscious institutional entity, was to have more direct participation in government than in the past. Seen in retrospect, this movement was a manifestation of a nascent Latin-style militarism, inasmuch as it "sought to increase by force the position of the military in the government for its own advantage."[95] Indeed, three years later, when the government headed by the UPM's civilian allies proved to be disadvantageous to the corporate interests of the military, the same officers who overthrew Isaías Medina ousted AD from power.

94. A detailed analysis of the relationship between professionalism and political activism in Latin American military institutions is found in Lieuwen, *Arms and Politics in Latin America,* 122–53.

95. Foreign Area Studies Division, *U.S. Army Area Handbook for Venezuela,* 537.

CHAPTER IV

THE NOVEMBER 24 COUP D'ÉTAT

The Revolutionary Junta of Government remained in power for over two years. With four of the seven Junta members *Adecos,* and with Rómulo Betancourt cast in the dual role of Junta president and party chief, the provisional government embarked on an ambitious reform program designed to reconstruct Venezuela from top to bottom.

The principal goals of the revolutionary government were to promulgate a new constitution and to sponsor free direct elections. The first step toward these goals was the calling of a constituent assembly to draft a constitution. In the election for assembly delegates held October 27, 1946, Acción Democrática outpolled its political opponents by a wide margin, enabling its delegates to forge a liberal constitution that closely reflected party doctrine. The next step was the election on December 14, 1947, of the President and Congress, in which AD won a smashing victory in both the presidential and congressional contests. The following February Rómulo Gallegos was inaugurated, and Venezuela returned to constitutional rule. But Gallegos governed a mere nine months; in November, 1948, the military high command ousted the Chief Executive and seized control of the government on behalf of the national armed forces.

Why did the same group of officers that had brought AD to power three years earlier overthrow the Gallegos regime? The answer is complex, but rooted primarily in hostility toward AD in the civilian and military sectors, which had been building since the October 18 rebellion.

The provisional government was closely identified with AD throughout the twenty-eight months it held power. The AD-controlled Junta bore the reformist stamp of the party. By prerevolution arrangement, the military members gave their civilian counterparts a free hand on all matters except those related to defense, internal security, and over-all political objectives; the officers did not involve themselves in social and economic policymaking or in routine political decisions.[1] On most issues, the Junta acted as a rubber stamp for the national executive committee of AD, the body that formulated party policy.

The tone of the regime was set by provisional President Betancourt. Born in 1908 in Miranda State, this student leader of the "Generation of '28" proved to be a tough-minded and able politician. As chief executive of both government and party, he exercised vast influence on the course of events during the provisional regime. Undismayed by the scope of his responsibilities, he threw himself enthusiastically into the tasks of governing, determined to restructure Venezuela's economy and society virtually overnight.

To Betancourt, the Junta was not designed to serve as a mere caretaker government. He was not of a mind to delay basic reforms until after a constitutional administration had been elected. On the contrary, he was determined that from the very start the Junta should operate as an active agent to cure Venezuela's social ills. Therefore, reforms were introduced almost immediately after the revolt, and Miraflores Palace was converted into a "decree machine."[2] The endless stream of executive decrees emanating from the office of the provisional President brought about changes in almost every area of Venezuelan public life.

Many Venezuelans, however, resented the manner in which the reforms were promulgated. Measures of sweeping significance were declared by the stroke of a pen. There was no national debate over critical problems; Congress was suspended, and the opposition parties were excluded from the decision-making process. AD's powerful national executive committee made the important decisions, which then passed on to the Junta for virtually automatic approval. The party's arbitrary methods thus angered and frustrated non-*Adecos*.

The AD reform program has been widely and learnedly discussed, and its details are available in a number of

1. John D. Martz, *Acción Democrática: Evolution of a Modern Political Party in Venezuela,* 63, 305. One exception to this general rule in the earliest days of the Junta was Capt. Mario Vargas, who, although his title was Communications Minister, appeared to the U.S. Embassy to be more of a "military vice president." (DFDS, 831.00/10-2645, Corrigan to Secretary of State, October 26, 1945.) Vargas, however, was the military leader most closely identified with the AD position throughout the *trienio*.

2. Martz, *Acción Democrática,* 64.

sources.[3] In essence, AD greatly expanded government efforts in education, health and sanitation, agriculture, economic diversification, and industrialization that the regimes of the last two Andean presidents had undertaken. Support for the vastly enlarged government expenditures in those areas came through an increase in the government's share of petroleum revenues. AD's much-vaunted attack on the country's basic social and economic problems did not represent a fundamental "social revolution," as *Adecos* and pro-AD writers have insisted, but rather represented an invigorated and expanded policy of domestic reform that had already been accelerating over the 1936–1945 decade. The real "revolution" was political: for the first time in Venezuela the political base of the ruling party now resided in the middle and lower classes, not in the elite.

As was to be expected, the Venezuelan armed forces were among the principal beneficiaries of October 18. The military budget rose in proportion to the increased government revenues after 1945. The first Junta budget allocated over 75 million *bolívares* to the military, compared to Medina's projected figure for that year of 40 million *bolívares*.[4] Two years later the defense budget had nearly tripled.[5]

The high level of military expenditures was justified on the basis of the "shocking" needs of the armed forces that were only discovered fully after the coup. According to the new military command, salaries and troop allowances were utterly insufficient, housing was substandard, and there was a woeful lack of modern equipment.[6] Consequently, a high percentage of the increased appropriations was devoted to improving the lot of military personnel. Within a year after

3. Sympathetic accounts of the reforms of the 1945–1948 period are contained in the already cited Martz, *Acción Democrática,* and Edwin Lieuwen, *Venezuela,* and in Stanley J. Serxner, *Acción Democrática of Venezuela: Its Origins and Development;* Robert J. Alexander, *The Venezuelan Democratic Revolution: A Profile of the Regime of Rómulo Betancourt,* and *Prophets of the Revolution: Profiles of Latin American Leaders.* For the most detailed, but highly partisan, exposition of the program, see Betancourt, *Venezuela,* Chapters V–XIV.

4. Venezuela, Ministerio de la Defensa Nacional, *Memoria: 1946,* 19.

5. *Revista de las Fuerzas Armadas* (June 1947), 316, and Isaías Medina Angarita, *Cuatro años de democracia,* 157.

6. Venezuela, Defensa, *Memoria: 1946,* 69–70.

the revolt, officer salaries had risen 37 per cent and troop allowances 57 per cent; the allotment for troop rations climbed 50 per cent, and the amount spent on pharmaceutical supplies rose 250 per cent.[7] In addition, matériel procurements increased substantially as newer and better equipment was purchased from the United States and other powers from their remaining World War II stock piles.

The new government promptly instituted reforms in military education. The enrollments in the service academies increased sharply, in proportions varying from 100 to 200 per cent over those of the previous regime.[8] Newly formulated plans for specialized schools for advanced studies achieved reality. Large numbers of students went abroad, particularly to Panama and the United States, to complete their technical education.[9] Foreign influence on the military became quite evident after the establishment and enlargement of U.S. military missions, which reorganized instruction in the academies along U.S. lines.

The new military commanders recognized that their predecessors had been severely wanting in professional ability, and they decried the lack of coordination between the services and between divisions within each branch. Thus, the Ministry of War underwent thorough reorganization. The new commanders cashiered all officers who had attained ranks above major before October 18, 1945, and UPM leaders assumed all key staff and command posts. Junta member Delgado Chalbaud became Minister of Defense, Pérez Jiménez headed the General Staff, and other leaders of the junior officer clique took command of the Navy and Air Force.

Major Pérez Jiménez, whose forte was military administration, directed the reorganization of the Ministry of War, the name of which was changed to the more contemporary Ministry of Defense. He introduced administrative centralization and modernized and strengthened the nerve center of the new ministry, the General Staff. The new command streamlined the system of regional garrisons, proposed a new headquarters for the Ministry of Defense, and began construction on new housing for officers and men. By 1948 the ministry had reorganized the Navy and had granted more

7. Venezuela, Defensa, *Memoria: 1946,* 6.
8. Venezuela, Defensa, *Memoria: 1946,* 7.
9. In 1947, for example, 66 officers and soldiers were sent abroad on study missions (Venezuela, Defensa, *Memoria: 1948,* 60–62).

autonomy to the Air Force, which formerly had been under the control of the Army. Whereas previously Army and Navy officers with no aviation experience filled command positions in the Air Force, officers trained within that branch now directed its affairs.[10]

Proceeding apace with socioeconomic and military reforms were AD's much-heralded constitutional and electoral reforms. The new AD-influenced Constitution provided for the direct election of the President and Congress. It reduced the presidential term from five to four years and prohibited re-election for two successive terms thereafter. The Constitution abolished the literacy requirement for voting. The sections dealing with social and economic matters were more or less formalized AD philosophy. Labor received additional rights and benefits. An enlarged role for government in business and public welfare was part of the document, along with a more nationalistic economic policy, which included more stringent restrictions on foreign enterprises operating in Venezuela. Finally, following Venezuelan tradition, the 1947 document was strongly centralist and granted sweeping powers to the chief executive.[11]

The framing of the Constitution was only one aspect of the Junta's regularization of political processes. All Junta members, soon after they assumed power, agreed to disqualify themselves as presidential candidates. In March, 1946, all constitutional guarantees were restored, and a new election law went into effect. AD's chief competitor was the Comité de Organización Política Electoral Independiente (COPEI)—the Christian Democrat party—which had been founded in January, 1946.[12] Although heterogeneous in composition and ideology, the party had a pro-Church, moderate-to-ultraconservative outlook, and received its most enthusiastic support from the traditionalist Andean region.[13] Its leading spokesman was Rafael Caldera Rodríguez, a young lawyer and sociologist who resigned as Attorney General in April, 1946, to lead his party into open opposition to AD.

AD's second strongest rival was the Unión Republicana

10. Venezuela, Defensa, *Memoria: 1948,* 83–84.
11. Russell H. Fitzgibbon, ed., *The Constitutions of the Americas,* 764–813.
12. See Manuel Vicente Magallanes, *Partidos políticos venezolanos,* 149–52.
13. Martz, *Acción Democrática,* 66–67, 69.

Democrática (URD)—the Democratic Republican Union. Founded in March, 1946, in opposition to the provisional government, URD was a nationally based middle-class party, with its greatest strength in the Oriente. Its membership included many former members of Medina's extinct PDV, including Jóvito Villalba, famed orator of the "Generation of '28," who soon became the party's secretary general.[14] Its doctrinal position was nebulous and was to remain so; however, during the *trienio,* the party's location on the political spectrum was to the right of AD, but to the left of COPEI.[15]

Also aligned against AD were the Communists. The PCV, founded in 1931, had operated underground until legalized by Medina in 1945. During the 1940s it split into two factions, reflecting the rival aspirations of two leaders, Gustavo Machado and Juan Bautista Fuenmayor. The two factions united for electoral purposes in 1946, but later split again into the so-called red and black divisions. Support for the Communists came mostly from intellectuals and from workers in the large urban centers and the oil fields of Zulia State.[16]

The result of the election for the constituent assembly was a landslide victory for AD. The party polled 78.4 per cent of the vote, compared to 13.2 per cent for COPEI, 4.3 for URD, and 3.6 for PCV.[17] This overwhelming triumph gave AD 137 of the 160 seats in the constituent assembly.[18]

The *Adecos* repeated their successful performance in the December, 1947, election for President and Congress. In the race for the presidency were Rómulo Gallegos for AD, Rafael Caldera for COPEI, and Gustavo Machado for the PCV. The outcome was another lopsided victory for AD. Gallegos received 74.4 per cent of the votes cast, as opposed to 22.4 per cent for Caldera and 3.1 per cent for Machado.[19] Gallegos' party also secured absolute majorities in both congressional chambers. Five months later, on May 9, 1948, in an election for municipal councilmen, AD continued its

14. Magallanes, *Partidos,* 167–69.

15. Martz, *Acción Democrática,* 319–21, and Lieuwen, *Venezuela,* 72.

16. Lieuwen, *Venezuela,* 72–73, and Robert J. Alexander, *The Communist Party of Venezuela,* 5–16, 138–39.

17. Boris Bunimov-Parra, *Introducción a la sociología electoral venezolana,* Cuadro Anexo II.

18. Martz, *Acción Democrática,* 69.

19. Bunimov-Parra, *La sociología electoral,* 73.

success at the polls by winning 70.1 per cent of the vote, to 21.1 per cent for COPEI, 3.9 for URD, and 3.4 per cent for the PCV.[20]

AD's ability to garner such an extraordinarily high percentage of votes in the three elections developed from at least five basic advantages that the organization enjoyed. First, it had a longer history than either COPEI or URD; its origins were in the old PDN of the López Contreras period. In their years of clandestine activity, party leaders gained valuable political experience, which was put to use in 1941, when the party began to operate freely under its new name. Members worked diligently at building a national organization during the Medina regime, whereas COPEI and URD did not organize until after October 18. The PCV had been in existence longer than COPEI and URD, but serious internal dissension had counterbalanced its broader experience in politics.

Second, AD outclassed its rivals in political organization. Guided by the master organizer Rómulo Betancourt, AD built an effective party apparatus on a national scale. Third, AD had a program that appealed to the Venezuelan masses, in particular the long-neglected peasant and laboring man. Fourth, AD made certain that it would reap maximum advantage from lower-class support by opening the suffrage to illiterates. Fifth, AD had the obvious advantage of being the incumbent party. It is quite likely that many Venezuelans supported AD at the polls because they accepted the general belief that in Venezuela the government never loses an election.[21]

While the *Adecos* viewed the election results with justifiable pride, opposition elements naturally saw them in quite a different light. The lopsided AD victories bred a sense of frustration and futility among the other parties, which boded ill for the future of Venezuelan democracy. Rival parties grew impatient with the *Adecos,* who appeared to be able to maintain themselves in power indefinitely. The rival parties expressed their resentment at first in the fiercely fought election campaigns and then in their grudging acceptance of the results. This frustration over successive defeats, compounded by a multitude of other grievances, provoked a highly

20. Martz, *Acción Democrática,* 75.
21. Bunimov-Parra, *La sociología electoral,* 246–50.

charged political crisis that the party in power was unable to solve.

AD, supported by its impressive election victories, confronted strong opposition from all political rivals, whose most frequently voiced charge against the party was excessive sectarianism. According to critics, AD was running the government unilaterally, paying no heed to outside opinion. The party's executive committee wielded an overwhelming influence on the operation of the government. In addition, although independents were represented in the Junta and Cabinet, *Adecos* monopolized the lower echelons of the bureaucracy. Betancourt seems to have tried to discourage party subordinates from excluding non-*Adecos* from government jobs, but they ignored his requests.[22] Consequently, the federal bureaucracy became the exclusive domain of one party. AD sectarianism also took the form of an uncompromising attitude toward political opponents. *Adecos* were often accused of harassing individuals critical of the party and of overzealousness in furthering their political interests.

On another front, COPEI, URD, and Communists accused AD public servants of a complete lack of governing ability. Charges of inefficiency, exorbitant spending, and administrative bungling were common. AD reformist measures, said their critics, were as arbitrary as they were disorganized. AD was now the target of the same complaints of peculation and corruption that it had lodged against previous regimes.[23]

There was more than a measure of truth to these charges. Inefficiency and waste were prevalent, despite attempts by the party leaders to reduce mismanagement and financial irresponsibility. But AD's enemies undoubtedly exaggerated these charges, as political adversaries invariably do. Such political transgressions, common to all Venezuelan regimes, in and of themselves would not have provoked the military intervention that ended the regime in 1948.

Aside from party rivals, the *Adecos* had to contend with the consequences of their hostility toward all former regimes.

22. Rodolfo Luzardo, *Notas histórico-económicas, 1928–1963,* 142. The U.S. Ambassador predicted a week after the revolt that continuing *Adeco* monopolization of government jobs would provoke "revulsion." See DFDS, 831.00/10-2645, Corrigan to Secretary of State, October 26, 1945.

23. See Luzardo, *Notas,* 158–59.

Medinistas resented AD because it had overthrown by force what they considered to be the most democratic and progressive regime in Venezuela's history. *Lopecistas* were angry because AD had snatched away their opportunity for electoral victory, and they were disturbed by the radical bent adopted by the new regime. Both factions felt they were victims of political persecution.

They felt persecuted, with reason. The revolutionary government had wasted little time in taking revenge against former public officials. Generals López Contreras and Medina were promptly imprisoned and later exiled; others were subjected to systematic harassment. In 1946 the Junta moved against members of the three immediately preceding regimes to recover all "illicitly obtained" wealth. They established a special court, the Tribunal of Civil and Administrative Responsibility, to try former public servants.[24] On the tribunal's list of those indicted for illegal enrichment were 168 names, including those of former Presidents López Contreras and Medina, many of their civilian and military colleagues, and surviving members of the Gómez clan.

Although few doubted that many of the indicted individuals were guilty of corruption, critical observers found fault with the tribunal on several counts. The list was too long, indiscriminate, and included many innocent persons. The tribunal was not a constitutionally established judicial body, but a seven-man commission hand-picked by the Junta and granted sweeping powers of decree; the defendants had no right of appeal, since all tribunal decisions were final.[25] The net effect of the peculation trials was to create more enemies for AD and to make martyrs of the former presidents, their families, and collaborators. The trials were a serious political mistake that cost the AD party the good will of a broad spectrum of Venezuelan society.

Further discontent was voiced by influential sectors of society and by foreign economic interests. They criticized the *Adecos* for trying to do too much too soon, for the arbitrary method in which the reforms were carried out, and for the

24. Venezuela, Ministerio de Relaciones Interiores, *Sentencias del Jurado de Responsabilidad Civil y Administrativa,* I, 4.

25. Luzardo, *Notas,* 138–39, 158, and Julio Diez, *Historia y política,* 30–35. A lengthy attack on the tribunal and a detailed personal defense are found in Eleazar López Contreras, *El Triunfo de la verdad: documentos para la historia venezolana,* 123–213.

radical nature and maladministration of the reform program. The Church, landowners, industrialists, manufacturers, and petroleum firms also had specific grievances, most of them centering on AD-inspired legislation that affected their interests.

AD's educational policy ran afoul of the Roman Catholic Church, which had always suspected the party of anticlericalism. Its suspicions were confirmed with the passing of several measures that it felt were prejudicial to the Church's educational system, including a controversial law that required certification by the government of all nonpublic institutions. Church schools were forced to comply with a whole series of regulations instituted by secular authorities, which circumscribed the freedom and autonomy that parochial education had long enjoyed.[26] The clergy feared that these were merely the beginning steps in a process that would lead to the nationalization of all levels of education. This fear was coupled with a conviction that AD was, at bottom, a Marxist front and militantly atheistic. The charge was unfounded, but the party's less than friendly attitude toward the Church did not reassure ecclesiastical authorities.[27] AD's unwillingness to reach a *modus vivendi* with the Church's hierarchy therefore resulted in the alienation of yet another powerful pressure group.

The government's role as an active agent of social change in general disturbed the traditionalist elements in society who wanted the government kept in the manicured hands of the educated elite. In addition to the rapid extension of welfare measures, the intrusion of labor and peasantry into national politics disturbed those paternalists who wanted change to come slowly, if at all, and under their own aegis.

The business community was beset with two major problems: the prolabor policy that the government habitually applied when arbitrating labor–management disputes and the rising labor costs that resulted from the gains made by labor under AD rule. Foreign companies, particularly the petroleum giants, futilely resisted attempts to make them turn over an increased share of their revenues to the national treasury. From time to time they raised, without substantial evidence, the specter of nationalization. Their hostility and the subtle

---

26. Luzardo, *Notas,* 145, 158.
27. Martz, *Acción Democrática,* 86.

use of their influence in the national economy contributed to the climate of discontent.[28]

Finally, the large landowners felt threatened by the Agrarian Reform Law. They became hostile to any government-fostered change, but it was the proposed land reform that solidified their opposition to AD. Even though little privately owned hacienda land was actually confiscated, the very threat of redistribution frightened the *hacendados,* and they too moved into outright opposition to the regime.[29]

AD might have overcome the broad and deep hostility from various areas of society if the most powerful political interest group had remained sympathetic, or at least neutral, to the regime. The party's inability to retain the military's loyalty proved its undoing. Unfortunately for the historian, constitutional prohibitions prevented armed forces personnel from making public their grievances against the prevailing regime; thus public utterances of discontent by military officers, during the *trienio,* are unavailable. Information on causes of military disaffection comes mainly from the high command's justification for the *coup d'état* written after the seizure of power in November, 1948.

The first detailed apologia for the *coup d'état* was in a communiqué issued on November 24, 1948, entitled "Exposition of the Armed Forces to the Nation." The document states that in October, 1945, the Army did not take power for itself, but instead placed it in the hands of the only party in opposition to the existing regime. The military's initial attitude, in spite of having two military representatives on the governing Junta, was "absolutely apolitical."[30] However, AD continued the same political vices that had characterized previous regimes: use of power for the party's benefit, political sectarianism, constant agitation, and creation of a state of complete disorder. Nevertheless, the armed forces put down every rebellious act committed against the government.[31]

28. Martz, *Acción Democrática,* 85–87.

29. For a critical appraisal of the agrarian reform by a former official of the provisional government, see Luzardo, *Notas,* 159.

30. Venezuela, Oficina Nacional de Información y Publicaciones, *Documentos oficiales relativos al movimiento militar del 24 de noviembre de 1948,* 19. Hereafter cited as Venezuela, *Documentos oficiales.*

31. Venezuela, *Documentos oficiales,* 19.

The communiqué continued by accusing AD of capitalizing on the election of the Constituent Assembly to draft a constitution that, although it included progressive measures, also contained dangerous clauses leading to the "abusive exercise of power."[32] Under that constitution the duly elected president took office and the military institution initially supported him fully. The President refused to act on his own, however; instead, he let himself be led by members of his party.

Then the "extremist" element in control of the party began "a series of maneuvers tending to dominate . . . the National Armed Forces, trying to sow among them discord and disunion."[33] The high command, in search of an effective remedy, set before the President their specific grievances, but the influence of the President in his own party was nil. Instead, the conduct of the military officials was interpreted as disaffection with the government, and "what could have been a problem of easy solution, was converted by the work of partisan intransigence and the indecision of the President, into a political crisis" that the armed forces never wished to create.[34]

In subsequent declarations by members of the Military Junta over the year following the *coup d'état,* the same—and additional—charges were leveled at the now-deposed AD government party. In the political realm they were accused of sectarianism, hyperaggressiveness, persecution of political adversaries, demagoguery, manipulation of elections, and the arming of a civilian militia as a counterpoise to the regular armed forces. In regard to public administration, the indictment charged AD with ineptness and dishonesty, an excessive number of incompetent bureaucrats, and the tendency to conceive of the party and the government as one and the same entity.

As for economic policy, the military accused AD of planning poorly, causing food shortages, and raising the cost of living. But the most interesting charge was that the Administration lacked nationalistic fervor in economic affairs. The military spokesmen stated that this lack was observable in two important areas. First, although AD had criticized the petroleum reform of President Medina for being "timid,"

---

32. Venezuela, *Documentos oficiales,* 19–20.
33. Venezuela, *Documentos oficiales,* 20.
34. *Ibid.*

one of the first acts of the revolutionary government was to assure the oil companies openly that the basic petroleum law would not be changed. Second, AD invited foreign capital into sectors of the economy where previously it had no access. Singled out was Nelson Rockefeller's International Basic Economy Corporation, which was given lucrative concessions in agriculture, cattle raising, and fishing.[35]

Finally, the military charged the AD leadership with hostility toward and harassment of the military command and of attempting to split the armed forces into rival factions. Those charges bring light to bear on the growing hostility between party and military as it unfolded during the *trienio.*

Although relations between the military and AD steadily worsened between 1945 and 1948, public statements by leaders of both groups failed to reflect the strength of the increasing tensions. For example, in an Army Day speech in 1946, provisional President Betancourt declared that the government fully supported the young officers in their efforts to make Venezuela's armed forces the best organized in Latin America.[36] In his writings, Betancourt insisted that he and his party had always had high regard for the national armed forces and felt the military had a legitimate function to perform in a democratic civilian administration. He asked only that the military stay out of politics, an area AD regarded as the exclusive domain of civilians.[37]

Military leaders also expressed themselves as favoring an apolitical army. Their statements disavowing political ambitions are legion. For example, in an editorial appearing in the *Revista de las Fuerzas Armadas,* Maj. Amable Andrade Niño stated emphatically that the October 18 movement contradicted the notion that "the military and civil government" were antagonistic. The idea that any member of the armed forces had aspirations to rule the country was unthinkable; on the contrary, the mission of the armed forces was "completely alien to politics."[38]

35. Venezuela, *Documentos oficiales,* 72. If military spokesmen were sincere about the two last charges, this would tend to weaken the more familiar argument that the military intervened on behalf of traditionalist groups and foreign interests against a regime that had become too radical for most officers.

36. *Revista de las Fuerzas Armadas* (July 1946), 22–23.

37. Betancourt, *Venezuela,* 551–52.

38. *Revista de las Fuerzas Armadas* (July 1946), 4.

The 1947 Constitution defined the armed forces as a "non-political institution, essentially professional, obedient, and not deliberative."[39] It prohibited active members of the armed forces from exercising the right of suffrage or joining political organizations. The legal and theoretical relationship between the civil and military authorities was thus explicit in the Constitution and was upheld in public declarations on both sides.

The course of civil–military relations obviously was not running as smoothly as might be deduced from official pronouncements. In reality, hardly a month passed without some form of subversive activity aimed at bringing down the revolutionary government. A mere sampling of the more serious plots reveals the precarious status of the regime. Already in January, 1946, a Maracay-centered plot surfaced; it allegedly implicated high officials of the López Contreras and Medina regimes.[40] A conspiracy of *Lopecistas* alone was foiled six months later.

The *cuartelazo* that came closest to succeeding was that of December 11, 1946, centered in Maracay and Valencia. It involved high-ranking officers of those garrisons and included the commandant of the Valencia base, Lt. Col. Juan Pérez Jiménez, brother of the Chief of Staff. Fighting raged for more than a day before the rebels were crushed.[41]

The following spring a crisis arose over the subversive activities of former UPM leader Maj. Julio César Vargas. He had been resentful of the new military command ever since his exclusion from the Revolutionary Junta. After the revolt he was appointed to the strategic post of Inspector General of the Armed Forces, but his outspoken political views caused constant embarrassment to the high command. In essence, he advocated a larger role for the military in the governing process and a concurrent restriction of AD influence. In the controversy that ensued, he was removed from his office as Inspector General and retired from active service. He then began conspiring to overthrow the government

39. Fitzgibbon, *Constitutions*, 779–80.
40. *El Nacional*, January 16, 1946.
41. Luzardo, *Notas*, 145. Civilians, including Jóvito Villalba, were arrested in connection with the conspiracy, but they were soon released and the extent of their complicity, if any, remains unclear (see *El Nacional*, January 11, 1947).

—allegedly even with exiled General López Contreras—but little came of his plots.[42]

In September, 1947, a conspiracy that included several military units and armed civilians was crushed by loyal forces. The movement centered in Caracas, but it extended as far as San Cristóbal in the West and Puerto La Cruz in the East. Rebel leaflets found in the port of La Guaira intimated that the Junta had betrayed the promises it had made in October, 1945, and therefore should be overthrown. The leaflets vaguely denounced the "sectarianism" of the *Adeco* members of the Junta and called on the armed forces to take control of the government in order to return Venezuela to the proper course.[43] The government denounced the movement as a reactionary plot and accused *Lopecistas, Medinistas,* and even members of the Gómez family of sponsoring it.[44]

Several anti-AD movements involved foreign interests. Money and arms for Venezuelan rebels came in from other Caribbean republics; Nicaragua and the Dominican Republic became asylums for Venezuelans who were fomenting the abortive uprisings. According to government sources, in January, 1948, the authorities thwarted a conspiracy that was to culminate in the bombing of key government installations in Caracas. Implicated in the plot, along with the Caribbean dictators Rafael Trujillo and Anastasio Somoza, was Pedro Estrada, a young Venezuelan civilian who later headed the National Security Police under Pérez Jiménez.[45]

These uprisings and conspiracies as well as other minor subversive movements drew the disapprobation of the military high command. Nevertheless, behind the public display of support for the government, stirrings of trouble in high places became noticeable early in the Junta period and increased in intensity after Gallegos' inauguration. Affecting government–military relations adversely was the uneven relationship between the three key military leaders and AD. Of the two military representatives on the Junta, the popular Mario Vargas had the closer ties to AD. The strongest defender of party policy in the military ranks, he managed to

42. *El Nacional,* April 7 and April 11, 1947.
43. *El Nacional,* September 13, 1947.
44. *Ibid.*
45. Luzardo, *Notas,* 145–46.

place a number of *Adeco* sympathizers in key command posts.[46]

Minister of Defense Carlos Delgado Chalbaud also was on good terms with AD initially. But, despite a reputation as a man of democratic, nonmilitaristic inclinations, he aroused suspicions of harboring great personal ambitions. He was, for example, falsely accused of being the central figure in a subversive movement previous to the November, 1948, coup.[47] It is true, nonetheless, that Delgado developed an aversion to the *Adecos* during the *trienio,* but—official pronouncements aside—the reasons for his change in attitude are unclear. His principal objective was probably to remain in a strong position vis-à-vis both the AD leadership and his military colleagues; in this he was generally successful.

The officer regarded by AD as the greatest threat to continuing civilian rule was Lt. Col. Marcos Pérez Jiménez. As one of the UPM organizers, Pérez Jiménez had the opportunity to make contact with numerous junior-grade officers. After October 18, he continued to court the friendship of fellow officers from his post on the General Staff, partly to keep abreast of their problems, but also to build up a personal following in the ranks. He was aided in this endeavor by his assistant chief, Lt. Col. Luis Felipe Llovera Páez. Llovera, a Tachiran like Pérez Jiménez, had returned from studies at Chorrillos following the revolt and, as he had not been directly implicated, he was more readily accepted by the officers who had not joined the UPM. He made valuable contacts with that faction, and thus a large following began to coalesce behind him and the Chief of Staff.[48] His and Pérez Jiménez' activities did not go unobserved by AD leaders; both were watched with suspicion, and there were several attempts, all futile, to remove them from their posts.

Since Delgado Chalbaud enjoyed more prestige in the civilian sector and Pérez Jiménez more prestige in the barracks, a mutually beneficial relationship developed almost

46. Unfortunately for the *Adecos,* Vargas' health was deteriorating steadily as a result of a pulmonary disorder, and he was finally forced to submit to treatment and a long rest at a sanatorium in Saranac Lake, New York. Consequently, AD was without the services of its most influential military supporter during the crucial months preceding the November 1948 coup.

47. Luzardo, *Notas,* 149.

48. Interview, Caracas, July, 1965.

automatically. Delgado frequently defended Pérez Jiménez and Llovera Páez before the *Adecos*, partly because of his relatively weak position in the officer ranks. Four handicaps put Delgado at a disadvantage in his relationships with his fellow officers: his entire military training had been non-Venezuelan, and consequently, he had few close friends in the Venezuelan armed forces; because of his training in engineering he was considered an engineer, or *técnico*, rather than a soldier; he belonged to the social aristocracy of the capital, a position that tended to alienate him from his provincial, lower-middle-class fellow officers; and finally, his aloofness and cold demeanor also kept his subordinates at a distance. Delgado Chalbaud had no personal following among the officers, and he had to rely on the Pérez Jiménez clique for the backing of the rank-and-file. On the other hand, Pérez Jiménez, distrusted and disliked by AD leaders, benefited from Delgado's support in the governing councils.[49]

At the core of the civil–military conflict was not only the issue of military intervention in "civilian" politics but also that of civilian intrusion into the military sphere for partisan purposes. In speeches and publications, armed forces spokesmen attacked this alleged interference, no matter from what source it came, but they singled out AD for attempting to undermine military professionalism.

According to military spokesmen, officers began to lose their enthusiasm for the regime when they discovered that AD was trying to win adherents to the party's cause inside the barracks.[50] AD officials denied having drawn the Army into politics. According to their version, what they sought was to win over as many officers as possible to the goal of a completely professional, apolitical army.[51] Undoubtedly that was the party's emphasis, but AD nonetheless attempted to gain support for its government within the military institution. Having fought hard to attain power, AD was unwilling to relinquish it. Sympathy within the Army for the regime was necessary, they felt, to counterbalance the growing hostility of other factions, both civil and military.[52] The net effect, however, was to introduce another divisive element into the military institution.

49. Interview, Caracas, July, 1965.
50. See Venezuela, *Documentos oficiales,* 29, 54–55.
51. Betancourt, *Venezuela,* 551–52.
52. See Lieuwen, *Venezuela,* 88.

The military hierarchy also condemned other civilian groups that tried to subvert armed forces personnel to their own ends. By 1947 the unrest could no longer be kept hidden. In public utterances, armed forces officials warned of the dire results of civilian intervention in the military sphere. It was even thought necessary for the Minister of Defense to address the Constituent Assembly on January 13, 1947, in reference to the subversive movement that had just been crushed. He said that the armed forces intended to remain firmly apolitical, but that they "could not remain indifferent to the attacks" on them and the "political maneuvers" that attempted to involve them in politics.[53] Delgado condemned "categorically and energetically those citizens who induce our companions in arms to conspire against the legitimate Government with fallacious arguments,"[54] including members of the previous regimes.

In April of the same year an article reprinted in the *Revista de las Fuerzas Armadas* carried essentially the same message. It noted that nonmilitary elements had been trying to draw the Army away from its professional course and had invited it to intervene in the bitter election campaigning as a kind of arbiter of national destiny. Those "seducers" sang the siren song of the "glory" of the young officer movement in 1945 in their attempts to incite them to desire more of the same kind of glory. But, the article continued, there was a better kind of glory—the glory of remaining true to their professional vocation.[55]

The fact was, though, that civilian pressure groups exerted considerable influence on members of the armed forces. One reason for their effectiveness was the almost constant campaigning that went on during 1946, 1947, and part of 1948; political passions remained at fever pitch throughout the entire period. Another reason was that politics was carried on in a completely uncompromising manner. AD, finally in control, assumed a recalcitrant attitude toward sharing power with other groups. Its rivals, COPEI, URD, and PCV, fretted under the yoke of one-party rule. They displayed the same sort of impatience that AD had under Medina.

53. *Revista de las Fuerzas Armadas* (January 1947), 27.
54. *Revista de las Fuerzas Armadas* (January 1947), 28.
55. "El ejército no es árbitro del destino nacional," *Fantoches* (Caracas), No. 1,093, reprinted in *Revista de las Fuerzas Armadas* (April 1947), 201.

Describing AD rule as a complete disaster and as leading Venezuela to ruin, they implied that the nation's political situation called for drastic action.

Their message was not lost on the officer corps. Constant election turmoil, exaggerated propaganda, demagoguery, and political agitation disturbed officers who, unaccustomed to the luxury of modern multiparty democracy, felt such a state of affairs was injurious to the best interests of the nation. It was natural for them to associate these adverse conditions with *Adeco* rule.

A third reason why officers fell prey to political propaganda was the composition of the officer corps. The majority of officers came, not from a privileged caste, but from the lower-middle class of the towns and cities of the interior. The Andean element still predominated, but whether the officer was from Táchira, Trujillo, or the Oriente, he was invariably a man of the people, not an aristocrat. He identified with his civilian compatriots and maintained social contact with them. As a result, he was constantly aware of the problems and attitudes of his fellow citizens, many of which were similar to his own. This close social and spiritual identification with civilian elements contributed to the over-all extrainstitutional pressure on the military and made it more difficult for the average officer to remain aloof from the political struggles raging about him.[56]

Civilian pressures on the military increased after Rómulo Gallegos' inauguration in February, 1948. Although a man of principle, Gallegos was an inept politician and administrator, a poor choice for Venezuela's first civilian constitutional president since Gómez' puppet presidents.

The opposition harassed his administration relentlessly in the press. *El Gráfico,* the COPEI daily, was especially savage in its attacks. To illustrate, a few weeks before the coup an article by a young COPEI leader, Luis Herrera Campins, addressed itself to the politico–military problem. The author was well aware, he said, that the "infinite majority" of the officers who had participated in the 1945 movement were discontented with the course the regime had taken. At the highest levels, however, he observed officers fulfilling politi-

56. Domingo Alberto Rangel, *Los andinos en el poder: balance de una hegemonía, 1899–1945,* 170–71. The traditionally close bond between the Venezuelan officer and his civilian peer was stressed in interviews in Caracas, in May of 1965.

cal and civilian functions. In such cases, those officers were faced with two alternatives: If the officer became dissatisfied with the "sectarian line" of the regime, he had a duty to retire from that position; if he stayed, it meant that he was giving his approval to the "arbitrary" policies of the government. Those officers, like the civilian officials, would some day have to answer for the "detour" the revolution had taken.[57] The article implied that the disaffected officers should rectify the situation.

Pressure from civilian sources could be both more direct and insinuating than journalistic propaganda. For example, women members of COPEI frequently sent intimidating letters to young officers, alluding to their lack of nerve, and even dispatched, along with the letters, items of women's intimate apparel as an insult to their masculinity.[58] COPEI was AD's most aggressive opponent, but URD, PCV, and independent elements all vied with each other in their attempts to promote revolutionary stirrings in the officer corps.

As matters came to a head, *Adecos* realized that the rival propaganda was affecting the officer corps and that hostility toward the ruling party was increasing at a dangerous rate. Military sources later claimed that AD began a campaign of outright antimilitary propagandizing among its membership when it realized that the majority of officers would not be seduced into supporting AD policy.[59] In trying to maintain close bonds with AD sympathizers in uniform, the party sowed the seeds of hatred against the Army among Venezuelan citizens by raising the specter of military dictatorship.

The military claimed that AD's hostility toward the armed forces was not confined to words alone. When the *Adecos* realized that they could no longer count on the military institution for backing, they sought to arm party members. The military charged, further, that AD, under Betancourt's direction, had begun training a paramilitary body, which the party supplied with arms in the hope of countering by force any military uprising. They cited the creation of this alleged AD militia as one of their principal reasons for overthrowing the

57. Luis A. Herrera Campins, "El mérito de una revolución traicionada," *El Gráfico* (Caracas), November 1, 1948.

58. Interview, Caracas, summer, 1965.

59. Venezuela, *Documentos oficiales*, 53–58.

Gallegos regime.[60] After the November 24 coup Delgado Chalbaud said that the Army had evidence that AD was arming its membership, but he did not produce any specific evidence at that time.[61] AD spokesmen denied all knowledge of such a militia; the charge, they said, was fabricated by the military hierarchy as a rationalization for the counterrevolution.[62]

A prolonged struggle over the allocation of Cabinet posts compounded the looming issue of alleged civilian interference with the military institution. As the AD–military rift widened, to keep the number of *Adecos* in the Cabinet to a minimum became military policy. Already at the time of the elections for the Constituent Assembly, a conflict arose over the key Interior Relations post, which had jurisdiction over the internal security and national police forces. The military members of the Junta emphasized to President Betancourt the importance to them of keeping the interior post out of the hands of party members. A civilian independent would be acceptable, but not an *Adeco*. Betancourt reluctantly acceded to their demand, which meant the removal of Valmore Rodríguez, a prominent party leader, from that position. As compensation, Betancourt allegedly sought to have Delgado Chalbaud ousted as Minister of Defense,[63] but quit his efforts in the face of military intransigence. Similar conflicts continued to plague the operation of the Cabinet for the remainder of AD rule.

By 1948 AD's animadversion to the military centered on the person of Lieutenant Colonel Pérez Jiménez, who, it feared, had an unquenchable thirst for power. Pérez Jiménez, on his part, asserted publicly in mid-1948 that he was a defender of the party in power. The first time he met socially with Laureano Vallenilla Lanz, *hijo* (later to be his Minister of Interior Relations), he intimated that he had defended the regime so firmly that many civilians thought he was an *Adeco*. He took credit too for having helped to crush all conspiracies against the government, including the one led by his own brother. He did not do it for love of the party, he said, but for love of country. He felt that subversive acts

60. Venezuela, *Documentos oficiales,* 29, 37.
61. Venezuela, *Documentos oficiales,* 37.
62. Betancourt, *Venezuela,* 561.
63. Venezuela, *Documentos oficiales,* 54.

were "crazy" and would produce a series of uprisings as had occurred elsewhere in Latin America. He concluded that, if it had not been for him, "those people [Adecos] would have been gone for some time."[64]

Pérez Jiménez had indeed used restraint to that point, but AD leaders feared that his attitude and that of the military hierarchy might change at the first opportune moment. Hence, they embarked on a project to get him out of the country. For months AD leaders maneuvered to send him on a mission to other Latin American countries, at the conclusion of which he was to be made military attaché in Rio de Janeiro. He finally made the trip (March 29–April 28, 1948), but Minister of Defense Delgado arranged that when he returned to Caracas he resumed his customary post.[65]

Army leaders reportedly learned in June, 1948, that the *Adecos* were compiling two lists of officers. The "white" list was composed of party sympathizers and the "black" list was of those hostile to the party. The white list was headed by Mario Vargas, the black, naturally, by Pérez Jiménez. The AD objective was to neutralize as many of the men on the black list as possible while favoring party sympathizers, or white-list men, with key positions.[66] According to military sources, the practice had been in effect since Gallegos entered office. Gallegos had immediately begun to recommend strategic personnel changes, a practice not without precedent in Venezuela. Army officials further conjectured that those shifts did not originate with Gallegos but were submitted to the President by AD's national executive committee,[67] which made the practice doubly objectionable.

By October the conflict between civilian and military branches of the regime was reaching a crisis. Homes and cafés were filled with rumors that AD and the Army were moving toward an open break. In this charged atmosphere the third anniversary of the "Revolución de Octubre" was to be celebrated with a large public gathering on the evening of October 18. As Delgado Chalbaud and Pérez Jiménez later declared, they would have participated in the meeting if they had felt assured that it was a national, nonpartisan celebra-

64. Vallenilla Lanz, hijo, *Escrito de memoria*, 278.
65. Luzardo, *Notas*, 149.
66. Ana Mercedes Pérez, *Síntesis histórica de un hombre y un pueblo*, 13.
67. Venezuela, *Documentos oficiales*, 55.

tion and not a political rally. But it was planned by AD, and although Gallegos purportedly had earlier declined to attend, he briefly addressed the crowd and renewed his expressions of adherence to party doctrine. The military suspected that the *Adecos* had designed the rally as a demonstration of mass support for the regime, which would in effect improve their bargaining position in the continuing struggle with the military over Cabinet posts as well as bolster their public image.[68] Whatever the case, the absence of the Minister of Defense tended to corroborate rumors of a serious rift between party and Army.

Several days later, President Gallegos hastily summoned the leaders of the Caracas garrison to a meeting in the Ambrosio Plaza cavalry barracks. Gallegos, in a state of extreme agitation, administered a tongue-lashing to the men, in the course of which he accused them of spreading slanderous rumors of AD's interference with the Army. In reality, he charged, instead of defending the party in power, the officers were reinforcing those rumors. He ordered an immediate stop to such practices and left the meeting abruptly.[69]

The President's intransigent attitude served only to worsen the situation. Minister of Defense Delgado, who was present at the meeting, tried to smooth matters over after Gallegos' departure, but the officers' anger and restlessness increased. In fact, their disaffection had become so great by that time that the high command itself was in danger. The lower-ranking officers were so strongly determined to oust the *Adecos* from power that, unless some solution could be found, they were resolved to remove Delgado, Pérez Jiménez, and other officials who acted as restraining influences.[70]

Consequently, they commissioned the Minister of Defense and the Chief of Staff to present an "ultimatum" to the President. The officers' object was not to force impossible demands on the Chief Executive in order to precipitate a crisis, but rather, to set forth clearly the military's position, in the hope that Gallegos would concede the requested changes. During an interview with Gallegos, Delgado and Pérez Jiménez formally presented the military's demands. The document's four points were: that Acción Democrática "abandon

68. Venezuela, *Documentos oficiales*, 56.
69. Pérez, *Síntesis*, 15–16; see also Vallenilla Lanz, *Escrito*, 281.
70. Interview, Caracas, summer, 1965.

its objective of interesting members of the Armed Forces in politics"; that there be changes in the Cabinet, preferably with independents substituting for *Adecos;* that the party militia be disarmed; and that Rómulo Betancourt leave the country for an indefinite period.[71]

Pérez Jiménez emphasized that the armed forces would remain squarely behind Gallegos so long as he ruled for all the people, not just for *Adecos.* The meeting was fairly cordial and Gallegos agreed to study the demands. Pérez Jiménez left the interview in an optimistic frame of mind and made a tour of the barracks, where he told his subordinates that there was a strong possibility Gallegos would accede to their demands.[72] But more than a week passed without any answer from Gallegos. During that time the President was reported to have interviewed individual officers to test their loyalty, and to have been disappointed in their reactions.[73] When finally he responded negatively to the "ultimatum," military rebellion appeared inevitable.

The public became aware of the gravity of the crisis a week before the coup. Beginning on November 17, there was a flurry of activity in Miraflores Palace; extra guards were posted outside the presidential barracks, and there were rumors of troop movements on the coast. On November 20 press aides of the President announced that, at a meeting with the high command of the armed forces, the latter had manifested their loyalty to the regime. Questioned by reporters upon leaving that meeting, Minister of Defense Delgado Chalbaud said only that "absolute calm exists in all the garrisons of the country."[74] Later the same day, however, a partial suspension of constitutional guarantees was decreed in the face of "a state of alarm affecting the economic and social life of the nation."[75] Thereafter the government censored all political news.

Meanwhile the *Adecos* and Adecophiles in the officer corps had been maneuvering to strengthen their position. Pro-AD officers urged Gallegos to arrest Pérez Jiménez and his clique; others urged Betancourt to take over presidential powers and do the same. Both refused. There was also a

71. Pérez, *Síntesis,* 18.
72. *Ibid.*
73. Pérez, *Síntesis,* 18–20.
74. *El Pais,* November 20, 1948.
75. *El Pais,* November 21, 1948.

move to oust Delgado Chalbaud from the post of Minister of Defense. On November 20 or 21 the commander of the strategic Maracay garrison, Lt. Col. Jesús Manuel Gámez Arellano, arrived in the capital to confer with Gallegos. Aside from Mario Vargas, Gámez had been the strongest backer of AD in the upper echelons of the officer corps, and he was a likely replacement for Delgado Chalbaud in the Ministry of Defense. Gámez requested authorization to take Delgado prisoner, a step he felt would derail the projected coup. Gallegos, however, refused Gámez' request, both because his action would have amounted to declaring Gámez the acting Minister of Defense—an appointment that, he knew, would precipitate an immediate military revolt—[76]and because he could not bring himself to believe that Delgado could betray him. Furthermore, he still hoped for salvation through negotiation.

The President urgently called on two men who he felt would be most successful at mediating the conflict between civil authority and the military. One was Lt. Col. Mario Vargas, hastily summoned from an upstate New York sanatorium to try to find some basis for compromise. Vargas arrived on November 20 and immediately conferred with the President.[77] Later, he took part in a series of conferences with military and civilian officials. He urged his fellow officers to refrain from violence in order to avoid needless bloodshed. But by the time he spoke to them, their mood was so militant that his efforts were futile. When the high command decided to act, he threw in his lot with his brothers in arms, hoping to exert a moderating influence on the new regime and to curtail the expected harsh reprisals against AD.

The other mediator summoned to negotiate for President Gallegos was the governor of the Federal Territory of Amazonas, José A. Giacopini Zárraga, a young lawyer who had been one of the few independents involved in the October 18 movement and who had served for a time as secretary general of the Revolutionary Junta. Gallegos selected him to

76. Luzardo, *Notas,* 155–56. One source claims that Gámez, after the President had expressed confidence in Delgado, asked two lieutenants he brought with him to give the President their opinion of the Minister of Defense. They both saluted Gallegos and declared, "He [Delgado] is a traitor." Interview, Caracas, August, 1968.

77. *El Nacional,* November 21, 1948.

serve as a mediator principally because of his close contacts with the military.

On November 22 Giacopini flew from Amazonas to consult with Gallegos. By that time the garrison at La Guaira had already rebelled and was restricting traffic in and out of Maiquetía Airport on the coast. Giacopini, however, was permitted to pass through, and once in the capital, he went directly to Miraflores to be briefed by Gallegos. At that point the President was so distraught he was unable to give a full explanation of the situation. For that reason, Giacopini offered to confer with the military and report back to the President. In the Miraflores barracks he found almost unanimous hostility against the regime among the junior officers. Determined to overthrow Gallegos at all costs, some of them attacked Giacopini solely for negotiating on behalf of the President. Nonetheless, two high-ranking officers told him they were still open to compromise if Gallegos would agree to certain demands.

After conferring with other officers, Giacopini arranged an interview with Lieutenant Colonel Pérez Jiménez for that afternoon. He had meanwhile learned that the military had made five demands of Gallegos in their latest effort to solve the crisis: that *Adeco* Cabinet members be replaced with independents; that the party militia be disarmed; that party head Betancourt leave the country; that Lt. Col. Mario Vargas remain abroad; and that Lieutenant Colonel Gámez Arellano leave the country. Actually, many officers were in disagreement over these demands, and, in any event, Vargas had already returned to Venezuela.

In his negotiations on the remaining demands, Giacopini told Pérez Jiménez that, in regard to reconstituting the Cabinet, the President had a special affection for Secretary of the Presidency Gonzalo Barrios, who had always been one of the most tactful and moderate of the *Adecos*. Giacopini asked if it would be possible for Barrios to retain his position, as a personal favor to the President, to which the General Staff Chief replied that not only could Barrios stay, but he would allow up to three *Adecos* in the Cabinet.

In regard to the disarming of party militias, Giacopini expressed the opinion that armed militias, as such, did not exist. He told Pérez Jiménez that it would be exceedingly difficult for President Gallegos to inform his fellow party members that their arms would be confiscated when the same measure would not be applied to other groups. Instead, he asked if it would be acceptable to disarm all citizens and revoke all weapon licenses universally. Pérez Jiménez again gave his assent.

As to the exile of the party president, Giacopini explained that it would be extremely embarrassing for President Gallegos to tell his comrade to leave the country. The mediator instead volunteered to discuss this demand with Betancourt confidentially, hoping to persuade him to leave of his own volition. Pérez Jiménez once again agreed, and added that, if necessary, he would be willing also to talk to Betancourt.

Although surprised by Pérez Jiménez' conciliatory attitude, Giacopini was encouraged. He learned, however, as he probed the situation, that the pressure for change that came from below was intensifying. The impasse had continued too long, and the younger officers were losing their patience. There was a real danger that these junior officers would overturn what they considered a weak and vacillating high command. Commandant Pérez Jiménez warned that the pressure could not be withstood for much longer. He reiterated his statement that the officer corps would be content with Gallegos' assurance that he would act as President of all Venezuelans and not rule as the head of a single party for the exclusive benefit of the party.

When Giacopini relayed his discussions with the military to President Gallegos, the latter was in anything but a conciliatory mood. Rather, he decried what he called military insurgency and rejected the modified demands. His solution to the crisis was to demand that the military apologize to him and then submit to disciplinary action. Displaying great emotional strain, Gallegos declared that he had always opposed the use of force in politics and thus would not be able to face his own family if he yielded to the military ultimatum. Giacopini responded that he would ask Rómulo Betancourt's cooperation in an effort to convince him that a more flexible approach was necessary to save the regime.

The negotiator then talked at length with *Adeco* leaders Betancourt and Valmore Rodríguez, president of the Congress, who revealed to him the depth of the hostility between party and armed forces. Betancourt felt that the military movement could be checked by calling a general strike and using the *Adeco* "militias" as "popular" forces, rather than as paramilitary units. He agreed to the demand that he leave the country; if his absence would contribute to political harmony he would leave of his own accord. In fact, he had already calculated that, if he did so, he would be able to return so well fortified politically that he could be a strong contender in the next presidential race.

That evening, at a secret meeting, military spokesmen Delgado Chalbaud and Llovera Páez conferred with Giacopini. When the latter related his conversation with the President, Llovera Páez reacted strongly against what he considered Gallegos' intransigence, and he judged the President as past the point of reason. The more diplomatic Delgado suggested that they call Betancourt instead and confer with him. Within a short time Betancourt appeared at the meeting, accompanied by AD leaders Alberto Carnevali and Gonzalo Barrios. Before they arrived, Llovera instructed Giacopini to present the military demands in a revised form. Instead of the three *Adecos* in the Cabinet that Pérez Jiménez had suggested, they would now permit up to six, with the rest independents; all they wanted was a non-*Adeco* majority.

The first matter for discussion was Betancourt's status. Alberto Carnevali broached the subject by saying that Betancourt was willing to go into voluntary exile but that he had not consulted the party; Carnevali felt the party would reject such a decision. Betancourt interrupted to say that, in a decision of such a critical nature, which might well alleviate a grave national crisis, the party could not impose its decision on him. He informed the group that he was determined to leave the country if the situation so demanded.

Next came the complex issue of altering the political composition of the Cabinet. After a discussion of individual members, Betancourt introduced what he considered the major objection to the reduction in the number of *Adecos* in the Cabinet: AD had received an overwhelming majority of votes in the elections, which gave the party the majority of seats in Congress. How could the party's leaders explain to party members and the Venezuelan people that they had suddenly agreed to a minority position in the Cabinet? He pleaded for the military to understand the party's situation. AD's president, however, was willing to compromise. His proposal was to leave an adequate *Adeco* representation in the Cabinet while changing a number of state governors and lower officials. He cautioned the men in the meeting that this measure was only his personal suggestion and therefore, before it could be implemented, he would have to discuss it with the President. At that point the meeting terminated, with agreement to meet again.[78]

After the civilians left, the mediator and the military representatives exchanged their impressions of the situation. Both Delgado and Llovera were pessimistic about the outcome. They felt it would be extremely difficult to arrange a settlement because of the ever-increasing impatience among the younger officers. In fact, the Minister of Defense considered the situation so critical that he wanted to notify the United States Ambassador of an impending crisis in the government. That proposal met the quick and vehement objection of Llovera Páez, who insisted that the Venezuelans could handle their own internal problems without any outside advice. He was quickly supported by two other officers who were present as aides, and consequently Delgado gave up his attempt to notify the Embassy.[79]

The next day, November 23, Giacopini and Mario Vargas continued their efforts to seek some realistic basis for a settlement. They met with the President, AD spokesmen, and the military command, but they were unable to reach a mutually acceptable compromise. The government, until the last moment before the take-over, assured the people that the situation was under complete control. Gonzalo Barrios went on the radio the day before the coup to assert that the government had complete confidence in the armed forces, which were obeying the orders of the Minister of Defense who, in turn, was taking orders from the President.[80] The same day, however, the entire Cabinet resigned "in order to facilitate the reorganization of the Cabinet in accord with the necessities of national interest."[81] They were not replaced; the two sides had not been able to come to final agreement on the

---

78. The foregoing information on the mediation efforts was obtained in confidential interviews, Caracas, summer, 1965. See also Vallenilla Lanz, *Escrito,* 282–85.

79. Interviews, Caracas, summer, 1965.

80. *El Universal,* November 24, 1948.

81. *Ibid.*

composition of a new Cabinet, and negotiations broke off that same day.[82]

The military movement got under way officially at noon on November 24. The immediate justification for the action was that, just when it appeared that the crisis was nearing solution, the AD-controlled labor confederation (presumably under Betancourt's direction) gave orders for a general strike. The strike would lead to economic disaster and civil war, the military command declared; to prevent nationwide chaos, immediate action to forestall it was imperative.[83]

In contrast to the 1945 affair, the November 24 *coup d'état* was brief and almost bloodless. The Ministry of Defense ordered all military units into action. Army, National Guard, and police units were stationed at strategic sites, and Miraflores Palace was ringed by tanks from the armored battalion stationed across the street. These forces detained President Gallegos at his residence. About an hour after the movement began, Chief of Staff Pérez Jiménez went on the radio with a brief explanation for the military action and a request for citizens to maintain order.

Garrisons in the interior automatically fell into line, and within hours the armed forces had control of the entire nation. Trouble was expected in only one location: the strategic compound in Maracay. AD apparently had hopes of setting up resistance headquarters in Maracay under the protection of the pro-AD commandant, Lieutenant Colonel Gámez Arellano. With that purpose in mind, Valmore Rodríguez and a handful of AD executives went to Maracay on the day of the coup. Maracay was not the haven they hoped for; Gámez, whose ambitious plans had been turned down by Gallegos at their Caracas meeting, was not prepared to lead the country into civil war. After a long telephone conversation with Mario Vargas, who had reluctantly joined the insurgents, Gámez refused to offer resistance;[84] with that decision the regime's last hope flickered out.

---

82. What exactly happened in the final hours before the coup to block a compromise solution is obscure. Most likely, two principal factors came into play. One was the continuing bitter intransigence of Gallegos, which neither Giacopini nor Betancourt and Barrios could soften. The second was that the momentum in the officer corps for a coup had probably built to a point of no return.

83. *El Universal,* November 25, 1948.

84. Luzardo, *Notas,* 155.

Rómulo Gallegos, outraged and humiliated, hastily penned a protest just prior to his arrest. The military coup, he wrote,

culminates an insurrectional process by the forces of the Caracas garrison and of the military high command, initiated ten days ago with the intent of exerting pressure in order to impose a certain line of political conduct on me. . . . Against such pretensions I have energetically fought in defense of the dignity of civil power, against which this blow has been directed in order to establish a military dictatorship.[85]

Nevertheless, in the opinion of one of the mediators, Lieutenant Colonels Delgado Chalbaud, Pérez Jiménez, and Llovera Páez were disposed to negotiate, and until the very end they used moderation and discretion. These qualities also held true for AD spokesmen Rómulo Betancourt and Gonzalo Barrios. The sole cause of the November 24 military movement was not the selfish ambitions of a clique of power-hungry Army officers. That some took advantage of the turn of events to advance their own interests is another matter.

The Gallegos regime fell because it had almost no support outside the AD party and its labor and peasant affiliates. The military very likely would not have intervened, in spite of their dissatisfaction, if the government had had broad-based civilian backing. But because of AD's alleged excesses and sectarianism, the opposition parties, officials of former regimes, and powerful economic interest groups incited the armed forces to intervene. The military, reluctant to maintain such a regime in power and alarmed by the threat of losing their institutional autonomy, tried to force a basic reorientation of the government, which would have resulted in a less partisan regime. Only when their efforts failed and when AD apparently was about to instigate an economic crisis through a general strike and possible civil war through use of party militias, did the high command depose Gallegos and the *Adecos.*

The military obviously had no constitutional sanction to intervene merely because it objected to government policy. The extrusion of the military beyond its legitimately prescribed bounds was inexcusable to constitutionalists. But

85. Venezuela, Presidencia de la República, *Documentos que hicieron historia: siglo y medio de vida republicana, 1810–1961,* II, 415.

such considerations had never stopped Venezuelan military men in the nation's history. To those who felt that Venezuela still needed the armed forces to exert a corrective function when the political system was in serious disequilibrium, the *coup d'état* was, within the Venezuelan political framework, a legitimate and justifiable solution to a crisis provoked by civilian blundering and intransigence. The civilians, it is clear, had not advanced very far beyond the military in their commitment to constitutionalism and democracy.

Military motivation for the coup was mixed. Multiparty political conflict, frequent election campaigns, and civilian rule were new experiences for the military, as they were for Venezuelans in general. The military failed to adjust to the new political circumstances, but many civilians also were unable to adjust. Civilian and military thinking coincided, then, in their alarm over the constant political warfare, violent campaign rhetoric, abuses of press freedom, the winner-take-all attitude of most *Adecos,* and the opposition to the reform program on the part of the elements that had traditionally dominated Venezuelan politics.

The problem of the relationship between military professionalism and the institution's political role had not been clarified, much less resolved. The most professional group in the pre-October 1945 army had intervened politically by force to impose its solution. It undoubtedly believed that it was taking that drastic action for all time, and in the highest national interest. This thinking was also operative in 1948. Officers believed that the attempted politicalization of the armed forces was destroying the atmosphere favorable to development of professional attitudes in the barracks: all political factions were inciting the military to one course of action or another. A quick and painless ouster of the floundering Gallegos-AD regime, they believed, would put an end to civilian interference and allow the military to prepare the way for a return to a civilian regime that would guarantee the institutional autonomy of the military. Armed forces leaders, however, soon discovered that the seizure of power was simpler to accomplish than the devising of a satisfactory formula for returning power to civilians.

Finally, personal ambition was not entirely absent from the motivation of the coup's leaders. Administering the military institution undoubtedly planted the notion in the minds

of certain military leaders that they could administer the
government as well and, as an added benefit, without the
constant agitation, campaigning, demagoguery, and other
luxuries of civilian democracy that a developing country like
Venezuela could ill afford.

CHAPTER V

A DECADE OF MILITARY RULE

From 1948 to 1958 Venezuela was ruled in fact or in name by the leaders of the national armed forces. The military command made national policy decisions; the government suspended representative institutions for part of the period or, when it permitted them to operate, used them only as rubber stamps for the executive; partisan political activity took place only under the restrictions imposed by a series of juntas, and the Pérez Jiménez dictatorship outlawed parties altogether. The course Venezuelan politics took during this period was largely determined by the changing political attitudes of the military leadership. Two events were strongly influential in bringing about the increased military control of government: the mysterious assassination of provisional President Carlos Delgado Chalbaud in 1950, and the invalidation of the Constituent Assembly election of 1952 and assumption of power by Colonel Pérez Jiménez on behalf of the armed forces. The transformation of the military from the hesitant leaders of 1948 into the authoritarian masters of Venezuela for a full decade is of interest here.

The first task of the coup's leaders in November of 1948 was to organize a provisional government. This provisional government, like its predecessor, took the form of a junta, but this time men in uniform formed it exclusively. The leading contenders for membership on the Junta, by virtue of rank, were Minister of Defense Delgado Chalbaud, Chief of Staff Pérez Jiménez, and Assistant Chief of Staff Llovera Páez. One other logical candidate was Mario Vargas, who still commanded respect in the civilian sector and in an important sector of the armed forces.

Late on November 24 the military command met to set up the new government. Vargas had already dissociated himself from any participation in the provisional regime. His conscience would not allow him to take part, even if his health would permit his undertaking the strains of such a position; the new leaders had forcibly overthrown a constitutional regime that he, Vargas, had defended and tried to save until its end.[1]

With the influential Mario Vargas now voluntarily removed from consideration, Pérez Jiménez proposed that the government be in the form of a military junta, with Delgado Chalbaud, Llovera Páez, and himself the three members. Delgado declined, on the grounds that he had been the Minister of Defense in the ousted constitutional government. Nevertheless, when Pérez Jiménez reminded him that he, Delgado, had made the final decision to revolt, Delgado is reported by Mario Vargas to have replied: "That is true, and I will form part of the junta, and preside over it, because I have the highest military rank."[2]

In another account, Delgado's actions seem even more abrupt and opportunistic. Many officers crowded outside the meeting chamber, uncertain about the composition of the new government and eager to know the decisions of the conferees. In the midst of the deliberations, an officer is said to have opened the door of the conference room to deliver a message. In a loud voice for all ears in the room and in the corridor, Delgado Chalbaud asked the officer if he recognized him as the head of the new government. Thinking that Delgado's choice was already a *fait accompli,* the officer answered in the affirmative.[3] Notwithstanding his expressed reluctance to preside over the government—noted by Vargas—Delgado, as in 1945, managed to emerge as leader through a daring stroke of opportunism.

The President of the Junta Militar de Gobierno was born in Caracas in 1909 to Gen. Román Delgado Chalbaud and Luisa Elena Gómez Velutini. His *Andino* father had won wide acclaim for having launched a daring invasion against Gómez in 1929; his mother was a leader of Caracas society. Carlos went to school in France, where he first received a degree in engineering and then attended the prestigious St. Cyr Military Academy for his military training. He served in a French engineering regiment in the late 1930s and also took advanced training. Before returning home, he attended the U.S. Army General Staff school at Fort Leavenworth,

1. Interview, Caracas, summer, 1965.
2. Rómulo Betancourt, *Venezuela: política y petróleo,* 562–63.
3. Interview, Caracas, summer, 1965.

Kansas. Once back in Venezuela, he was assigned to the engineering battalion stationed in Caracas. In July, 1943, he was appointed Chief of the Third Section of the General Staff, and the following December he was named Academic Director of the Military School, a post he filled until the October 18 revolt. From that time until November, 1948, Delgado served as Minister of Defense for both the Revolutionary Junta and the Gallegos administration.

Delgado Chalbaud was widely admired in civilian circles. In addition to his family connections and superior training, Delgado's personal qualities had furthered his career. He was tall, handsome, and possessed of the charm and good breeding of the Latin aristocrat. Scrupulously honest and intellectually gifted, he was one of the best-qualified men ever to lead the Venezuelan armed forces. Furthermore, as President, his acquaintance with almost every important person in the country was a great advantage both to him personally and to the military in winning popular acceptance for the provisional government.

The second-ranking member of the Junta presents an interesting contrast to Delgado. Marcos Evangelista Pérez Jiménez was born in 1914 in the small town of Michelena, Táchira. His parents were Juan Pérez Bustamante, already elderly at the time of Marcos' birth, and Adela Jiménez, a much younger woman, of Colombian origin. Marcos had one sister and two brothers, one of whom, Juan, also pursued a military career. Marcos' father died when the boy was still a child, and his mother taught school to maintain the family. While in elementary school, Marcos and Juan wrote letters for illiterate peasants to augment the family income.[4]

For his secondary schooling Marcos was sent to the Instituto de Gremios Unidos in Cúcuta, Colombia, a school associated with the Colombian Liberal party. He immediately established himself as a serious student by winning high scholastic honors.[5] He then entered the Military Academy of Venezuela in 1931 and graduated in 1934 with one of the best records compiled at the institution, having finished first in his class every year.[6]

4. Laureano Vallenilla Lanz, *hijo, Escrito de memoria,* 301.
5. Federico Landaeta, *Mi general: breve biografía del General Marcos Pérez Jiménez,* 20.
6. See Venezuela, Ministerio de Guerra y Marina, *Memoria: 1935,* 110–11.

Peruvian influence

While continuing his military studies at the Superior War School of Chorrillos, he met a number of outstanding South American officers, including Manuel Odría, the future strongman of Peru. These years in Peru and the associations there were formative for the young officer; he perceived that tha Peruvian military style was applicable to the Venezuelan Army and that an able officer could effect changes in his country's military institution just as the Peruvian officers had in their own.[7] Furthermore, his admiration for the modernization and development the beautiful Peruvian capital had undergone led to a desire to modernize and beautify the city of Caracas, in 1945 still a small, unimpressive, slow-moving city of 300,000.

Upon his return to Venezuela, Captain Pérez Jiménez rose steadily in the military institution. He served as professor of automatic weapons and artillery in the Military School and in January, 1944, while still a captain, he was named head of the First Section of the General Staff. During the years of Acción Democrática rule, Pérez Jiménez served as Chief of the General Staff. In 1946 he was commissioned to pay a courtesy visit to the United States to inspect its military establishment, and in the spring of 1948 he led a Venezuelan military delegation on the already-mentioned tour of eight Latin American countries.

The third member of the military triumvirate was Lt. Col. Luis Felipe Llovera Páez. He, like his long-time friend Pérez Jiménez, was a Tachiran by birth and had received advanced training in Chorrillos. A man of superior intelligence, his wit, tact, and friendship with Pérez Jiménez secured him the second position on the General Staff after the victorious revolt. Unlike Delgado and Pérez Jiménez, Llovera was always content to remain near the top; his ambitions reached no further.

Once the composition of the Military Junta had been decided, a constituting act of the Provisional Government was issued by the high command.[8] The signatories of the act included the Junta members, the commanding officers of the four services, and the Junta's civilian secretary. In a succession of decrees, the new leaders suspended constitutional guarantees, suspended the Congress and state legislatures,

7. Interview, Caracas, July, 1965.
8. See Appendix B, Document 2.

discarded the 1947 Constitution, and reactivated the 1936 Constitution (as amended in 1945). The substitution of the older document represented an about-face for the military, inasmuch as that same group of officers had previously attacked the López Contreras constitution and partially justi-fied their revolt of 1945 on the basis of the necessity for con-stitutional reform.

Since, however, the military government was only provi-sional, Delgado announced that elections would be held for delegates to the Constituent Assembly. In the first weeks after the coup, he repeatedly assured the nation that free elections, with universal suffrage, would be held. All that was needed for the electoral process to begin was a return to normal conditions.[9]

Whether the military's declared intention to restore demo-cratic constitutional government was sincere or not, the Junta was determined that the AD party would never again play an active part in Venezuelan politics. Military spokes-men expressed no outward hostility toward civilian govern-ment in general. Instead, their criticism was directed exclu-sively against AD, particularly against the supposed hard core of "extremists" who controlled the party. Viewing the party as a threat to their own power, the new military gov-ernment initiated a policy of harassment and repression, its objective being the total elimination of AD from Venezuelan politics.

In the first days after the coup, AD leaders were rounded up and imprisoned. Some, like Gallegos and Betancourt, went into exile; others were detained in Venezuelan prisons for varying lengths of confinement. Then, on December 7, 1948, the Junta decreed the dissolution of AD throughout the country, closed its offices, and suppressed all its publica-tions.[10] Although the decree was enforced with a vengeance, AD maintained a skeletal organization and continued clandes-tine opposition to the military regime.[11] It was to rise again,

9. Venezuela, Oficina Nacional del Información y Publicaciones, *Documentos oficiales relativos al movimiento militar del 24 de noviembre de 1948,* 25, 35.

10. See Appendix B, Document 3.

11. For information on AD underground activities, see John D. Martz, *Acción Democrática: Evolution of a Modern Political Party in Venezuela,* 132–46, and Domingo Alberto Rangel, *La revolución de las fantasías,* 13–27.

phoenixlike, in the election campaign of 1958.

The Military Junta initially was considerably more tolerant toward other political organizations. The very night of the coup, Jóvito Villalba and Rafael Caldera, heads of URD and COPEI, respectively, paid visits to the Ministry of Defense to announce their adherence to the newly constituted government.[12] Leaders of both Communist factions also declared their support of the country's new government. Subsequently, a number of *Urredistas* and *Copeyanos* were appointed to state governorships and subordinate posts in the government. Although the new regime may have been anathema to the persecuted *Adeco* leaders, most members of other political organizations were far from unhappy with the turn of events. At that point in Venezuela's political development, the forcible overthrow of a constitutional president was not so repugnant to them as the continued presence in powerful positions of their despised opponents.[13]

But once having consolidated its power, the Junta rarely consulted with party spokesmen on political issues. Nor did *Copeyanos* and *Urredistas* play prominent roles in the new administrative hierarchy. The Junta generally selected political independents and former officials of the López Contreras and Medina regimes for high civilian posts. The upper bourgeoisie had more representation than it had experienced under AD, and as a result, the tone of the new administration, with respect to social policy, became more conservative. Civilians still held a majority in the Cabinet, but the posts of Minister of Interior Relations and Minister of Communications, as well as Minister of Defense, were filled by officers.

The reasons for the military's shift in political philosophy from 1945 to 1948 are difficult to assess, owing in large part to military secrecy on this issue. According to one widely accepted explanation, probably of military origin, they wanted to avoid making the same mistakes twice. To the military, AD rule had been a disaster, but since they had turned over power to AD in October, 1945, there was little they could legitimately do to effect a change. They finally decided that there was sufficient justification for a *coup*

12. Vallenilla Lanz, *Escrito,* 291.
13. Vallenilla Lanz, *Escrito,* 291, and Betancourt, *Venezuela,* 569–70. URD's position vis-à-vis the coup is in a lengthy communiqué that appeared in *El Nacional,* December 23, 1948.

d'état. Hoping to avoid the same predicament, they cautiously decided to delay restoring the government to civilians. They were reluctant to initiate an electoral process that would lead to a situation comparable to that which prevailed from 1945 to 1948.[14]

Furthermore, after three years of operating the military institution according to their modern theories, certain ranking officers were eager to try their hand at operating the entire government. To them, the government could and should function on much the same basis as the armed forces. They also felt that military men, given their superior organizational ability, their respect for efficiency and hierarchy, and their technical expertise, were better public administrators than were civilians. These reasons, plus the seemingly inevitable ambitions for personal power, caused the provisional regime to drag its feet on the matter of swift restoration of constitutional normalcy.

Important decisions were not made by the Junta until the military command had been consulted. The so-called Gran Consejo Militar, composed of the Defense Ministry's highest officials, General Staff chiefs, and commanders of the four services, became the chief advisory body to the Junta.[15] The military triumvirate felt a justifiable need for consulting the armed forces before taking action, lest backing from the instrument of coercion be withdrawn.

Although the Junta continually stressed its provisional status, it proceeded toward the announced goal of new elections at a snail's pace. Elections could not be held until constitutional guarantees had been restored, but these guarantees would not be restored until members of the dissolved AD party ceased subversive activities. A number of plots were uncovered, and all, claimed the government, pointed to the work of *Adecos.* It was merely a question of timing; when conditions returned to normal, a free, open election would be held.[16]

14. Some undoubtedly felt that they should have heeded President Medina's advice to one of his captors on October 19, 1945, that they should not turn over the government to any political party (Isaías Medina Angarita, *Cuatro años de democracia,* 176).

15. Ramón Díaz Sánchez, "La evolución social de Venezuela," in Mariano Picón-Salas and others, *Venezuela independiente: 1810–1960,* 296.

16. Venezuela, *Documentos oficiales,* 75.

It soon became obvious to observers, however, that the course of political events depended upon the respective political attitudes and skills of the two key figures in the new government: the Junta's President and the Minister of Defense. Their opinions on such matters as universal suffrage and the ultimate political objectives of the military governed the possibility and the timing of the elections. More importantly, the political situation was affected by the extent of their personal ambitions. Were they content to remain military leaders or did they have grander designs? Speculations about the relationship between these men and about their personal ambitions were rife at the time. Delgado's subsequent murder added the ultimate question mark.

In the early months of the Military Junta Delgado emerged as a more moderate figure than his colleague. An idealist as well as an opportunist, he had twinges of conscience over the November 24 affair and was more lenient than Pérez Jiménez in the purge of the *Adecos*. Delgado, for example, had given orders to treat Gallegos with the respect due a chief of state. The day after the coup, when it was learned that Betancourt had found refuge in the Colombian Embassy, some subordinate officials offered to assassinate him. When their scheme came to Delgado's attention, he exploded. Such an action was unthinkable, especially at a time when the regime was seeking diplomatic recognition. He fumed that he was the last person to have any part in such a plot: "Up to a short time ago I ate with Betancourt and we worked at the same table!"[17] Some have concluded that Delgado's moderation was a calculated effort to build civilian support, with the objective of becoming constitutional president by way of the ballot box. Quite possibly he was trying to determine the best timing for the elections, while assembling a political base, when death suddenly intervened.[18]

Delgado was not unaware of the ambitions of his colleague Pérez Jiménez. The latter lacked the good looks, brilliance, and civilian connections of the President, but these handicaps were compensated for in other ways. While Delgado made contacts with the Caracas elite, Pérez Jiménez strengthened his ties with his uniformed companions. He pushed forward

17. Vallenilla Lanz, *Escrito,* 295.
18. Betancourt, *Venezuela,* 580–81.

his modernization plans for the military and increased the authority of the chief of the General Staff. Along with his erstwhile companion Llovera Páez, he continued to build support among his colleagues by befriending officers and placing loyal subordinates in key command posts. After 1948, culminating a process that had begun in 1945, all factions in the armed forces coalesced behind Pérez Jiménez. Delgado had disbanded the UPM immediately after the 1945 revolt, since his hold over it was more precarious than that of Pérez Jiménez. The latter, however, tightened his hold on the young officer clique after the 1948 coup, and with the death of Mario Vargas in 1949, he picked up support from the last nucleus of officers still aligned with another leader.[19]

Previous to the November 24 movement, while Pérez Jiménez remained in the background, Delgado was receiving considerable public recognition. Nevertheless, Pérez Jiménez, although he made a poor showing in public and at first impression seemed wanting in intellectual gifts, was not to be taken lightly. Behind the scenes he was planning circumspectly and skillfully, relying on meticulous organization to build support for himself. Whether or not he was content to control only the Army or aspired to grander things is not easy to answer. In the light of subsequent events the latter possibility would seem the stronger. But it should be remembered that Pérez Jiménez had taken a back seat to Delgado for five years. A man possessed of "extraordinary patience,"[20] there was little to indicate that he was about to change.

It is difficult to assess which of the two was in the stronger position at the time of the President's death. Those who give the edge to Delgado Chalbaud state that Pérez Jiménez was no match at wits with him and that the slower-thinking *Andino,* filled with self-doubts and indecision, was losing strength, relative to that of the provisional President. In this frame of theory, Pérez Jiménez was being slowly eased out of power by the deft maneuvering of his rival.[21]

On the other hand, other observers believe that Delgado Chalbaud was little more than a front man for the two military-oriented members of the Junta. With the balance of

19. Interview, Caracas, July, 1965.
20. Rangel, *La revolución,* 52.
21. Rodolfo Luzardo, *Notas histórico-económicas: 1928–1963,* 168–69.

power in their hands, Pérez Jiménez and Llovera were able to force Delgado to do their bidding.[22] Delgado was retained, goes the theory, solely for his prestige in civilian circles and his valuable ties to powerful economic interest groups.

The truth lies somewhere between these two theories. At the time of his death, Delgado was in the ascendancy politically because of his greater rapport with the civilian sector, but Pérez Jiménez was the real military leader, and the Army was firmly under his control. Both enjoyed power, and quite possibly their conflicting ambitions would eventually have led to a power struggle that far overshadowed the election issue.

On November 13, 1950, all speculation as to who was Venezuela's real strongman came to an abrupt end. On the way from his private residence to Miraflores Palace, provisional President Delgado Chalbaud was seized by a band of thugs, taken to an unoccupied house in a residential section of Caracas, and murdered. Over twenty men were involved in the assassination, the alleged ringleader being Rafael Simón Urbina, famous in Venezuela for his revolutionary expedition against Gómez in 1931. Evidence presented at the subsequent inquest unmistakably pointed to Urbina as the leader of the band of assassins. He never stood trial because he was shot by guards while purportedly attempting to escape on the way from jail to the military hospital.[23]

Certain evidence presented at the inquest and later published by the government was damaging to Pérez Jiménez, the obvious beneficiary of the deed. First, Urbina had sought asylum in the Nicaraguan Embassy after the shooting, and while there, he wrote a note to Pérez Jiménez that read, in part: "As I told you . . . I want no other President but you. Delgado was mortally wounded, although I did not want them to kill him. . . . I pray that you come to my aid in the Embassy of Nicaragua, where I am badly wounded."[24] Pérez Jiménez acknowledged having received the note and let it be entered in the official record.

Also, Delgado's aide reported at the inquest that, in the car on the way to the house, Urbina said, "Now we've got him. Pérez Jiménez is informed of everything," to which the

22. Tad Szulc, *Twilight of the Tyrants,* 279.
23. *El Nacional,* November 15, 1950.
24. Martín de Ugalde, "¿Quién mató a Delgado Chalbaud?" *Elite* (February 8, 1958), 48.

startled Delgado replied, "That is a lie."[25]

The circumstances of Urbina's death also pointed to guilt in high places. While driving to the murder scene, one of the assassins accidentally shot Urbina in the right foot, wounding him severely and preventing him from taking active part in the crime. While hiding in the Nicaraguan Embassy afterward, Urbina lost a considerable amount of blood from his wound; he fainted at least four times and was in a very weak condition when he was turned over the authorities. His foot had been completely smashed, so that to stand cost him great effort. The autopsy showed that most of the blood loss had been through his foot and not through the wounds in his torso from shots fired by the guards.[26] This raises the question: How could Urbina run from his captors, when he could barely walk and was probably near death from loss of blood? Since he could not have attempted escape, a logical conclusion is that, in a brutal application of the "law of flight," he must have been shot to prevent him from talking. The official summary of the inquest proceedings was later removed from circulation by order of Pérez Jiménez.[27] To some who studied the record, it seemed incredible that he had allowed its circulation even briefly.[28]

In all fairness, however, it must be added that other observers, including detractors of Pérez Jiménez, read the same records and came to the conclusion that the conspiracy went no further than the mad schemings of Urbina. According to one harsh critic of the future dictator, most people mistook a coincidental for a causal relationship; because Pérez Jiménez was the person who benefited by the shooting, people assumed that he ordered it.[29] Another account reported that, while at the murder house, the band ordered Delgado to bring the other Junta members there on any pretext, the idea being to kidnap all three of them. Delgado refused and thus forced the assassins to depart from

25. Ugalde, "¿Quién mató?" 48, and Betancourt, *Venezuela,* 582–86.

26. J. A. Oropeza Ciliberto, "Así mataron a Rafael Simón Urbina," *Elite* (June 19, 1965), 14–15, and interview, Caracas, May, 1965.

27. I was unable to locate a copy of the *Sumario del juicio seguido a las personas indiciadas de haber cometido el asesinato del Coronel Carlos Delgado Chalbaud* (Caracas, 1951).

28. Interview, Caracas, May, 1965.

29. Luzardo, *Notas,* 168.

their original plan, which seems to have been nonviolent.[30]

Pérez Jiménez appeared to be sincerely grieved by his colleague's death. He was one of the first to express his sympathy to the President's widow, and on that occasion he seemed deeply moved. He took charge of the lying-in-state and burial; it was he who urged that the deceased be promoted posthumously to full colonel. Delgado's widow was at the time of the tragedy appreciative of his aid and sympathy, although she later turned against him.[31]

About three years later, when reports reached the President that the Delgado Chalbaud family was accusing him of the murder, Laureano Vallenilla Lanz, *hijo,* the Minister of Interior Relations and confidant of the dictator, reported that Pérez Jiménez was deeply hurt by the accusation. The latter claimed that he had always been at Delgado's side during the Revolutionary Junta period and that "the intriguers failed in their attempts to alienate us. . . . At all times I tried to bolster his authority and surround him with respect."[32] Whatever the case, if Pérez Jiménez did have a hand in the crime, it has not been definitively established and perhaps never will be.

With the death of Delgado Chalbaud, Pérez Jiménez was in a position to become *Número Uno* both in fact and in name. Sensing that his immediate assumption of the presidency would have been incriminating, given the mystery surrounding Delgado's death, he sought instead to appoint a civilian as head of the Junta, while he and Llovera stayed on as the two military members.

Although Pérez Jiménez was not yet prepared to assume the highest office, he was unwilling to elevate any military colleague to the Junta presidency for fear of losing personal control. The situation called for the selection of a civilian figurehead, whose appointment would serve to placate popular opinion and remove the stigma of exclusive military rule. After discarding various proposals of candidates for the post, at the suggestion of the Junta secretary the military chose a Caracas lawyer named Germán Suárez Flamerich.[33]

Suárez Flamerich had been a legal adviser to the 1948

30. Luzardo, *Notas,* 168.
31. Ugalde, "¿Quién mató?" 48, 68.
32. Vallenilla Lanz, *Escrito,* 326.
33. Vallenilla Lanz, *Escrito,* 323–25, and interview, Caracas, August, 1968.

Military Junta and was currently serving as Venezuelan Ambassador to Peru. A member of the "Generation of '28," a former dean of the Central University Law School, and ex-president of the Caracas Municipal Council, he nonetheless was relatively unknown to the public and his personality was far from exciting. The public rightly regarded him as a puppet of the military chiefs.[34] With Suárez Flamerich as figurehead, the new Junta continued the basic policies of its all-military predecessor. Pérez Jiménez remained Minister of Defense and Llovera Páez, Minister of Interior Relations.

One of the reconstituted Junta's most pressing problems was the maintenance of public order. The assassination of Delgado brought in its wake a wave of disturbances. Student riots led to a temporary closing of secondary schools and the Central University. A plot to assassinate Pérez Jiménez was allegedly discovered.[35] Those political parties still permitted to function carried on increasing agitation for free elections.

The Junta, in the face of mounting opposition, was determined to maintain order at all costs. The new political undesirables crowded the national prisons, and a new prison camp was built on the island of Guasina in the delta of the Orinoco. Hundreds of men, all incarcerated for political offenses, were confined to the low-lying, disease-ridden enclave and forced to do manual labor in the fierce tropical heat.[36] When complaints about the prison reached him, Pérez Jiménez said, "If we are hard now, tomorrow, or in a short time, we will be able to ease up. If we do the opposite, we will have a civil war or anarchy on our hands."[37] Although Guasina was closed by 1953, it remained a nightmare for those who had survived it.

As the "proper" atmosphere for elections and the restoration of civil liberties receded further into the future, the government stood firm in the face of growing public clamor for elections. Unlike Delgado Chalbaud, Pérez Jiménez was extremely reluctant to restore civilian constitutional rule. His main objection, he stated, was to the idea of enfranchising

34. Vallenilla Lanz, *Escrito,* 330–31, 336.
35. *El Nacional,* April 15, 1952.
36. For a prisoner's account of conditions in Guasina, see José Vicente Abreu, *Se llamaba S.N.*
37. Vallenilla Lanz, *Escrito,* 328–29.

minors (18 to 21) and illiterates, who made up the bulk of the population.[38]

A change had come over Pérez Jiménez since 1945. He had not attempted to interfere with the three major elections held from 1946 to 1948; why then was he so cautious about holding an election at this juncture? The most plausible answers are that, first, he was apprehensive about a repetition of the commotion, demagoguery, and bitterness that had characterized the elections under AD sponsorship. Also, he may have anticipated that the outlawed *Adecos* would throw their secret support to one of the opposition candidates in order to defeat the government. More fundamentally, he had come to believe that the military were better suited to the task of building Venezuela materially than were the politicians. National development took time, and an atmosphere of order and stability was necessary for its growth. The military could best provide such conditions. Finally, he probably harbored continuist intentions. Power suited him, and he was reluctant to loose the reins of authority.

As months of rule by decree stretched into years, the excuse that the requisite orderly atmosphere was still lacking sounded more 'and more feeble. And despite the adoption in April, 1951, of an electoral law providing for compulsory voting for all citizens from 21 to 65, including illiterates,[39] another year elapsed before most constitutional guarantees were restored and the campaign to elect members to the Constituent Assembly could get under way.

A restrictive political party act was passed in conjunction with the electoral law. The act required all political organizations to register with the government in order to receive approval to campaign. The two leading parties not under banishment, COPEI and URD, both received government certification and began to campaign, although a number of provisions circumscribed their activities. Under the act's provisions, they had to furnish detailed information to the government regarding party-sponsored public meetings, membership rolls, and finances. If irregularities in party records surfaced, the government was empowered to impose

38. Leo B. Lott, "The 1952 Venezuelan Elections: A Lesson for 1957," *Western Political Quarterly,* 10 (September 1957), 542.
39. *El Nacional,* April 19, 1951.

heavy fines or to restrict the party's campaigning. The act required the parties to obtain a special permit for every public assembly at least two days in advance; to campaign in a subdued fashion; to refrain from disrespect toward or overly severe criticism of the authorities. The parties could not use broadcasting media for propaganda purposes.[40] Both parties agreed that "not even a minimum of respect for liberty or guarantees existed in the unfolding electoral process."[41] There was evidence of harassment of the opposition by forces supporting the regime; activities of COPEI and URD were given only limited coverage in the press, and even that was subject to censorship.

In support of the regime, several groups organized into a collective party known as the Frente Electoral Independiente (FEI)—the Independent Electoral Front. Like the other parties, FEI sought to elect delegates to the Assembly; however, a movement closely related to it began to wage a campaign supporting Marcos Pérez Jiménez for President. This Movimiento Pro-Adhesión gathered force in the last weeks of the campaign. The election was slated for November 30, 1952, and by November 5 over 1.5 million persons had reportedly signed petitions in support of Pérez Jiménez for President. A week before the election, the Movimiento Pro-Adhesión merged with FEI to become a single force. FEI's propaganda stressed the material progress made under military rule and advanced little else in the way of political doctrine or programs of social betterment.[42]

AD was of course omitted from the electoral process. As far as the government was concerned, the party no longer existed, but from exile, party leaders published a manifesto shortly before election day, denouncing the election as a farce. The document stated that AD would be willing to participate in any free election, but the voting process elaborated by the Junta was worthless. It charged the government with seeking only to legitimize a *de facto* regime. Since no dissolved party could participate, AD leaders asked the party membership to abstain from voting.[43] It appears, however, that Betancourt reversed that policy a few days prior to the

40. Lott, "The 1952 Elections," 543–45.
41. Lott, "The 1952 Elections," 545.
42. Lott, "The 1952 Elections," 546–48.
43. Acción Democrática, Comité Ejecutivo Nacional, *Acción Democrática ante la farsa electoral*, 3–4.

election and secretly urged *Adecos* to cast their votes for URD.[44]

The election itself was conducted in strict fairness and order. The authorities took stringent precautions against possible violation, and impartial observers agreed that "the voters were able to cast their ballots in complete secrecy."[45]

Trouble began the day after the election, when the Supreme Electoral Council published preliminary figures, based on about a third of the results. At that point URD led the FEI by almost 150,000 votes, while COPEI lagged far behind in third place.

Already on election day, the military hierarchy had begun to suspect that the vote was not going its way. His principal political advisers had persuaded Pérez Jiménez to hold elections, and they had convinced him that the government would assuredly win. Following their advice was one of Pérez Jiménez' worst political blunders. As even a key adviser admitted, the government had lost much of its dynamism and prestige since the lackluster Suárez Flamerich had replaced Delgado Chalbaud at the head of the Junta; Pérez Jiménez and his colleagues should have realized the extent of the hostility to the regime in recently politicized Venezuela.[46]

Late on election day, the military began to weigh alternate courses of action, in the event FEI was defeated. After much discussion the senior officers agreed not to relinquish authority under any circumstances. They had the power to enforce their decision; all they needed to do was to stand firm and united. Orders went out to all garrisons to be on the alert, with special attention to the vital Maracay command. The military determined that, if necessary, the armed forces would take over the government by force.

The next morning, with the election still undecided, Laureano Vallenilla Lanz, *hijo,* suggested a possible course of action. His scheme was for the Junta to resign. They would present their resignations to representatives of the armed forces, from whom they had secured their power in the first place. Then the military high command would select Pérez

---

44. Ana Mercedes Pérez, *Síntesis histórica de un hombre y un pueblo,* 24. Others insist that the decision by *Adecos* (and Communists) to vote the URD ticket was entirely spontaneous; see Luzardo, *Notas,* 170–71.

45. Lott, "The 1952 Elections," 548.

46. Vallenilla Lanz, *Escrito,* 336, 344.

Jiménez to be interim President until the Constituent Assembly, in turn, would elect him constitutional President.[47]

Pérez Jiménez, indecisive at other crucial junctures in the past, wavered at taking so drastic a step. He appeared perplexed as to whether he should accept the outcome of the election or overturn the results and seize command of the country. When a National Guard official advised him to take power and dissolve the Junta, Pérez Jiménez, showing great emotion, is reported to have answered:

> If you men help me, I'll remain. . . . I could leave the country, but I believe that Venezuela still needs me. . . . I do not have personal ambitions. . . . If I resolve to remain here it is for the country, exclusively for the country.[48]

The Junta's resignations were drafted by Vallenilla, signed by the three members, and presented to the commanders of the four services. The military then delivered presidential powers into the hands of the self-abnegating Pérez Jiménez, who would remain as provisional President until a new constitution was adopted.[49]

When subsequent returns showed the FEI badly trailing URD, all election news coverage was suspended. On December 2, Pérez Jiménez announced over the radio that the Junta had returned its powers to the armed forces, which had in turn designated him interim President.[50]

The final figures published on December 13 revealed the following results:[51]

FEI	788,086
URD	638,336
COPEI	300,309
Others	41,259

---

47. Vallenilla Lanz, *Escrito,* 348.

48. Vallenilla Lanz, *Escrito,* 347.

49. Arturo Aguilar, *Tierra sin justicia: historia y política contemporáneas,* 26.

50. Early the same day Pérez Jiménez sent a telegram to URD leaders Villalba and Ignacio Luis Arcaya, accusing their party of collaborating with and being the vehicle for the electoral victory of AD and the PCV. The use of the words "triunfo electoral" suggests that Pérez Jiménez acknowledged the URD victory (Iván Claudio, *Breve historia de URD,* 56–57, and Betancourt, *Venezuela,* 675–76).

51. Lott, "The 1952 Elections," 549.

To those who voted against the regime, these figures added up, not to an FEI victory, but to a *golpe de estado* in the tradition of 1945 and 1948. For the third time in seven years, the Venezuelan armed forces took direct action to circumvent the constitutional process for transfer of authority.

URD leader Jóvito Villalba, who had fully expected victory as a result of the early returns, was called to a meeting with the newly appointed Minister of Interior Relations, Laureano Vallenilla Lanz. Villalba condemned the regime for its flagrant violation of the democratic process and added that the Constituent Assembly could not convene, for lack of a quorum, since both URD and COPEI were determined to boycott it.

When his initial protest brought no reaction, Villalba, in a more conciliatory tone, proposed an alternate scheme. URD would be willing to have the Assembly elect a political independent as provisional President, and the party would even permit Pérez Jiménez to continue as Minister of Defense. URD would have an effective voice in the government but would refrain from all reprisals against the military.

When Vallenilla rejected the proposal, Villalba lashed out again, declaring that the government had lost because it had supported Pérez Jiménez as presidential candidate. "The country is sick of the *tachirense* monopoly,"[52] he added. The bitter Villalba was arrested as he left the Ministry, and on December 16 he and six other URD leaders were "invited" to leave the country "temporarily" by the provisional government.[53]

Despite an official boycott of the Constituent Assembly by COPEI and URD, enough of their delegates defied party orders to constitute a quorum. The Assembly was nonetheless controlled by proregime delegates who easily pushed through their own programs. First, they gave Pérez Jiménez full powers of government until decreed otherwise; second, they framed and adopted a new constitution that met acceptance by the military; and, third, on April 17, 1953, they elected Col. Marcos Pérez Jiménez constitutional President for a five-year term.

One of the initial objectives of the new regime was to develop a philosophy that would justify its existence and

52. Vallenilla Lanz, *Escrito,* 367.
53. *El Universal,* December 17, 1952.

proclaim its goals. Venezuelans thus soon began hearing and reading the phrase, "The New National Ideal." Generally attributed to Laureano Vallenilla Lanz, *hijo,* the slogan was an updating or, to some, a parody, of the theory of "Democratic Caesarism" evolved by Vallenilla's father, an eminent historian and sociologist. In his *Cesarismo democrático*[54] and other works, the elder Vallenilla Lanz had advanced the theory that Latin America was not ready for the Anglo-Saxon brand of representative democracy. More suited to the continent were benevolent, paternalistic dictators who ruled autocratically for the welfare of the people. He gave extensive biological, sociological, and historical bases for the theory as it applied to Venezuela. Since Vallenilla was a defender of General Gómez, many believed that his social philosophy amounted to an intellectual justification of the Gómez dictatorship.

The New National Ideal, however, was never put in concrete and systematic form. Kept deliberately vague, the regime claimed that it was founded on "our historical tradition, our natural resources, and our geographic position," and had for its objectives "the rational transformation of the physical environment and the moral, intellectual, and material betterment of the country's inhabitants."[55]

In practice, the regime emphasized "material betterment" of Venezuela to the detriment of the moral and intellectual. Although Pérez Jiménez still claimed adherence to the ideals of the 1945 revolution, gone were the noble words about democratic fulfillment. Democracy now was to be judged by its "practical accomplishments" rather than by its origins or methods.[56] Political activity was outlawed. The aim of the regime now was to rid Venezuela of the scourge of partisan

54. Laureano Vallenilla Lanz, *Cesarismo democrático: estudio sobre las bases sociológicas de la constitución efectiva de Venezuela.* In an interview, Caracas, August 1968, I learned that Pinzón, not Vallenilla, had originated the "New National Ideal." Whatever the case, Vallenilla acknowledged that Pinzón, who was legal counsel to President Pérez Jiménez, wrote most of the dictator's speeches (Vallenilla Lanz, *Escrito,* 392).

55. República de Venezuela, *Venezuela bajo el nuevo ideal nacional: realizaciones durante el tercer año de gobierno del General Marcos Pérez Jiménez,* 8–9.

56. República de Venezuela, *Cinco discursos del General Marcos Pérez Jiménez, Presidente de la República, pronunciados durante el año 1955 y obras realizadas por el gobierno en 1955,* 104.

politics and concentrate national energies on material progress, carried out in an atmosphere of political stability.

In his self-concept, Colonel Pérez Jiménez was more in the tradition of Guzmán Blanco—the civilizer and builder—than that of his *Andino* predecessor, Juan Vicente Gómez. He once told Vallenilla Lanz: "I do not want to be compared to the Well-Deserving [Gómez]. . . . He headed a static government. . . . At his death we inherited the same Republic that Guzmán Blanco left us, the same capital, the same schools and almost the same roads."[57]

Pérez Jiménez saw as his mission the material development, modernization, and beautification of Venezuela. He wanted his homeland to be the showcase of Latin America. He admired the material accomplishments of such Latin strongmen as Manuel Odría, Juan Perón, Rafael Trujillo, and Getúlio Vargas, and he was obsessed with surpassing them. For example, the luxurious complex, Círculo de las Fuerzas Armadas, on the outskirts of Caracas was little more than an attempt to outdo the costly officers' facilities in Peru.[58]

Venezuela underwent impressive development during the decade of military rule, especially after 1953. Pérez Jiménez showed signs of being an excellent administrator. Under his administration the government pushed forward huge public works projects and constructed thousands of miles of highways, including the Pan-American highway and the Caracas-La Guaira expressway. Construction was begun on a steel works and a petrochemical plant, and Caracas was transformed into a glittering, modern capital city. The ultramodern University City was completed and scores of high-rise "superblocks" for the housing of working-class families were erected.

Much criticism has been heaped upon the Pérez Jiménez administration for concentrating on valueless, showy public works projects instead of socially constructive programs. Such criticism is not entirely justified. Public planning was

57. Vallenilla Lanz, *Escrito,* 305. On another occasion he told Vallenilla: "I want to be a true revolutionary, the man who carries civilization to the entire nation. It does not matter if they call me a tyrant tomorrow, if a great work remains to defend me" (*ibid.,* 337).
58. Interview, Caracas, May, 1965. A more sociologically oriented explanation is advanced by John J. Johnson in *The Military and Society in Latin America,* 173.

somewhat disorganized, but that had been the case before his administration and has been since. The administration sacrificed the interests of the interior to those of the capital, but that too was in the Venezuelan tradition. The agricultural sector was sadly neglected, but, with the possible exception of the AD *trienio,* during no other period had any substantial headway been made in revitalizing Venezuelan agriculture.

The Army assumed a larger role in public administration than it had exercised under Medina, the Revolutionary Junta, and Gallegos. In essence, the Army's public role was merely an intensification of the trend that began in 1945, reversing the civilianizing efforts of López Contreras and Medina. Pérez Jiménez, unlike Medina, was well aware that his power derived from the armed forces, not from the Constituent Assembly or Congress. At least for the first few years he accurately judged the mood of the armed forces and was able to keep them relatively content.

The President's first gesture toward the armed forces was to emphasize to the point of exaggeration their strategic importance. He stressed the noble traditions of the national army that originated in the Liberating Army of Bolívar. For example, while still Minister of Defense, he told the troops: "We feel ourselves honored to be the depositories of a heroic and permanently victorious tradition, written by our forces on the soil of half a continent."[59] Moreover, Pérez Jiménez seems to have had designs on making Venezuela first among South American nations, not only on the historical basis of its leadership in the struggle for independence, but also because of its strategic geographical position.[60]

Second, he advanced the interests of the institution through his policy of heavy spending on defense matériel. The Army was given tanks, artillery weapons, automatic rifles, and other matériel in large numbers. The Navy likewise was strengthened. The Venezuelan Navy had not been of great effect since the time of the wars for independence, and at times it had been nonexistent. Pérez Jiménez now developed a fleet of destroyers, added new ships of lesser size, and reconditioned others. The naval build-up increased morale among the sailors and placed the service more nearly

59. Marcos Pérez Jiménez, *Pensamiento político del Presidente de Venezuela,* 19.
60. Interview, July 23, 1965.

on a par with those of other Latin American countries. The Air Force, too, was modernized and its effectiveness increased by the addition of modern bombers, jet fighters, and transport planes. The National Guard was the recipient of much new equipment, and FAC cadets attended classes in a specialized school.

Third, military education underwent a process of expansion and refinement. Before Pérez Jiménez, three academies had existed—the Military School in Caracas, the Naval School in Maiquetía, and the School of Military Aviation in Maracay. The dictator put a new system into effect. A two-year basic school was opened in Caracas for cadets from all branches of the service. Afterward, the cadets went to their respective service academies for specialized work. In addition, the Superior War School was opened at the El Valle military complex in Caracas with a more advanced curriculum, including command and general staff courses.

Furthermore, the number of military personnel going abroad for advanced studies continued to increase. Up to 1945 only 49 officers had ventured outside Venezuela to continue their training; between 1946 and 1955, 455 officers went abroad.[61] In the year 1957 alone, 133 officers were on missions of study abroad, including 51 in the United States, 25 in Italy, 21 in Peru, and 14 in England. In addition, 261 noncommissioned officers, cadets, and soldiers were spending the year on various study missions outside Venezuela.[62]

Fourth, the Pérez Jiménez regime paid heed to the material welfare of the officers and men. The administration built modern barracks and other facilities throughout the country, including plush officers' clubs, like those in Caracas and Maracay. The Social Assistance Fund expanded, and favorable loan and mortgage arrangements contributed to the material comfort of the personnel.

The oil boom of the 1950s helped the military regime to increase its defense spending without enlarging the share of the national budget going to the armed forces. In 1955, for instance, 8.8 per cent of the national budget was allocated to the Ministry of Defense,[63] down slightly from the first year

61. Venezuela, *Cinco discursos,* 80.
62. Venezuela, Ministerio de la Defensa Nacional, *Memoria: 1957,* 142, 178.
63. Venezuela, *Cinco discursos,* 38.

of Pérez Jiménez' constitutional term, when it amounted to 9.4 per cent.[64] In comparison, the López Contreras regime had devoted an average of approximately 12 per cent of the total budget to the Ministry of War,[65] although government revenues were much lower in the 1936–1941 period.

Officer participation in nonmilitary government functions increased after 1948. The percentage of military personnel in state governorships rose. In 1955, of the governors of the twenty-one states, the two territories, and the Federal District, five were full or lieutenant colonels (two in retired status). Again in 1957, five of the twenty-five governors had military backgrounds. Under General Medina, in contrast, no active officers had held those posts, and the all-civilian policy had continued under AD. Other high posts were held by officers, including the presidencies of the Línea Aeropostal Venezolana, the Compañía Venezolana de Navegación, and other autonomous government agencies. Such posts, however, had been traditionally entrusted to military men.[66]

In the Cabinet, officers occupied two posts: Defense and Communications. After 1952, the Ministry of Interior Relations was again in civilian hands; the legislative branch of government had long since eliminated the military from any influence.[67]

In the 1945–1955 decade, no promotions to general had been made. All generals appointed before October, 1945, had been retired by decree of the Revolutionary Junta. In 1948 the high command that toppled the Gallegos regime was still composed of lieutenant colonels. In 1950 Delgado Chalbaud

64. Ladislao T. Tarnói, *El nuevo ideal nacional de Venezuela,* 236. The regime's last budget allocated 8.6% to the Ministry of Defense. In that same year (1958), Brazil devoted 29.1% of its national budget to its armed forces, Colombia 26.3%, Peru 21.9%, Argentina 21.5%, and Mexico 8.4% (*El Nacional,* December 27, 1959).

65. See Chapter II.

66. Under AD rule (1945–1948), for instance, both the Línea Aeropostal Venezolana and the Compañía Venezolana de Navegación had military presidents. Lt. Col. Mario Vargas was Minister of Communications and later Minister of Interior Relations. A few officers held high posts in the Interior Ministry, and an army lieutenant headed the Federal District Police. The only state president with a military background was a retired lieutenant colonel who served as president of Táchira State.

67. See Leo B. Lott, "Executive Power in Venezuela," *American Political Science Review,* 1 (June 1956), 423.

was promoted to colonel posthumously. The following year Pérez Jiménez achieved the rank of colonel, and in 1955 he became the first officer in more than ten years to be promoted to brigadier general. By 1958 the Venezuelan armed forces had a dozen generals, and a concomitant swelling of commissions in the colonel bracket kept pace with that increase.

The renewal of promotions to the rank of general was one factor that accounted for the increased presence of military men in civilian positions of government. A general needed a job worthy of his rank; since there were not enough high-level posts within the military establishment, these officers were given prestigious assignments in the civil administration. Pérez Jiménez here was falling into practices employed by pre-1945 regimes—the same practices he had previously deplored.

Another reason for military intrusion into normally civilian posts was the belief, held by Pérez Jiménez and most officers, that military men were better suited for public office than civilians because they had the technical training and sense of order and hierarchy needed for administrative positions. The politician could not get things done; the professional soldier could, and that was all that counted. In a phrase reminiscent of Porfirio Díaz, Pérez Jiménez asserted: "Governing is administering, and not politicking."[68]

Again, this movement of the military into civilian posts was a complete reversal of the aims of the UPM movement and in line with a whole change in attitude exhibited by the new military chiefs. It was caused by a combination of known and unknown factors, including disillusionment with the AD's governing experiment; a budding sense among the military of intellectual superiority fostered by advanced technical training; continuist intentions on the part of Pérez Jiménez and seduction by power; initial insincerity; and a lingering inability to face squarely the political implications of genuine professionalism.

Critics of Pérez Jiménez have emphasized the degree of military predominance in his regime, but they have also denounced the continuing *Andino* influence.[69] To some crit-

68. Luis Cova García, *Fundamento jurídico del nuevo ideal nacional,* 142.
69. See Betancourt, *Venezuela,* 580.

ics, Pérez Jiménez was in the direct line of Castro, Gómez, López Contreras, and Medina. They also believe that he surrounded himself with Tachiran advisers, both civilian and military, and ruled for the benefit of his region to the detriment of the nation as a whole. Such a generalization is not supportable.

General Pérez Jiménez was not a typical Tachiran. Although a native of the state, he left the provincial environment at an early age. His Colombian mother sent him to Cúcuta, across the border, for his secondary education. Directly after leaving the Gremios Unidos School he entered the Military Academy in Maracay, which at the time served as the political and military headquarters for Venezuela. Once graduated from the Academy, Pérez Jiménez continued his studies in Peru, where he came in contact with new and different ideas. The rest of his career he spent in Caracas, broken by brief trips to other Latin American countries and the United States. Little, except a few nostalgic reminiscences, remained from his boyhood days to influence his thinking along regional lines. Although Pérez Jiménez did much for the material improvement of the state of Táchira, he did the same for other areas of the country. His master plans for public works projects reveal no predisposition to favor Táchira.[70]

Nevertheless, it is true that General Pérez Jiménez had many Tachiran friends in the military who exerted a strong influence on him, a situation that resulted from the composition of the officer corps of the Army, still heavily *Andino*. Applicants for the military schools from the economically depressed Andean states continued to outnumber those from the rest of the country. Although there undoubtedly was a certain amount of regional favoritism that brought Tachirans to high military posts with more frequency than non-*Andinos,* this pattern was no more nefarious than the pervasive tradition of southern dominance in the United States Army. Even if one accepts the assumption that an Andean clique controlled the dictator, it is relatively meaningless; the *Andino* officers of the "Generation of '45" and later were not a provincial breed. Intensely nationalistic, their attention to

70. Interview, Caracas, June, 1965. If anything, Pérez Jiménez gave more attention to the Federal District than was normal even for a Venezuelan president (see Betancourt, *Venezuela,* 755–60).

national and international problems far outweighed any concern they might have had for the area of their birth.

There are references also to a mysterious, but powerful, clique of civilian advisers who hailed from Táchira, called the Grupo Uribante. Reportedly, members of this exclusively Tachiran group put pressure on the President to place them in important governmental positions, while they lined their own pockets in the bargain.[71] Actually, the Grupo Uribante consisted mainly of Táchira professional men and students residing in Caracas who gathered for discussion of problems affecting their native region and the country. Their purpose was largely cultural. One of their main objectives was to counteract the pervasive anti-*Andino* sentiment of the time by showing the Venezuelan people that *Andinos* were not all barbarous caudillos or soldiers, but cultured and educated men, equal in urbanity to any comparable group in Venezuela.

This group of young Tachirans published a periodical that appeared for the first and last time in September, 1945. Of the editors and collaborators of *Sumario de Occidente,* the name farthest down on the list was that of Marcos Pérez Jiménez.[72] A month later the *golpe de estado* brought an end to the periodical, and the Grupo Uribante never met as such again. Some of its members later became collaborators of the dictator and perhaps exerted an influence on him as individuals, but others, such as Ramón J. Velásquez, served long prison terms for opposing the regime.[73]

Pérez Jiménez' principal advisers were non-*Andinos.* His two closest political confidants, Laureano Vallenilla Lanz and Pedro Estrada, were from Caracas and the Oriente, respectively. In the sensitive post of Federal District governor, Pérez Jiménez placed retired Lt. Col. Guillermo Pacanins, a *Caraqueño.* On economic matters, such wealthy *Caraqueños* as Fortunato Herrera and Napoleón Dupuy advised the dictator. Clearly, the extent of regionalist influence in the administration of Pérez Jiménez has been highly exaggerated. The "Andean hegemony," such as it was, had ended definitively in 1945.

71. Betancourt, *Venezuela,* 580.

72. *Sumario de Occidente,* I (September 1945). Only volume published.

73. Based on interviews in May, June, and July, 1965.

*   *   *   *   *

Between 1948 and 1958 Venezuelan militarism reached its zenith. The elimination of the moderate Delgado Chalbaud in 1950 and the nullification of the 1952 election paved the way for the outright military dictatorship presided over by Gen. Marcos Pérez Jiménez. If Delgado had lived, or if the military command had been unable to unite behind the solution of the election invalidation, the Venezuelan military institution might have a very different record and reputation today. Perhaps the political role of the Venezuelan armed forces would have evolved into that of "protector" or "guarantor of the constitution," similar to that of some other Latin American military bodies. But such conjecture, fascinating as it may be, is ultimately fruitless.

The military under Pérez Jiménez consolidated power at the end of 1952 and kept a firm grip on the government for five years. Not since General Gómez had there been such total suppression of political activity and civil liberties. Pérez Jiménez, unlike some of his military contemporaries, made no pretense about ruling Venezuela democratically. The earlier advocate of an apolitical military institution and austere professionalism had now become the supreme military politician, under whom his officer colleagues dominated decision-making in many key areas of policy. With no organized civilian power base to count on, Pérez Jiménez ruled in the name of and on behalf of the military. Insofar as he was able to keep his fellow officers united behind him and contented with their material lot he was successful in his militarist experiment. But when military disaffection eventually matched civilian discontent with the regime, Pérez Jiménez' rule was doomed.

CHAPTER VI

THE JANUARY 23 INSURRECTION

Despite the impressive material progress made during the decade after the fall of Gallegos, Venezuela's military rulers had, by 1957, succeeded in alienating almost every sector of society. At one point or another, the unemployed, the *campesinos,* labor, the business community, professionals and intellectuals, the students, the Church, and the military either moved into outright opposition or remained neutral while the regime struggled to maintain itself in power. Politically inept, corrupt even by Venezuelan standards, Gen. Marcos Pérez Jiménez met the mounting opposition with increasing repression, committed needless political blunders and, finally, fell because he lacked the will to remain in power.

Security was one of the most vexing problems for the military government. In Venezuela, internal security, public order, and political procedures were under the domain of the Ministry of Interior Relations. At the time of the December 1952 "coup," Colonel Pérez Jiménez raised Laureano Vallenilla Lanz, *hijo,* to that sensitive Cabinet post. A prominent member of Caracas society, Vallenilla was young, intellectually gifted, and a francophile. His political philosophy followed closely that of his positivist father, whom he greatly admired. Contemptuous of both the lower classes and professional politicians, he favored a Platonic government of philosophers, but settled for its vague Venezuelan approximation of lower-middle-class Army officers and creole oligarchs. Although an able administrator, his repressiveness, arrogance, and thievery made Vallenilla Lanz one of the most hated men in Venezuela.

The second ranking official in the Ministry of Interior Relations was Pedro Estrada. A man of charm and intelligence, he was nonetheless thoroughly ruthless in handling opponents of the regime. For seven years (1951–1958) he supervised the feared Seguridad Nacional (SN), or National Security Police, which had been created in 1946 by act of the

Revolutionary Junta.[1] The national security forces had been completely reorganized after the October 18 revolt. All Medina appointees were cashiered, and pro-AD men substituted. After the 1948 coup the SN underwent another shakeup that eliminated all *Adeco* influence. Inasmuch as the principal qualification for membership in the SN was to have the correct political loyalties, many of the men hired after 1945 were otherwise unqualified for police service, and most were totally inexperienced. Frequently their acts were inept rather than cruel;[2] nevertheless, SN agents gained a notorious reputation for abuse of authority and for repression, especially after 1948. The security force, sustained by a huge budget, rose to over 5,000 employees under Pérez Jiménez, with thousands more working as part-time informers. The government planted spies everywhere, from private homes to military barracks.

All political parties came under the wary eye of Vallenilla and Estrada. Acción Democrática and the Communist party were the principal victims of Pérez Jiménez' repressive machinery, although the dictator later reached a *modus vivendi* with a minority faction of the Communists.[3] Initially, COPEI and URD fared better than the other parties, but after December, 1952, they, too, had to curtail all open activity, and such opponents of the regime as Jóvito Villalba and other URD leaders had to abandon the country after the 1952 election. COPEI leader Rafael Caldera lived a precarious existence in Caracas for several years, was eventually confined, and finally forced to leave the country. All active politicking was outlawed, with severe reprisals meted out to

1. In a confidential interview with a high civilian official of the military and Suárez Flamerich provisional governments, summer, 1968, I learned that Pérez Jiménez had informed the interviewee he refused to appoint *Andinos* to those unpopular posts. He did not want to give *Andinos* a bad name; those jobs were better suited to "s.o.b.'s" such as Vallenilla and Estrada.

2. Interviews in San Cristóbal, June, 1965, and in Caracas, August, 1968. The Táchira division of the SN followed a policy of restraint during the decade of military rule. Whereas Estrada had to flee the country upon his dismissal, the SN chief in Táchira, Enrique Benavides, continued to live in the state after the fall of the regime without any molestation.

3. The position of the "Black" Communists vis-à-vis the military regime is described in Robert J. Alexander, *The Communist Party of Venezuela*, 29–38.

offenders. As a result, by the late 1950s, all political organisms, with the exception of one Communist faction, were working clandestinely against the dictatorship.

Opposition grew, not only among political parties, but among civilians on all levels of Venezuelan society. Working-class citizens were aroused by the government's cavalier treatment of organized labor. Two months after AD was disbanded, the Confederación de Trabajadores de Venezuela (CTV)—the Venezuelan Workers Confederation, met the same fate. The official replacement, the Confederación Nacional de Trabajadores (CNT)—the National Workers Confederation, was nothing but a government mouthpiece. Moreover, in contrast to the prolabor stance of the AD regime, Pérez Jiménez was largely indifferent to labor demands. The government closely restricted strikes, collective bargaining, and organizing activities. The regime, nonetheless, attempted to curry favor with the Venezuelan workingman by building facilities such as the "vacation city" of Los Caracas on the Caribbean and an imposing labor center in Caracas, but these gestures were small compensation for the strangling of the labor movement;[4] despite prosperity in certain sectors of the economy, the rising cost of living ate into wages and created conditions in which many laborers were worse off than before the boom of the 1950s.

Venezuelan workers became resentful also of the vast influx of foreigners who flooded the Venezuelan labor market during the 1950s. Approximately 700,000 Europeans—mostly Italians, Spaniards, and Portuguese—flocked to Venezuela to take advantage of the high wages paid in the booming construction industry. Although the vast public works projects undertaken by the regime created a heavy demand for construction workers, a relatively small percentage of native workers benefited, in the face of the government's deliberate encouragement of foreign labor. Competition for jobs with non-Venezuelans, then, provoked profound discontent in the labor sector.

Another urban group had reason to join the opposition. This was the growing mass of unemployed who lived in the hillside *ranchos* circling the capital city. These slums were

4. See Rómulo Betancourt, *Venezuela,* 629–49, and Mauro Barrenchea, "Militarismo y sindicalismo: un caso aleccionador," *SIC, Revista Venezolana de Orientación,* 32 (February 1969), 68–71.

the product of dramatic social changes that were taking place during the 1945–1958 period. Between those dates, Caracas grew from an easy-going city of 300,000 to a metropolis of 1 million inhabitants. Lured by the unparalleled construction activity centered in the Federal District, thousands of landless rural workers flocked to Caracas. Within little more than a decade, this movement reversed Venezuela's urban-to-rural ratio to the point that it was by 1958 a predominantly urban nation. A large percentage of the rural migrants to Caracas and other big cities were, however, shut off from lucrative jobs in construction trades and related occupations because of the influx of foreign labor, their lack of skills, illiteracy, and inability to adapt to urban life. As they endured a hand-to-mouth existence in their humble *ranchos,* they contrasted their plight with the ostentatious wealth of the more privileged. Caracas provided a dramatic contrast between the glitter of that part of society which benefited from petroleum and the Ministry of Public Works, and the squalor of that other largely forgotten society, sprawled helter-skelter over the hillsides. Smoldering discontent among these slum-dwellers burst into open opposition to the governing elite by 1958.[5]

The Venezuelan *campesino* also fared badly under the regime. The AD agrarian reform program, such as it was, came to a halt, and almost no further land redistribution took place. As they had organized urban labor, AD had been the first party to organize and incorporate the peasant into the body politic. Under the Pérez Jiménez regime, the close connection between AD and peasant confederations (which also were dissolved) worked to the disadvantage of the rural worker. In addition, the government's intensified concentration on developing the capital as a showcase made more vivid the neglect and lack of interest accorded the agricultural sector.[6] The contrast was all too apparent to *campesinos* who were alert to national problems.

5. See Domingo Alberto Rangel, *La revolución de las fantasías,* 70–83.

6. The regime did not entirely neglect rural Venezuela. Large-scale agricultural colonization projects were undertaken, including the 100,000-acre Turén colony in Portuguesa State, and the smaller Unidad Agropecuario de los Andes in Táchira. Projects such as these, however, benefited only a small percentage of the rural populace and they did little to bolster Venezuela's over-all agricultural production.

Initially, the military regime had the full support of the business community, which was relieved to be done with the turbulence and agitation of the AD years. Those who benefited most from the military regime were contractors, engineers, and other professionals involved in the construction industry. Political stability, combined with an oil boom, allowed for prosperous years during the 1950s. For example, production of crude oil rose from 482,299,000 barrels in 1949 to 1,014,424,000 in 1957. Exports of crude rose from 460,-013,000 (1949) to 940,311,000 (1957). Iron ore production went from 1,269,600 metric tons in 1951 to 15,295,500 metric tons in 1957, with iron ore exports rising comparably. The value of total exports climbed from 3,360,000 *bolívares* in 1949 to 7,928,000 in 1957.[7]

Yet, by the late 1950s, the business sector had withdrawn much of its support of the regime. A variety of causes account for this change. First, the overambitious public works policy of the regime created a fiscal crisis. When the oil boom tapered off about 1957 a descending spiral contracted the whole fiscal structure. Foreign creditors began demanding repayment of loans and became impatient with delays. Contractors were caught in the squeeze. The result was that large-scale liquidation took place in the last months of 1957.

Second, Domingo Alberto Rangel suggests, after 1956 the United States looked less enthusiastically on the Pérez Jiménez regime than it had previously. At the 1956 Panama Conference of American Presidents, the Venezuelan delegation proposed the establishment of a hemispheric multilateral aid fund. The sincerity of the Venezuelan proposal is a matter of dispute, but the Eisenhower Administration definitely frowned on the multilateral approach to foreign aid. From that point the Pérez Jiménez regime lost the confidence of Washington. And when U.S.-oriented Venezuelan business leaders became aware of the Americans' change in attitude, they withdrew their confidence also.[8]

A third cause for discontent was political favoritism. A number of important officials of the regime, taking advantage of their position and the easy money of the 1950s,

7. Guillermo Morón, *A History of Venezuela,* 226, 230, and Edwin Lieuwen, *Venezuela,* 114, 140.
8. Rangel, *La revolución,* 42–43.

became major entrepreneurs. Once they had gained control of financial institutions, the regime rewarded them with government business, to the detriment of more established businessmen who did not enjoy the special favors of the men in power. The unfavored businessmen became less enthusiastic in their support of a government whose arbitrary policies operated to their disadvantage. In addition, a process of capital concentration took place during the 1950s, which resulted in a number of major industries coming under monopolistic control, the outstanding example being the Mendoza-Vollmer group. Those less skilled and aggressive in the entrepreneurial arts had no special reason to continue support of a regime that allowed such practices.

Fourth, the 1950s were years of impressive economic growth, but it was a growth tied to a favorable set of circumstances in the world economy: nationalization of Iranian oil, the Suez crisis, the rebuilding of Europe, the Korean War, the U.S. arms build-up. By 1957 Venezuelan businessmen realized that the intense oil-induced economic development had already peaked. The perils of overdependence on oil and world markets now became obvious. But government had done little to protect native industries or to encourage local agriculture and industry as resources in such circumstances. The problem was this: If the regime continued to follow the same economic policy much longer, conditions could become so grave as to threaten the nation with basic social upheaval. To salvage their position and to recapture control of the economy, Venezuelan businessmen concluded that a change of regime was necessary.[9]

Fifth, for some inexplicable reason, the Pérez Jiménez administration began to stall on paying its financial obligations in the post-1956 period. The government delayed payments to contractors, which caused general financial embarrassment and occasional bankruptcy. Often, the desperate businessman would be forced to pay exorbitant bribes in order to have his payment released. But, oddly enough and contrary to what some critics of the regime have stated, the government treasury was by no means empty in 1958. When the books were examined immediately after the dictator's

9. Rangel, *La revolución*, 43–44.

fall, there was a reserve of close to $700 million.[10]

Blame for the practice of withholding payments seems to rest squarely with Pérez Jiménez himself. In late 1957 Minister of the Treasury Pedro Guzmán complained to Minister of Interior Relations Vallenilla Lanz that the government had become notorious for defaulting on debt obligations. He stated that all domestic debts outstanding amounted to less than $150 million, while the Treasury had a reserve balance of over $700 million. Yet his pleas to the President went unheard. The Minister of Interior Relations replied that he too had been unable to solve this unnecessary problem; when he had approached the Chief Executive, his plea for financial reform had been swept aside.[11]

At first the Venezuelan business community acted cautiously, but in the last days of the regime it moved into outright opposition. Two circumstances prompted their new determination. First, business was given assurance by the two most powerful opposition leaders, Rómulo Betancourt and Jóvito Villalba, that their return to power would not bring any basic structural change to the country. Second, an Air Force revolt on January 1, 1958, startled them into realizing that the regime was fast decomposing. From that point on, businessmen, many of whom had been fortunate beneficiaries of the regime, converted to dedicated revolutionaries.[12]

By the last year of the dictatorship, the Roman Catholic Church also had developed serious reservations about the impact of the Pérez Jiménez regime. Inasmuch as relations between the Church and AD had been hostile, the overthrow of Gallegos caused the Church's hierarchy little grief. Indeed, large measures of clerical good will were bestowed on the new military rulers, partly because Catholic education received considerable impetus during the military regime. Due to constant political conflict with students at state institutions, the dictator embarked on a policy of fostering paro-

10. Interview, May, 1965, and letter, Caracas, May, 1966. The balance did not include revenues still to be collected from the income tax and oil royalties. See Laureano Vallenilla Lanz, *hijo, Razones de proscrito*, 57, 238.

11. Laureano Vallenilla Lanz, *hijo, Escrito de memoria*, 449, 452–53.

12. Rangel, *La revolución*, 46–47.

chial education as a "counterpoise" to the secular institutions.

Church–state relations cooled, however, over the Pérez Jiménez years. Church leaders discreetly criticized the low moral tone of the regime, its widespread corruption, and its obsession with material progress at the expense of social betterment for the faithful. The most vocal cleric was Monsignor Rafael Arias Blanco, Archbishop of Caracas. His official position on Venezuela's socioeconomic problems was expounded in a pastoral letter dated May 1, 1957.[13] A week earlier, the President had made an important public address boasting of the material accomplishments of his regime. In reply, Arias' Labor Day message listed the serious problems facing the working class and implied that the Venezuelan laborer's economic position was deteriorating. Noting the difficulties that arose from the flight of thousands from farm to city, he described the cities as enclaves of unemployed slum-dwellers. His letter, read in churches throughout Venezuela, encouraged the forces working to undermine the regime.

From that moment mutual hostility and incriminations characterized church–state relations.[14] Although warned by Vallenilla Lanz, Arias and other clergy continued to preach social justice from their pulpits. Many became active participants in the resistance movement. Clerics were harassed, jailed, and subjected to numerous indignities, to the extent that the cynical Minister of Interior Relations expressed more concern over the effects of the regime's repression of dissident clergy than was normal for him. "The Church is eternal and wise," he mused, "it does not associate with lost causes."[15]

Also arrayed against the dictatorship were the traditional Latin American revolutionaries—students and intellectuals. The latter complained of the lack of freedom of expression,

13. Pertinent excerpts from the letter are in Appendix C, Document 1. The full text of the letter is included in Presidencia de la República, *Documentos que hicieron historia: siglo y medio de vida republicana, 1810–1961,* II, 420–29.

14. For an account of the Church's role in the overthrow of Pérez Jiménez, see Gabriel García Márquez, "La iglesia en la lucha contra la dictadura," in José Umaña Bernal, *Testimonio de la revolución en Venezuela,* 91–98.

15. Vallenilla Lanz, *Escrito,* 454.

violations of civil liberties, maladministration of public funds, and the regressive educational policy of the government. The students at the Central University, unimpressed by the construction of the ultramodern University City, protested against rigid controls on political activity, official censorship, and many other restrictions. The students, the most vociferous of the regime's critics, caused constant turmoil, and in retaliation, the government closed the university for much of the period.

Inasmuch as all the above groups were hostile to the regime and all were denied the right to dissent openly, it was inevitable that attempts should be made to unite them in a clandestine resistance movement. Such a step was taken in June, 1957, at the instigation of Fabricio Ojeda, an obscure newspaperman on the staff of *El Nacional*. Ojeda, a member of URD, brought together a small nucleus of conspirators pledged to absolute secrecy. Out of this group emerged the Junta Patriótica (Patriotic Junta), which was to play a vital part in the struggle against the regime.[16]

The Patriotic Junta sought to enlist the support of every sector of society, and by the end of 1957 its objective had been almost fulfilled. In addition to two representatives from each of the four major parties, the junta consisted of representatives from industry, commerce, labor, professional guilds, clergy, students, and women's associations. Also included were representatives of the *Lopecistas* and *Medinistas*. The junta, working through these larger groups and through their subdivisions, was remarkably efficient; orders could be transmitted and put into operation within a matter of hours.[17]

The Patriotic Junta's stated objectives were threefold: to restore respect for the Constitution; to oppose the re-election of Pérez Jiménez and convoke free elections for president; and to establish a democratic government respectful of civil liberties.[18] One of the organization's main activities was the issuing of propaganda expounding these objectives.[19]

Pérez Jiménez, whose presidential term was to expire in

16. Umaña Bernal, *Testimonio,* 199.
17. Interview, May, 1965.
18. Umaña Bernal, *Testimonio,* 72.
19. Antiregime propaganda, originating both from the Patriotic Junta and other sources, is collected in *Así se fraguo la insurrección: documentos clandestinos, 1956-1958.*

April, 1958, was facing the problem of succession to the presidency. For a solution he consulted his principal political adviser, Vallenilla Lanz, who suggested three alternatives: a free election with all parties included, all political prisoners freed, and all exiles permitted to return; a rerun of the 1952 election with an official candidate running against some restricted party opposition; or a return to indirect election by Congress.[20] The President showed little enthusiasm for any of the proposed schemes, especially the open election. He professed to believe that the Venezuelan people were not yet ready for a free democratic election. More to the point, he feared that the very announcement of such an election would provoke a military coup. He was convinced, perhaps with some justification, that military leaders would not tolerate the election of a civilian.

Instead, Pérez Jiménez put forth a counterproposal: a plebiscite, in which he would be the only candidate and the electorate would be given the choice of voting for or against him. The plebiscite scheme had been discussed vaguely at an earlier time, but Vallenilla opposed the idea because it smacked of a "caesarist flavor" and because of the strong possibility that the President would receive more negative than affirmative votes.[21]

Pérez Jiménez' insistence on the plebiscite (a violation of his own 1953 Constitution), was the ultimate evidence that he had completely rejected his earlier democratic attitudes. Psychologically incapable of relinquishing power, he told Vallenilla simply: "I believe that I ought to continue in power for a period."[22] Yet, in the peculiar tradition of Latin American dictators, he felt the need to "legalize" his power. In this circumstance he chose the transparent device of a single-candidate election.

The President insisted that the Ministry of Interior Relations organize the plebiscite, but he wanted it kept from the public as a surprise until the last possible moment. Vallenilla drily replied that surprises could work both ways and that he, for one, thought the Venezuelan people were tired of receiving so many. Underestimating public opinion and the effec-

---

20. Vallenilla Lanz, *Escrito,* 447–48.

21. Vallenilla Lanz, *Escrito,* 448. However, it was generally believed at the time that Vallenilla Lanz was the inspiration behind the plebiscite. See Tad Szulc, *Twilight of the Tyrants,* 297.

22. Vallenilla Lanz, *Escrito,* 448.

tiveness of propaganda, Vallenilla felt, was the regime's "greatest error."[23]

As soon as plans for the plebiscite were announced, the Patriotic Junta began a propaganda campaign urging abstention. When Caracas students rioted in protest against the plebiscite, the government countered with newspaper pledges of support for Pérez Jiménez, listing tens of thousands of names. The dictator was later accused, with justification, of obtaining the signatures by threats and coercion.

The plebiscite was scheduled for December 15. All citizens above eighteen years of age were permitted to vote. In addition, the election law enfranchised foreigners who had lived in Venezuela for two or more years, an inclusion that enraged Venezuelan nationalists. Matters worsened when the Italian Ambassador violated diplomatic protocol by urging the large Italian colony to vote for Pérez Jiménez.[24]

On December 20 final tabulation of the voting was made public: 2,374,790 voters had cast affirmative ballots, 364,182 negative, and 186,013 were invalidated.[25] Government spokesmen called the result a great vote of confidence for the regime; the same day Pérez Jiménez was proclaimed President for another five-year term.

A somewhat different interpretation of the plebiscite's result was provided by a Patriotic Junta communiqué: "The Plebiscite has failed. The people did not vote. . . . Down with usurpation!"[26] A lengthier manifesto amplified the claim, stating that the official totals were complete fabrications by the Ministry of Interior Relations. The junta was, in fact, encouraged by the "poor showing" at the polls.[27]

Far greater encouragement than voter apathy came less than two weeks later when a surprise rebellion by the Air Force and some Army units nearly succeeded in toppling the regime. Never sure where civilian loyalties lay, Pérez Jiménez attempted to muster his support from the military; his real popularity had always been in the armed forces. He was not an attractive public figure and never attempted to build up a counterpoise to the Army in the civilian sector, as his friend Juan Perón had done with labor in Argentina. He

23. Vallenilla Lanz, *Escrito,* 449.
24. Szulc, *Twilight,* 298.
25. *El Universal,* December 21, 1957.
26. Umaña Bernal, *Testimonio,* 75.
27. See Umaña Bernal, *Testimonio,* 135–37.

discovered to his dismay that when the military withdrew its backing, he had no support left but his security forces. Effective as they were, they were not sufficient.

Pérez Jiménez and the military high command proclaimed the unity of the armed forces until the very end of the regime. Most Venezuelans believed that this much-heralded unity was an established fact, since internal dissension was kept within the thick walls of the barracks. But grounds for discontent with the regime were many. First, the luxurious life that Pérez Jiménez led after 1950 resulted in his estrangement from his officer associates. He developed a craving for material wealth and maintained a style of life completely contrary to that of a dedicated professional soldier. He augmented his income illicitly through the usual devices, and his thievery soon took on enormous proportions. A privileged coterie of high military and civilian officials surrounding him were also exploiting their positions for personal gain. Was the junior officers' repudiation of corruption in high places based strictly on moral precepts, or was it also tinged with envy? The real problem, perhaps, was that little of the abundance was trickling down into the pockets of junior officers.[28] Rangel suggests that envy among the officers, produced by the fabulous enrichment of their middle-class compatriots, was an important cause of discontent in the barracks. From 1948 to 1958, while most officers increased their standard of living gradually and modestly, a significant percentage of the urban middle class was growing wealthy on government contracts, buying mansions and luxurious cars, and, in general, flaunting its often ill-gotten wealth in the face of their less affluent officer peers.[29]

Another source of discontent was Pérez Jiménez' fear of potential military rivals for power. After Delgado's death, he stepped up his practice of making appointments on a highly personal basis. Repeating the error made by earlier Tachiran presidents, he distributed key posts on the basis of personal loyalty rather than on professional merit. As a result, many of those appointments were exceedingly poor choices. For example, he rejected for the most responsible posts outstanding members of the 1945 UPM group and substituted men of

28. United States Embassy, Caracas, Confidential Political Report, August, 1957, read to me.
29. Rangel, *La revolución*, 58–59.

mean ability. Furthermore, his police imprisoned a number of his former associates among the junior officers for opposing questionable practices of the regime.

Grumbling the loudest about the dictator's capricious military police were junior officers, since they had a related grievance. Their story was by now familiar: Many had trained abroad and had obtained an education far superior to that of Pérez Jiménez and the 1945 "Peru" generation.[30] In technical preparation these men held considerable advantage over the high command. They complained about the same situation the young officers in the UPM had lamented under General Medina. The problem of maintaining loyalty in the younger generation of Academy graduates, unsolved by Medina, remained to plague Pérez Jiménez.[31]

A few specific examples should suffice to illustrate the breakdown of armed forces unity. First, a number of officers of the 1945 generation, disturbed by the dictatorial and corrupt turn taken by the regime, were eased out of high posts and subjected to a variety of punishments. One such officer was Maj. Edito J. Ramírez, who had been largely responsible for winning over Major Delgado Chalbaud to the UPM.[32] He was sent abroad for a period, lost his active status, and after his return was kept in enforced seclusion for the remainder of the regime.

Another charter member of the UPM who ran afoul of the regime was Lt. Col. Martín Márquez Añez, who in 1954 was serving as a professor in the Superior War School. Angered by what he considered a policy of excessive political repression and by the notorious corruption that went unchecked, he decided to take his complaint directly to the President, a former classmate at Chorrillos. In his audacious attempt to confront the dictator with the seriousness of the situation, he reportedly told him:

30. The United States became the dominant military influence on the Venezuelan armed forces after World War II. U.S. army, naval, and air missions were established, and a high percentage of Venezuelan officers and cadets went to the U.S. for advanced military training.

31. Interview, July, 1965. The perennial complaint of inadequate remuneration probably played some role in military discontent under Pérez Jiménez also; see Arístides Bastidas, "La verdad sobre el 23 de enero," *El Nacional,* January 22, 1959.

32. "No era 'monolítica' la unidad de las Fuerzas Armadas de Venezuela," *El Universal,* January 24, 1958.

Mr. President, my personal opinion is that instead of maintaining such a vast service of vigilance against the officer corps and against citizens of estimable reputation, what ought to be watched more effectively is the management of public funds . . . which according to general belief, are enriching without measure certain elements supported by the regime.[33]

His warning was not ignored. He was escorted out of Miraflores by SN agents and spent the next few years in a federal prison. In late 1954 certain officers attempted to get the SN to transfer Márquez Añez to military jurisdiction, but their request was futile.[34]

Another old friend of Pérez Jiménez was subjected to similar treatment. Col. José León Rangel, one of the principal organizers of the 1948 coup, fell from grace four years later. Once his loyalty came under suspicion, he was relieved of his post as Director General of Services of the Ministry of Defense and imprisoned in Caracas' Cárcel Modelo for two years, after which he was confined to his home. Other ranking officers whom a mistrustful Pérez Jiménez removed from important posts were FAC Commandant Oscar Tamayo Suárez, Air Force Chief Félix Román Moreno, and Gen. Roberto Moreán Soto, chief of the Third Section of the General Staff.

Not only individual officers suffered. A more serious breakdown in the unity of the armed forces developed in the form of interservice rivalry. Pérez Jiménez tended to favor the ground forces since he, an Army man, felt more confident of their loyalty. Although all branches of the service underwent technical improvement under Pérez Jiménez, the rate of progress in the Navy, Air Force, and National Guard was slower than in the ground forces.[35] In addition, for political reasons all Air Force installations were within the reach of strong Army garrisons. As for the Navy, Pérez Jiménez took liberties with personnel appointments there also. Capt. Wolfgang Larrazábal, who signed the constitutive act of the 1948 military junta as commander of the Navy, subsequently filled such nonstrategic sinecures as the presidency of the National Sports Institute and the directorship of the Caracas

33. "Euforia en Miraflores," *Elite* (February 1, 1958), 36.
34. "No era 'monolítica'," *El Universal,* January 24, 1958.
35. Interview, May, 1965.

Officers' Club. Although he was reinstated as commander shortly before Pérez Jiménez' fall, the popular Larrazábal's relegation to inconsequential posts was looked on with disfavor by Navy personnel.

Another factor was far more important, however, in the ultimate withdrawal of military support for the regime: the growing predominance of the SN. Although Pérez Jiménez continued to rule in the name of the armed forces, he increased his reliance on the Vallenilla–Estrada machine, subordinating the military. In previous years the SN had kept interference with the armed forces to a minimum. But Estrada's tentacles penetrated everywhere, including the barracks. Well aware of growing military disaffection, he knew that to maintain tight control, vigilance was at least as necessary in the military sector as in the civilian. Greater interference, as should have been anticipated, bred greater resentment. Moreover, the status-conscious military suspected that the SN, with its enormous budget and elite status, had become Pérez Jiménez' favorite; the police, who were little more than a gang of thugs, had come between the President and the armed forces. The military had not exaggerated the position of the police: Before any military official could be received by the President, he was stopped and searched by SN agents. Professional military men resented the practice as demeaning and humiliating; to them it symbolized the growing separation between the Commander-in-chief and his uniformed subordinates.[36]

In late 1957, as curiosity mounted in the barracks about the dictator's plans for the presidential succession, Pérez Jiménez informed the men personally of his decision to remain in power. He scheduled a series of conferences with officers, the first held at the Military School. To justify his decision to stay in office, the President declared that Venezuelans still were not prepared to assume the responsibilities of partisan government and that he needed another term to complete his most ambitious public works projects. After his speech he invited written questions. Many asked about the postponement of debt obligations, to which he gave a very unsatisfactory reply. In effect he shut off all dialogue, leaving the officers with the impression that he was treating them like chil-

36. Umaña Bernal, *Testimonio,* 68, and interview, July, 1965.

dren.[37] A second meeting, held in Maracay, produced similar results. Evaluating those meetings, Vallenilla thought the dictator had simply used the wrong tactics; he should have invited small groups of officers to Miraflores for informal discussions about the problems that were troubling them.[38]

The first major armed attempt to overthrow Pérez Jiménez broke out on New Year's Day, 1958. For a number of weeks conspiratorial conversations had been taking place in the military installations. One pocket of discontent was in the Urdaneta barracks in Caracas. Those young officers soon made contact with officers in the Páez barracks in Maracay, and the movement quickly spread to other installations at Maracay. This junior officer group, seeking support in the higher ranks, made contact with Lt. Col. Hugo Enrique Trejo, the assistant chief of staff, who accepted their offer and assumed the leadership of the movement. They also made contacts with civilians, but not with the Patriotic Junta, which remained unaware of the conspiracy.

Despite the failure to reach the major resistance movement, plans progressed and the conspiracy gained new recruits, including high-ranking officers of the Army and Air Force. At the last formal meeting of the plotters, on December 29, Trejo announced that two Army units in Caracas could be counted in as well as the Army and Air Force units in Maracay. The revolt was set to commence on January 5 at 4 A.M.[39]

As in 1928 and 1945, the conspirators' plans again became known and they were forced to act ahead of their schedule. On the morning of December 31, two high officers suspected of implication in the plot were arrested: Gen. Hugo Fuentes, commander of the ground forces, and Col. Jesús María Castro León, chief of staff of the Air Force. Their detention alerted the rebels, and they decided to act immediately. Unfortunately for the effectiveness of this premature action, the movement had been planned haphazardly, amidst a great deal of dissension and poor coordination between units. After frantic discussions the conspirators, at the urging of Lieutenant Colonel Trejo, agreed to move the next morning. On the afternoon of December 31, Pérez Jiménez delivered

37. Vallenilla Lanz, *Escrito,* 451.
38. Vallenilla Lanz, *Escrito,* 451; see also Rangel, *La revolución,* 59–60.
39. *La Esfera,* January 3, 1959.

his New Year's message to the Venezuelan people. It was a boastful harangue, delivered in a tone that even the haughty Minister of Interior Relations considered arrogant.[40] The President had been informed of the arrests, but he apparently thought his security apparatus had a firm grip on the situation. At any rate he went through with his plans to entertain a large gathering at his residence that evening, and like many other holiday celebrants, did not retire until the early hours of the morning.

Near dawn, the President was awakened by a phone call informing him that the entire Air Force was in revolt. He rushed to his office, as did his principal civilian and military aides. For a while their position looked grave. At 7:00 or 7:30 A.M. Maracay-based Air Force planes began a series of bombing and strafing raids. Among their targets were Miraflores Palace, the Ministry of Defense, and La Carlota military airport in east Caracas. The bombing and strafing inflicted only minor damage but it unnerved the authorities. Pérez Jiménez ordered a trusted aide, Air Force Major Martín Parada, to Maracay to investigate and report back to him. Shortly thereafter, the President, the high command, and civilian advisers took shelter in the basement of the Miraflores barracks across the street.[41]

That afternoon an officer came from Maracay to tell the astonished dictator that the leader of the movement in Maracay was none other than Martín Parada, the officer he had sent there hours earlier to investigate. Owing to an appalling lack of coordination, however, the Air Force was not receiving aid from units in Caracas. Finally, around 5:00 P.M. the rebels in the Urdaneta barracks received a desperately needed supply of ammunition. The logical maneuver then would have been to make a direct attack with their tanks on Miraflores, but for some inexplicable reason, their leader, Trejo, decided instead to march to the town of Los Teques, on the road to Maracay, hoping to reinforce the Maracay rebels the next day.

Meanwhile, Pérez Jiménez ordered detachments from the interior to march on the rebel stronghold in Maracay. Within a short time he learned that the column headed by Trejo had entered Los Teques, where it set up headquarters. The Presi-

40. Vallenilla Lanz, *Escrito,* 458.
41. Vallenilla Lanz, *Escrito,* 461.

dent then commissioned two colonels to go to Los Teques to persuade Trejo to rejoin the loyal forces. One of the colonels went over to the rebels, but the other reported that, although Trejo and his officer aides refused to submit, the troops seemed indecisive.[42]

While the Caracas column hesitated in Los Teques, loyal columns led by Col. Roberto Casanova advanced on Maracay. Casanova had crushed a minor revolt in Monagas State a few years before, and once again he did his job efficiently. He met little resistance and soon had complete control of all installations. By the early morning hours of January 2 the revolt in Maracay had ended. By that time the Air Force pilots who had led the raids on Caracas had given up all hope of receiving reinforcements from Army units. Their raids, which continued until nightfall, had received no support from the capital. The government remained in charge of all Caracas units except Urdaneta barracks, and the radio stations also stayed in government hands. The Air Force rebels were also unaware that Trejo's rebel column was already in Los Teques and was broadcasting revolutionary propaganda. Faced with a desperate situation, the rebel aviators took Pérez Jiménez' presidential plane and, piloted by Major Parada, flew off to Barranquilla, Colombia, where they remained until the collapse of the regime three weeks later.

The officials assembled in the basement headquarters breathed a collective sigh of relief at the news that the main thrust of the rebellion had been blunted. Nevertheless, there remained Trejo's force at Los Teques. Knowing that the rebel troops were confused and demoralized, an aide suggested that an airplane scatter leaflets over the rebel camp to urge them to surrender. Shortly after the leaflets fell among the rebels, they surrendered.[43]

On January 2 General Pérez Jiménez announced the rebels' defeat to the public. He praised his loyal officers and troops; they were victorious, he said, because they knew their cause was just. He proclaimed that the failure of the rebellion had demonstrated the fundamental unity of the armed forces, which had withstood the divisive attempts of a few unprincipled, unprofessional conspirators to undermine it.[44]

42. Vallenilla Lanz, *Escrito,* 464.
43. Vallenilla Lanz, *Escrito,* 465.
44. *El Universal,* January 3, 1958.

The dictator spoke confidently, but he was clearly disturbed by the open rebellion of the military. So long as outright opposition was confined to students and the usual partisan activists, he felt he could maintain control indefinitely. But his anxiety mounted with the realization that he could no longer trust his own companions in arms. Once he had surmounted the New Year's crisis, a psychological reaction set in. After January 2, Pérez Jiménez seemed to go adrift mentally. Always an emotional person, his fits of temper increased. In a seeming loss of confidence in his own abilities, he came to rely more heavily on the men surrounding him—mediocre men who were even less able and more disoriented than he. Although reasonable men advised the President to introduce drastic, long-overdue reforms in order to save the regime, he closed his ears and depended for advice on sycophants and third-rate generals.[45]

Accounts conflict about the nature and order of events between January 3 and 23, those concerning developments within the armed forces being especially vague. Civilian activity, however, was more open. The Patriotic Junta continued to function, despite the concerted efforts of the SN to crush it. The junta advocated a general strike to paralyze the economy, organized a series of demonstrations, issued propaganda, and negotiated with military malcontents. On January 9, 10, and 14, its committees organized demonstrations in various parts of the capital, which were promptly broken up by the police. Virtually daily clashes took place between students and the police. In one courageous act, a large delegation representing the women's committee of the Patriotic Junta and led by Irma de Medina, the widow of the former President, marched in front of the SN headquarters.

Pérez Jiménez was confident that his security apparatus would hold the workers, the unemployed, and the students at bay, but he feared the growing hostility of the professional and business classes. Traditionally, they did not move against the prevailing regime until they had completely lost confidence in it. But on January 10 a Declaration of the Intellectuals was distributed, calling for the restoration of individual rights, the return to morality in government, and the elimination of the repressive machinery.[46] The list of signers

45. Interview, July, 1965. See also, Szulc, *Twilight,* 254–55.
46. Umaña Bernal, *Testimonio,* 118–19.

mounted into the hundreds. Within the space of a few days, antiregime manifestoes were published by the lawyers', engineers', doctors', and business associations. Especially upsetting to the dictator was the Manifesto of the Engineers, which provided a detailed criticism of the regime's much-heralded public works program.[47]

The Patriotic Junta, which had issued two manifestoes in October and December, came forth with a third. This document praised the military for valorous action on January 1 and urged them to throw out the nefarious "triumvirate" of Pérez Jiménez, Vallenilla Lanz, and Estrada. It declared that the January 1 movement had exposed the deepest split in the armed institution since 1945.[48]

The Patriotic Junta meanwhile carried on a quieter campaign of negotiations with all branches of the military in an attempt to cement a firm civil–military alliance. The tendency of most officers was to back any government in power, despite personal reservations, until the situation became intolerable both in the barracks and in society generally. Thus, in January, 1958, the officers needed to be convinced that the regime was totally unacceptable to a great majority of the people as well as being prejudicial to the best interests of the military institution. The junta capitalized on the causes of the abortive New Year's Day revolt, thus encouraging dissident elements in all four branches. Adding fuel to the fire, Vallenilla and Estrada began cracking down on military personnel more freely than ever; resentment rose dangerously, and frustrated officers, most of them junior grade, moved closer to an alliance with the junta.

The organization's main liaison agents with the military were Blas Lamberti, a prominent engineer, Oscar Centeno Sucinchi, a pharmacist, and Fabricio Ojeda, the junta's president. Centeno had already established some contact with young officers in late 1957. About the same time, a conspiratorial nucleus, unrelated to the January 1 Air Force insurgents, formed in the Military School. Lamberti and Centeno eventually made contact with that group and with other Army and Navy junior officers.

The role of the Navy during the first three weeks of January is not entirely clear, except that it moved into open revolt

47. Umaña Bernal, *Testimonio,* 123–24.
48. See Appendix C, Document 2.

some time before January 21. Some Navy units had been pledged to come to the assistance of the Air Force on January 1 but had been unable to act because of technical difficulties. In the aftermath of the government's triumph, a number of conspirators in the Navy were arrested. Pérez Jiménez also ordered the small fleet of destroyers to disperse so as to eliminate the threat to the capital their long-range guns represented.

On January 8 the fleet returned to La Guaira, and the next day the dictator sent two emissaries to the port. The first was Chief of Staff Gen. Rómulo Fernández, whose mission was to placate the rebellious young officers and to determine the scope of the conspiracy. He invited the ringleaders to return to Miraflores, ostensibly to talk things over, but on their arrival in Caracas they were arrested.

Later that day General Llovera Páez left Caracas on a special mission to the coast, armed with a column of tanks and heavy artillery. His orders were to disarm one of the destroyers, but instead, he ordered all ships to surrender their ammunition. For the Navy insurgents his order precipitated a crucial decision, fraught with anxiety. Surrendering the ammunition would neutralize the destroyers during the projected revolt, but any resistance at that point would have been crushed by Llovera's tanks and artillery. The officers reluctantly handed over the ammunition, but through deft maneuvering they managed to hide some ammunition on the ships.[49]

While enemies of the regime mobilized for a decisive blow, the President frantically sought to keep his government from disintegration. Pressure from military officers, who were now taking the offensive, forced him to reorganize the Cabinet and make personnel changes in the upper echelons of the bureaucracy. The first to go were public enemies one and two, Minister of Interior Relations Vallenilla Lanz and SN chief Estrada, whose presence had become intolerable to the armed forces, both because of their violations of the institutional integrity of the armed forces and because of the public outcry against them.

Dismissal of Vallenilla Lanz was an easy gesture for the President. After the scare on January 1, Pérez Jiménez had

49. Bastidas, "La verdad," *El Nacional,* January 22, 1959, and Elvira Mendoza, "Las fuerzas navales dieron el golpe mortal," *Elite* (February 1, 1958), 50.

become extremely hostile toward his long-time confidant. On January 9 the President informed his Minister of Interior Relations that the military command had delivered an ultimatum, backed by garrisons throughout the country, demanding that Pérez Jiménez either make changes in the Cabinet or resign. The President told Vallenilla that he had accepted the first alternative; he asked him to collect resignations from all Cabinet members. Vallenilla dutifully collected the signatures, drafted the collective letter of resignation, and then rushed to the Italian Embassy.[50] As soon as he could arrange passage, he fled the country. Estrada's exit followed the same pattern.

The dictator's precarious hold on power is best illustrated by the ouster of Vallenilla and Estrada. If he had tried to retain them, his military colleagues would have forced his resignation. Instead, he parted with his two most efficient subordinates. Their security forces still had a firm grip on the citizenry, and neither man was afraid to take any measure necessary to preserve order. With their removal the political police lost much of its potency, making the work of the rebels correspondingly easier.[51] Faced by this dilemma, Pérez Jiménez chose to placate the armed forces in an attempt to win their support.

Now Pérez Jiménez acceded to the military's ultimatum and increased the military representation in the Cabinet to seven. General Llovera Páez moved from Communications to the post vacated by Vallenilla Lanz and Gen. Rómulo Fernández moved up from chief of staff to head the Ministry of Defense. In addition, a Navy captain was named governor of the Federal District, and the chief of the military police took over as director of the SN.

The dictator blundered sadly in his new appointments. His new Minister of Education, Gen. Néstor Prato Cárdenas, was an exceptionally poor choice. Corrupt and ignorant, he had no prestige whatever in the civilian sector at large, much less in academic and student circles. The public outcry over his appointment forced the dictator to dismiss him and turn instead to Dr. Humberto Fernández Morán, a brilliant young

50. Vallenilla Lanz, *Escrito,* 473–74. The Italian Ambassador was reluctant to offer asylum to Vallenilla and his wife; they were transferred to the Brazilian Embassy, where they were more hospitably received.

51. Interview, May, 1965.

scientist, but the change came too late to benefit the regime. Since Llovera Páez' appointment as Minister of Interior Relations also was unsatisfactory, Pérez Jiménez turned next to his cousin, Antonio Pérez Vivas, the long-time governor of Táchira. Although well liked in his home state for his relatively benign rule, Pérez Vivas was completely unknown to the *Caraqueños* and came unprepared to assume the most sensitive post in the Cabinet.[52]

For approximately forty-eight hours it appeared that the dictator had met his match in General Fernández, the new Minister of Defense. Fernández had been instrumental in framing the military's ultimatum, and some thought he represented a large segment of the armed forces hostile to the dictator. But Fernández, a military mediocrity, lacked prestige in the ranks, and was known to have acquired enormous wealth through peculation of Army funds. His dominance was brief; Pérez Jiménez outmaneuvered him and, two days after appointing him to the Cabinet, sent him abroad on a "special mission." The President then took charge of the Ministry of Defense, "to assure the maintenance of the unity of the Armed Forces."[53]

Pérez Jiménez resorted to wholesale arrests as the regime entered its last days. No one escaped suspicion. A number of officers in Cabinet posts and state governorships were forced to resign after a few days in office and were immediately arrested. In addition, the SN made scores of arrests among lesser officials. But these desperate moves were ineffective administratively and they damaged any positive remnants of the regime's public image.

While clashes between the popular forces and Caracas police continued to erupt, the Patriotic Junta developed plans for a general strike, to take place on January 21, at noon. Exactly at 12:00 factory sirens, car horns, and church bells sounded, signaling the start of the strike. All industrial and commercial activity came to an abrupt halt. No newspapers appeared that day. Any business establishment that remained open suffered the wrath of the Caracas mobs. In the after-

52. Interview, June, 1965. An additional mistake was the appointment of Héctor Parra Márquez, president of the Supreme Electoral Council, as Minister of Justice. Parra Márquez, as head of the Council, was chiefly responsible for the carrying out of the December plebiscite.

53. *El Universal,* January 14, 1958.

noon the police broke up a large demonstration in the downtown El Silencio area. The government then imposed a dark-to-dawn curfew. The Patriotic Junta urged the public to maintain the strike throughout the next day, and they exerted strong pressure on recalcitrant storekeepers who feared financial hardship.[54]

By this time the resistance leaders felt the moment had come to bring the military into the revolt. The forming of an effective civil–military alliance had been slowed by the inability of the junta to establish contact with the National Guard, although sympathy for the movement was not lacking there. Consequently, a major obstacle was hurdled when Col. Miguel Angel Nieto Bastos, commandant of FAC, agreed to join the rebels, on the condition that they spare his brother Eladio, the less-than-popular Chief of Police in Caracas.[55] But a new problem arose when junta liaison officers Blas Lamberti and Oscar Centeno discovered that the Navy was preparing to move unilaterally.

On the night of January 15 Centeno met with representatives of the Navy, Air Force, and the Military School in attendance; Centeno was the sole civilian representative. Only at this meeting were precise plans laid for bringing all branches of the service into one coordinated movement. Those present agreed that the revolt should begin between January 16 and 21. On January 20 another crucial meeting was held in Centeno's pharmacy, at which the conspirators decided to act at midnight of January 21. The civilians and officers present also came to agreement on the composition of the junta of government that would replace the dictatorship. They unanimously selected Wolfgang Larrazábal, commandant of the Navy, to be president, with Manuel R. Egaña, a Cabinet officer under López Contreras, and Pedro Emilio Herrera, a prominent engineer, as the other two members.

The Patriotic Junta anxiously awaited the start of the military movement, but midnight of the twenty-first came and went with no hint of action. Junta leaders became alarmed when morning came and all remained quiet. Afternoon came before they discovered that serious coordinational failures had forced the military to stay their hand.[56]

54. Interview, May, 1965.
55. Bastidas, "La verdad," *El Nacional,* January 23, 1959.
56. *Ibid.*

After more hurried meetings the plotters agreed to move at 6:00 that evening (January 22). All units were alerted as rapidly as possible, but with such short notice the movement did not commence with military precision. In fact, if the government had acted more forcefully, the rebellion could rather easily, if only temporarily, have been put down.

The Navy moved into active rebellion at 6:00 P.M., and the Military School joined in shortly thereafter. The conspirators at the school were still unsure of what attitude the school's director, Col. Pedro José Quevedo, would adopt at the critical moment, although his behavior had been lenient up to that point. Quevedo, a personal friend of Pérez Jiménez since school days, finally informed the assembled rebels that he would not let his affection for the President interfere with his duty to the country and the military institution.[57]

Quevedo acted immediately. The government still had control of all communications, and it was difficult to get messages through to other installations. He learned directly from Pérez Jiménez by phone, however, that the Navy had rebelled and that the government had begun to take defensive measures. Armed with that information, Quevedo toured several military installations to persuade uncommitted units to join the rebellion.[58]

On his part, the President limited his defense to telephoned pleas for loyalty, with some success. The commander of the Bolívar armored battalion, for one, remained loyal to the dictator to the very end. He had command of the tanks, the heavy weapons, all that was needed to put up stout resistance and thereby to keep other units from defecting. He asked permission to march on the Military School with his full force. Although willing to attack, he felt that the mere threat of a heavy barrage would force the cadets, equipped only with rifles, to submit. For whatever reason, Pérez Jiménez did not give the order.

Throughout the evening the President called Larrazábal, commander of the Navy, to arrange a compromise. The Admiral had never been in the confidence of the President, but he made no overt moves against the regime. A widespread myth identifies Larrazábal as the key figure in the revolt, but it seems clear that he acted only after the tide had

57. Bastidas, "La verdad," *El Nacional,* January 25, 1959. See also Rangel, *La revolución,* 95–100.

58. Bastidas, "La verdad," *El Nacional,* January 25, 1959.

irrevocably turned. He finally showed his hand late that evening, after the third call from the dictator. When the latter asked him, "Are you with the Navy?", Larrazábal replied, "No, the Navy is with me."[59]

Later, Larrazábal telephoned two tough-minded colonels, Roberto Casanova and Abel Romero Villate, both of whom had played key roles in the crushing of the January 1 revolt. It was important to gain their support for the movement or at least to neutralize them; therefore Larrazábal invited them to join the insurrection. They agreed, on the condition that they be included in the provisional junta. Larrazábal accepted these terms and then advised the President to leave the country.[60]

The once-powerful caudillo in Miraflores Palace, lacking the will to fight and incapable of negotiating a settlement with his military subordinates, decided to flee. He hurriedly packed his bags, assembled his family and close associates, and headed toward the La Carlota military airport, where a plane was already warming its engines. It took off at 3:00 A.M. and deposited its passengers in Ciudad Trujillo, Dominican Republic, three hours later.

While the dictator was hurriedly packing, a junta was already being organized in the Military School. Exclusively military in composition, it consisted of representatives from each of the services: Rear Admiral Wolfgang Larrazábal, president, Army Colonels Roberto Casanova and Pedro José Quevedo, Air Force Col. Abel Romero Villate, and FAC Col. Carlos Luis Araque. This obviously was not the junta agreed upon by the civil–military committee several days earlier. Neither Larrazábal nor the colonels had consulted the Patriotic Junta about an all-military provisional governing council. Such a device was completely alien to the objectives of the civilian resistance fighters. The four colonels were simply the highest ranking officers available at that moment.[61]

The startling news came over radio and television about

59. Bastidas, "La verdad," *El Nacional,* January 25, 1959.

60. Umaña Bernal, *Testimonio,* 14.

61. Interview, May, 1965. Rangel agrees, but he states also that the dictator, just prior to his hasty exit, had the presence of mind to propose a tough all-military junta, which would prevent any basic changes or inordinate reaction against his regime (*La revolución,* 100–101).

2:00 A.M., January 23, that General Pérez Jiménez had been deposed. On learning that the long dictatorship was over, the people became euphoric. Thousands marched to the downtown Caracas area, car horns honked, and church bells pealed triumphantly. Later communiqués, however, revealed that the dictator had been replaced by a military junta. This later news dampened the victory celebration, since the idea of an all-military junta was strongly opposed by both junior officers and the Patriotic Junta.

Throughout the day the debate raged over the composition of the provisional junta. Colonel Casanova in particular was taking advantage of the multiple tasks that occupied Larrazábal in order to consolidate his position on the junta. For a while, prospects were so bleak for the democratically minded forces that some junior officers, who had been involved in the movement from the start, were worried that their own coup had already been overthrown by a counter coup.[62]

Nevertheless, both the civilian and military organizers of the rebellion were determined to change the composition of the junta. Orders were given to the people to keep up their massive opposition until the two most objectionable officers could be forced out and replaced with civilians. The mobs demonstrated against Casanova and Romero Villate the entire day. In the meantime, earlier candidates for the junta were discarded and Blas Lamberti, a leader of the Patriotic Junta, and Eugenio Mendoza, the country's leading industrialist, were substituted.

Mendoza, who was one of the principal beneficiaries of the fallen regime's public works program, flew from New York to Caracas in the early hours of January 24 and went immediately to the home of a friend, Antonio Requena, the representative of the professional guilds on the Patriotic Junta. Several members were already at Requena's residence, and they urged Mendoza not to accept appointment to the provisional government until Casanova and Romero Villate had been ousted. Mendoza complied. Dr. Requena was commissioned to present the Patriotic Junta's demands to the military. The person most necessary to be convinced was Lt. Col. Jesús M. Castro León, the Air Force's chief of staff, who had been jailed from December 31 to January 23, and whom Larrazábal had just designated as acting Minister of Defense.

62. Bastidas, "La verdad," *El Nacional,* January 25, 1959.

At 1:00 A.M., January 24, Requena met with Castro León and a large assembly of officers. The majority agreed with Requena that Casanova and Romero Villate should be dropped. Castro León agreed to dismiss the two officers, and he informed them of the assembly's decision.[63] Romero Villate acquiesced and left the country voluntarily, but Casanova, the toughest and most stubborn principal in the January, 1958, affair, threatened to support his position with force. It was only when he became convinced that the others were determined to resist him that he, too, took the route to La Carlota and thence abroad. With the removal of the two colonels, Mendoza and Lamberti were sworn in, creating a junta of government, composed of three military representatives and two civilians. They immediately proceeded to the difficult tasks confronting them.

*   *   *   *   *

General Pérez Jiménez' failure to crush the insurrection was essentially a failure of will. If he had conducted himself in 1958 as he had eight or ten years earlier, he might have extended his time in power. But he had lost the toughness he had acquired in the life of the barracks. He became self-indulgent, overly fond of luxury, and out of touch with the thinking of the men in the very institution that was sustaining him. He surrounded himself with men of mediocre ability who were totally lacking in political insight, and he listened to their self-serving advice while rejecting the counsel of those who advised reform and purification.

In the military sphere Pérez Jiménez closed his ears to those who, out of loyalty, begged to fight for him. He made only feeble attempts at conciliation. His indecisiveness in the last stages of the revolt may also be ascribed to his lack of technical preparation. He excelled in administration rather than in strategy and tactics, a peculiarity he shared with General Medina. Pérez Jiménez had not participated in combat before his ouster, except for that thirty-hour period spent in the basement of Miraflores barracks on January 1 and 2. He let himself be convinced that his position was untenable and then fled the country; no one forced him out.[64]

63. Interview, May, 1965.
64. Based on interviews, May, June, and July, 1965.

A military victory would have gained him only time. He would have had to initiate drastic reforms in order to placate the opposition, including a free election in the immediate future. There is no indication that he was willing to carry out such reforms.

In general, civilian insurgents acted with greater purpose and determination than the military. The Patriotic Junta worked with greater precision than the conspiratorial committees of the armed forces. Furthermore, in the two weeks prior to January 23, hundreds of civilians gave their lives and over a thousand were wounded in battles with the police, whereas the entire military institution during the same period suffered but one casualty, a lieutenant who was accidentally slain on January 22. Most officers did not join the rebels until they were convinced the regime could no longer be saved. Admiral Larrazábal remained passive until he realized the whole Navy was ready to rebel. Colonels Casanova and Romero Villate defected only when the dictator was preparing to escape and when they were guaranteed a share of the rewards of power. Colonels Quevedo and Araque, too, most likely would not have changed sides at the last moment if they had not become aware that the regime was fast crumbling.[65] When the spoils were ready to be divided, there was no lack of uniformed leadership for the rebellion, but prior to that time the military hierarchy had acted somewhat less decisively. Only the activist junior officers showed the determination that characterized their civilian counterparts in the struggle against the dictatorship.

Finally, much has been made of the Táchira clique that surrounded Pérez Jiménez during his entire career. That coterie of favored officers was supposed to have exercised a nefarious influence on him and was alleged to have embittered other officers against the *Andinos.* Logically, after Pérez Jiménez' ouster, Tachiran influence should also have diminished considerably. But who overthrew him? Larrazábal, to be sure, was a non-*Andino,* but Hugo Fuentes, Hugo

65. Ex-President Gallegos, in exile in Mexico, was informed on the twenty-third that Pérez Jiménez had been overthrown and that a military junta had replaced him. Gallegos expressed his skepticism of a government composed exclusively of "the collaborators and subalterns of Pérez Jiménez." At that moment he wondered whether the insurrection was worth the blood and sacrifice it had cost (*El Universal,* January 24, 1958).

Trejo, Martín Parada, J. M. Castro León, Pedro Quevedo, and Carlos Araque were all *Andinos*. The new military high command was composed of Castro León, a Tachiran, heading the Ministry of Defense; Col. José M. Pérez Morales, a Tachiran, as chief of staff; and Lt. Col. Hugo Trejo, from Mérida, as assistant chief. This imbalance resulted from the circumstance that the percentage of *Andino* officers was still disproportionately high. The proportion of *Andinos* among the military was subsequently to be lessened, but that process began more than a year later. The fall of General Pérez Jiménez, like the fall of General Medina, had little relation to regional animosities. Rather, the conflict of a new generation with the old and the determination of broadly based civilian and military elements put an end to a regime that had outlived its function in the life of the nation. Electoral democracy, so often scorned, never seemed so attractive to Venezuelans as it did in January, 1958.

The Junto de Gobierno created January 25, 1958, was the fourth junta to govern Venezuela in little more than a dozen years. The three previous juntas had increased military participation in national politics; the fourth differed markedly in this respect. At the end of a year of this junta's rule, the military presented less threat to civilian supremacy than it had at the beginning. Further, it permitted the peaceful transfer of power, by popular election, to an old foe: Rómulo Betancourt. This accomplishment resulted as much in spite of as because of the policies and decisions of the provisional government. Indeed, the determined support by most Venezuelan citizens—civilian and military—for a return to democratic civilian government had as much effect on the final result as did overt acts of the Larrazábal Junta. Nevertheless, the Junta made two important contributions to Venezuela's political stabilization: the demilitarization of politics and the institution of free elections within the year.

Initial declarations of the short-lived all-military junta had a familiar, vaguely ominous, ring. Rear Admiral Larrazábal, addressing the nation on January 23, declared:

> The National Armed Forces have assumed the Public Powers of State and have constituted a Junta of Government with the triple objective of saving the unity and institutional sense of the military element, of satisfying the unanimous clamor of the people represented in all sectors, and of conducting the Republic toward a juridical and political organization in accord with universal practices of democracy and law.[1]

Although he went on to discuss restoration of human rights and liberties, he said nothing specific about the means by which the government would accomplish these ends. Also, since he had emphasized military unity as an objective, Venezuelans suspected that this revolution was to be a repetition of the 1948 coup. However, the ouster from the Junta of

1. *El Universal,* January 24, 1958.

two military members, Romero Villate and Casanova, and the inclusion of two distinguished civilians in their stead encouraged those citizens who were concerned about continued military dominance. Another hopeful note was struck at the swearing-in ceremony for Eugenio Mendoza and Blas Lamberti; Larrazábal reiterated his promise that the Junta would rule democratically, "[convoking] elections at the earliest possible date."[2]

The provisional government, unlike the 1948 Junta Militar, held true to its word. In preparation for a return to representative government, it first dismantled the political machinery of the previous regime. Through a succession of decrees, the Junta abolished the Seguridad Nacional, permitted political exiles to return, reinstated political parties, voided the December plebiscite, and dissolved all legislative bodies organized under the dictatorship.

On February 22, just a month after the overthrow of Pérez Jiménez, the Junta named a commission to write a new electoral law, which was presented to the public three months later. The law provided for the election of President, Congress, state legislatures, and municipal councils. Electoral provisions were similar to those in effect in 1947: universal adult suffrage and a secret ballot, with colored ballots to extend the vote to illiterates. The campaign officially opened in mid-November and general elections were held December 7; on February 13, 1959, Rómulo Betancourt was inaugurated Constitutional President of the Republic.

The speed and fairness with which the electoral process unfolded reflect credit on Admiral Larrazábal and his colleagues on the Junta; they completed the election in less than half the time the Revolutionary Junta required after the fall of Medina. The provisional government also resisted the temptation to continue itself in power. To balance the new regime's merits, serious weaknesses existed, located first in the qualifications of Junta President Larrazábal.

The handsome "hero" of January 23 was personable, popular with the masses, and flexible in his dealings with both civilians and military. He was inept, however, at administration and economic planning. His humane approach to socioeconomic problems did not produce the optimal results,

2. *El Universal,* January 26, 1958.

for his solutions were often superficial and, occasionally, counterproductive.

The Junta's determination to remain in power only for the minimum time necessary to restore constitutional procedures also produced unhappy results for the country. Aware of its impermanence, the regime neglected long-range development plans, often turning instead to easy and expedient remedies. An example was the controversial Emergency Plan announced on March 13.[3] To combat rising unemployment owing to the shut-down of construction projects, the government provided for unemployed laborers to receive the same wages they would have received if working. This solution to the stresses of unemployment caused a steady drain on the Treasury's balance and led to a multitude of abuses. Its only possible justification was that it may have prevented a violent social upheaval erupting from a desperate proletariat, a highly unlikely eventuality.

Another failure of the provisional regime was its inability to maintain law and order. The hated SN had been eliminated and its functionaries were refused jobs in the new organization that replaced it. Built without foundation, the Junta security police, as well as other police forces, employed many incompetent as well as untrained men in its service; the crime rate, kept relatively low by the omnipresent Pérez Jiménez police, rose sharply. Maintenance of public order was complicated by masses of newly unemployed workers roaming the streets and by the disorderly, almost anarchical, mood that gripped the masses in the wake of the insurrection.

The most glaring example of this prevailing disorder was the Nixon episode in mid-May. Communist-led students and unemployed workers, taking their cue from the disturbances that interrupted Vice President Richard M. Nixon's visit to Peru, halted the motorcade that was bringing the distinguished visitor to Caracas, swarmed over his car, smashed its windows, and subjected Nixon and his wife to various indignities. Washington considered the situation so grave that the United States Government dispatched military and naval reinforcements to the Caribbean and devised a plan to rescue the Vice President, if necessary, by force.[4]

3. *El Nacional,* March 14, 1958.
4. *El Nacional,* May 14–16, 1958.

The Junta incurred sharp criticism in many quarters for its handling of the affair. Many felt that the Nixon party had been deprived of adequate police protection, although local police authorities claimed that their plan to offer maximum protection had been rejected by a publicity-conscious FBI.[5] Whatever the case, U.S.–Venezuelan relations suffered a serious setback, adding to the already long list of problems confronting the Junta.

The breakdown of public order had another unfortunate effect. An unending series of massive demonstrations, riots, and parades put undue pressure on the Junta and prevented it from making decisions with the calm and objectivity that would have produced more effective and less politically expedient policies.

The fiercely partisan spirit that again characterized Venezuelan politics also contributed to a potentially explosive political climate. While unity was the watchword of the regime, it was manifest only when democracy itself seemed threatened. The three most prominent civilian leaders—Betancourt, Villalba, and Caldera—had met in New York after January 23, where they created the so-called Venezuelan Civilian Front. The front was a political device aimed at maximizing cooperation among the major parties to forestall the kind of bitter political in-fighting that so disturbed the military during the AD *trienio*. Fearful of another *golpe de estado* in the style of 1948, the three men agreed to search for a unity candidate whom they could all support as president.

Once back in the volatile atmosphere of Caracas, however, they found that it was harder to work together for unity than it was to proclaim it as an ideal in the comparative calm of New York. During the summer a round of conferences took place between leaders of AD, URD, and COPEI in an attempt to find an acceptable candidate.[6] As the time for the election campaign approached, the prospects for unity receded, and it became clear that some other method of choosing a candidate was necessary.[7] At the end of October, Cal-

5. See Numa Quevedo, *El gobierno provisorio: 1958,* 109–15.
6. The Communists were included in the talks initially, but they soon dropped out, on their own volition.
7. Fascinating information on the futile search for unity, from the point of view of a left-wing *Adeco,* is in Domingo Alberto Rangel, *La revolución de las fantasías,* 233–42.

dera played host to a conference of AD, URD, and COPEI leaders at his residence, Punto Fijo, out of which came the Pact of Punto Fijo of October 31. In the document the party leaders admitted that the best weapon "against tyranny and against the forces ready to regroup to sponsor another despotic adventure"[8] would have been a single unity candidate. Since they could not agree, they promised to support the winning candidate, to establish a coalition government, and to implement a common minimum program of government. Their inability to create even a temporary national front, especially in the face of the very real danger of military insurgency, proved that unity, for the most part, was no more than an empty slogan. In fact, the major parties fought tooth and nail on the lower levels during the entire period.

The organization that did more than any other to promote harmony and mobilize support for the provisional government was the Patriotic Junta. Although some alleged that the Patriotic Junta had no useful function, once Pérez Jiménez had been ousted,[9] its leaders were proud of the services it rendered during the tumultuous months of provisional rule. This was the time of the "weekend coup." No one knew when he left work on Friday if the provisional government would be in power when he returned on Monday. Rumors of conspiracies were in constant circulation, and many had a basis in reality. The task of quelling disturbances and threatened conspiracies fell mainly to the members of the Patriotic Junta. They spent so much time flying from place to place to stamp out political flare-ups, they earned the title "firemen of the regime." Working in conjunction with local juntas set up throughout the country, they settled partisan disputes and discouraged military and civilian plotters from rebelling.[10]

The Patriotic Junta received little support from the political parties out of fear that it would convert itself into a "super party" that would engulf all the others. Although this fear was groundless, criticism of the Patriotic Junta increased after the major crises had been weathered. Once it appeared that stability had been established, opponents of

8. Venezuela, Presidencia de la República, *Documentos que hicieron historia: siglo y medio de vida republicana, 1810-1961,* II, 446.
9. Robert J. Alexander, *The Venezuelan Democratic Revolution: A Profile of the Regime of Rómulo Betancourt,* 53-54.
10. Interview, May, 1965.

the unity organization eagerly awaited its dissolution, seeing it as "a tremendous competitor to their own prestige."[11]

Civilian tensions were dangerously taut, but the most serious threat to order under the regime came from the military. Larrazábal and his Junta colleagues, fully aware of the potential for disturbance from this source, embarked on a policy designed to maximize military content and loyalty to the regime. An awareness of the military's aims was already apparent in the multiservice composition of the Junta. While military members of all previous juntas had come from the Army, in 1958 the Army was allotted only one representative, as were the Navy and Air Force.

In June, the Junta signed a decree that replaced the old General Staff (Estado Mayor General) with the Joint Staff (Estado Mayor Conjunto). Pérez Jiménez, imitating the Peruvian model, had organized the General Staff in such a way as to give predominance to the ground forces. He had also made the office of Chief of Staff, traditionally an Army appointment, extremely powerful, thereby advancing his personal ambitions. After the January 23 movement, Air Force and Navy officers resolved to put an end to domination by the Army. Under the leadership of Castro León, an Air Force man and the principal exponent of the joint staff organization, the new system began operation. Its effect was to give complete administrative and budgetary autonomy to each branch of the service under the over-all supervision of the Minister of Defense.[12] In addition, the Escuela Básica (organized by Pérez Jiménez to bring together cadets from all branches for the first two years of training) was closed, a reflection of the proautonomy sentiment in the Air Force and Navy.[13]

Finally, the Junta granted an increase in base pay to all military personnel and promised improvements in living conditions and increased fringe benefits. This policy was motivated, at least in part, by political considerations. Even

11. Speech by Antonio Requena, president of the Patriotic Junta, January 23, 1959. Mimeographed copy in my possession.

12. Venezuela, Ministerio de la Defensa Nacional, *Memoria: 1959*, 109.

13. The Escuela Superior, or Staff College, also was temporarily closed after the crisis of July 22–24 for allegedly being the center of military discontent with the government. Foreign Area Studies Division, *U.S. Army Area Handbook for Venezuela*, 539.

though most of the senior officers loyal to Pérez Jiménez had left the country, a large number of *Perezjimenistas* remained in the armed forces, and their presence forced the regime into a policy of exaggerated concern for the military institution.

Reciprocal assurances of support for the Junta were immediately forthcoming from the armed forces. On January 27 Minister of Defense Castro León addressed the Junta of Government in a televised ceremony at Miraflores Palace. He said that as spokesman for the armed forces he could assure the Junta and the nation "that the several Armed Forces are united and that they support the present Government in the most determined and absolute form."[14] He continued:

> Personally, and speaking in my capacity of Minister of Defense, I want to assure the country that by virtue of my absolutely institutional training and convictions, the people of Venezuela can rest in the security that the best and most constant of my desires will always be the maintenance of the unity of the Armed Forces.[15]

He said, further, that the military would provide a sure guarantee that the liberties recently won would be respected and maintained. At a press conference a few weeks later, Castro León again declared his support of the regime and his faith in democracy. He pledged the armed forces' unquestioning support of any democratically elected government, a position that was contrary to that taken by the military in the past.[16]

A new tone crept into Colonel Castro León's remarks early in April. On April 2 the Minister of Defense initiated, with an important address, a television series entitled "Venezuela: Know Your Armed Forces." His talk was, in effect, a reply to newspaper attacks that implied that the military were still militaristic and that the *Perezjimenistas* retained considerable influence in the armed forces. Castro León declared that retaliation against the armed forces for permitting the Pérez Jiménez tyranny to persist so long would lead only to rancor, hatred, and anarchy. If officers were guilty of collaboration with the corrupt dictatorship, there was an equal necessity to recognize "the limitless guilt of the unscrupulous politician." It was time, he continued, to call a halt to

14. *El Nacional,* January 28, 1958.
15. *Ibid.*
16. *El Nacional,* February 21, 1958.

demands to purify the military institution. Implying that the institution was a law to itself, he claimed that the military could regulate its members without any "outside interference." In regard to civilian concern over the threat of military intervention in politics, Castro León declared that the Army had given the lie "once and forever to the threat of military takeover." That "threat" was nothing but the fabrication of sick minds.[17]

The speech created a furor in civilian circles and prompted a protest by professionals, businessmen, and students, who sharply condemned the Minister's attitude, his insulting language, and his thinly veiled support for the concept of military superiority and iron-clad autonomy. His remark that the military institution could solve its own problems was particularly resented. The protest expressed the concern that, as a result of such statements and attitudes, the "artificial tension" that had built up between civilians and military sectors during the dictatorship would revive, to the detriment of both.[18]

In the face of growing uneasiness among civilians, Castro León continued in the Defense post. Meanwhile, a series of crises that did not involve him directly contributed to the civilians' concern about political activity inside the barracks. On April 29 it was announced that Lt. Col. Hugo Enrique Trejo, one of the principal leaders of the January 1 uprising, had been relieved of his command as Assistant Chief of Staff and designated Ambassador to Costa Rica. Admiral Larrazábal had ordered the shift because of Trejo's constant interference in political affairs after January 23. In the months after the fall of Pérez Jiménez, Trejo, one of the most gifted of the young officers, had made numerous public statements in which he freely, and at times critically, commented on the general political situation. Worse, some indiscreet remarks, made privately, became general knowledge, including his suggestion that, since the armed forces had eliminated their strongman (Pérez Jiménez), the political parties should remove their veteran caudillos also. Caldera, Villalba, and especially Betancourt were apprehensive that this sentiment might exacerbate the generational and person-

17. Jesús M. Castro León, "Venezuela: conoce a tus FF.AA.," *Revista de las Fuerzas Armadas* (March–April 1958), 3.
18. *El Nacional,* April 13, 1958.

alist splits within their own parties. Politicians in general were also becoming increasingly alarmed over Trejo's oratorical skill, demagoguery, and popular appeal and their possible effect on the public. Since he was the only military man whose attractiveness approached Larrazábal's hold over the popular imagination, the Admiral saw in Trejo a potentially dangerous rival. There was even some speculation that, with the right combination of forces backing him, Trejo could convert himself into the Perón of Venezuela. The Junta finally confronted him with two choices: leave the country or go to prison. Trejo chose to leave.[19] Terming himself a firm defender of the provisional government, he left for gilded exile in Costa Rica, at the same time urging his companions in arms to continue to defend Venezuelan democracy. His wife, however, made a more revealing remark as a parting shot: "Hugo and I put up with ten years of dictatorship, but we could not abide three months of democracy."[20]

The next crisis came in the wake of the Nixon fracas in May. Many Venezuelans were shocked by the adverse comment the incident provoked in the international press. Pro-American, anti-Communist elements worried about the possible negative effect on U.S.–Venezuelan relations, and saw it as another sign of increasing Communist influence in national politics. The handling of the Nixon affair, among other reasons, prompted the resignation from the Junta of the civilian members, Eugenio Mendoza and Blas Lamberti. Their joint letter of resignation implied that they were weary of the prolonged bickering among the Junta's members. More explicitly, they cited as the immediate cause for their resignation Admiral Larrazábal's decision to exclude them from the consultations he had held with the military high command concerning the Nixon crisis. They felt that by virtue of their positions in the ruling council they should have been included.[21] Another explanation was that the military had forced Mendoza off the Junta on account of his allegedly obsequious response to Washington's threat to send U.S.

19. Rangel, *La revolución*, 164–77. See also *New York Times*, May 11, 1958.
20. José Umaña Bernal, *Testimonio de la revolución en Venezuela*, 258.
21. Umaña Bernal, *Testimonio*, 259–60.

forces to rescue the beleaguered Vice President.[22] There was also a rumor that Mendoza and Lamberti were concerned about Larrazábal's political ambitions and wished to dissociate themselves from his presidential aspirations.

As replacements, the remaining Junta members selected Junta secretary Edgar Sanabria and Minister of the Treasury Arturo Sosa. On May 26 the entire Cabinet resigned to permit the Junta to make desired changes. The reorganized Cabinet included some new faces, although Castro León continued as Minister of Defense. The government seemed to have regained its equilibrium.

Stability, however, was more apparent than real. In early July a flurry of rumors began to circulate concerning alleged subversive activities among the military. In fact, Arturo Sosa was approached by a group of high-ranking officers who proposed to make him president of a new junta, which they would impose by force. Sosa did not accept the offer, but he neither repudiated them nor informed Larrazábal of the proposal.[23]

On July 21 Larrazábal received an ultimatum directed at the Junta by the recently promoted General Castro León. Castro León, asserting that he spoke in the name of the national armed forces, listed a long series of grievances among the military.[24] The ultimatum declared, first, that the Nixon incident proved the government's inability to keep order; the rioting had given Venezuela a bad international image. The government also seemed to be soft on communism, since leftists allegedly involved in the fracas had been dealt with leniently. More generally, succeeding points declared that governmental irresponsibility on the highest levels had filtered down to the lower echelons, especially in matters dealing with the maintenance of order and the suppression of crime. Police laxity and corruption threatened personal security and had produced a lack of respect for private property. Another complaint concerned the influence

22. Laureano Vallenilla Lanz, *Razones de proscrito,* 153. See also *New York Times,* May 25, 1958.

23. Umaña Bernal, *Testimonio,* 261, and Rangel, *La revolución,* 221–22. Sosa claimed that he did not inform the Junta immediately because of a "conflict of conscience" (*New York Times,* July 28, 1958).

24. The full text of the ultimatum is found in Umaña Bernal, *Testimonio,* 262–63.

of organized labor on the government and protested the constant turmoil caused by strikes and disorders. Further, the Junta's economic policies had left thousands unemployed and had led to a business recession.

An important section dealt with the allegedly pervasive influence of AD and the PCV in the government and communications media. The document charged that almost all key government positions were going to *Adecos* and Communists, that these appointments followed a deliberate policy of favoritism, and that the policy was producing a bad psychological climate for the impending election campaign. Furthermore, all means of communications were in the control of the two parties, who used them for their partisan ends, strangling freedom of thought through biased news accounts. The armed forces also expressed alarm that international opinion considered Venezuela's government to be under strong Communist influence.

Item 9 focused on the causes of Castro León's and the military's dissatisfaction. It charged that the armed forces, their individual members, and even their families were insulted daily by radio, television, and press; that the authority of the armed forces went unrecognized; and that lack of respect for the military went uncensured by the government. Also, the AD party in the Federal District and two important states had requested that officers unacceptable to them be removed from their commands; these requests constituted intolerable interference with military autonomy.

The ultimatum demanded three immediate rectifications. First, that there be a change in government personnel to prevent "favoritism" in the national elections, and that all parties be given equal opportunity; second, that an executive decree order all communications media to exclude all articles, news, or commentaries that could be interpreted as prejudicial to the armed institution or to its component members; third, that all those who provoked or led actions that tended to defy the above decree should be immediately prosecuted.

These demands, in essence, reflected the same thinking that had prevailed in the armed forces during the AD *trienio* over a decade earlier. Once again the concept was advanced that the military should be immune from outside interference of any kind. The declaration also reflected strong anti-AD and anti-Communist biases. Underlying the statements was refusal to accept the realities of party politics. The document indicated that at least some leaders of the military institution still regarded themselves as overseers of national politics and felt justified in intervening directly when they felt the prevailing regime was injurious to national and military interests. Those two interests, according to the armed forces, were by definition synonymous.

Curiously, the author of the ultimatum was not an Army man seeking to preserve the Army's supremacy; neither was he a relic of the Gómez army or a member of the aggressive 1945 generation. Instead, Castro León was an intelligent, competent Air Force officer who had received a first-rate education, including more than a year of advanced aviation training in the United States. In the past he had opposed Gómez and had played a leading role in planning the Air Force uprising of January 1 against Pérez Jiménez. He made his first demands in good faith, convinced that he was right and certain that the changes demanded would be beneficial to the nation and to the armed forces.[25]

D. A. Rangel presents an interesting and well-balanced profile of Castro León. A man of honor and generosity, he was a *golpista* only so far as virtually every Venezuelan officer since 1945 was a potential *golpista*. He was definitely not a reactionary. From his public statements and letters he appeared to be cast more in the nineteenth-century liberal mold than in the contemporary militarist mold. Rangel sums up Castro León's political convictions by describing him as an advocate of "a controlled democracy, with respect for law and a certain reverence for the armed forces."

Castro León's disaffection with the regime and its lax and floundering policies provided welcome material for skillful use by a powerful nucleus of *golpistas* who had little or no respect for civilian democracy. Impatient for a return to stern military rule, these _gorilas_ surrounded Castro León while spreading their conspiratorial net throughout the Ministry of Defense and strategic garrisons. They in effect isolated him from the more democratically inclined elements in the military, particularly junior officers, and fed him a steady diet of antiregime propaganda.

25. The wording of the document, however, gave rise to the belief that the ultimatum sought to curry favor with the United States with its strong anti-Communist line, and with URD, COPEI, and independents with its anti-AD pitch.

Their cause advanced considerably when anti-AD politicians, principally Jóvito Villalba, took up the old charge that AD was dominating the bureaucracy. Villalba went so far as to suggest that an *Adeco* should not be President. This was what the *golpistas* wanted to hear; it gave them a ready issue and the appearance of support in the civilian sector. They also implicated Larrazábal in their criticism for taking no action to check AD's allegedly aggressive designs.

Despite Castro León's personal desire for a peaceful solution, the *golpistas* drove him toward armed action until it was too late to turn back. By early July the conspiracy had the support of the commanders of the Military School, most of the Caracas installations, the Air Force and Army battalions located in Maracay, and some FAC units. With this powerful force behind them, why delay longer? They prepared and delivered their ultimatum.[26]

The document convinced Larrazábal that only immediate and decisive action could forestall the coup that lurked behind the ultimatum. Late that night (July 21) he, with the other Junta members, Cabinet members, and other high officials, drove to the coast, where they conferred in the presidential villa at Macuto, under the direct protection of the loyal Navy. It was there that the government's strategy for victory was decided. Larrazábal obtained pledges of loyalty from Navy officials and from the commander of the National Guard. He himself advocated taking a firm stand against military insubordination and in this the entire Cabinet enthusiastically seconded him. Navy Commander Carlos Larrazábal, Wolfgang's brother, formulated plans to bombard rebel installations in Caracas with the Navy's long-range guns. He told the Junta that the Navy was ready to risk civil war to put down an unjustified insurrection, and to demonstrate that he meant business, he distributed 5,000 rifles to La Guaira dock workers.

arms workers

Shortly thereafter, Col. José María Pérez Morales, the chief of Joint Staff, joined the seaside conclave. To that point he had remained neutral; Larrazábal therefore judged that he had been sent as an emissary by the Minister of Defense to see if the Junta was willing to negotiate. The President realized that if the *golpistas* had negotiation on their minds, they were not at all sure of victory. This knowledge strengthened

26. Rangel, *La revolución,* 215–22.

the Junta's determination not to yield. Pérez Morales, his mission having failed, returned to Caracas.[27]

The next morning General Castro León went to his office at the Ministry. According to his version of the affair, he sincerely wanted to avoid a conflict—in fact, had later attempted to descend to the coast to confer with Larrazábal personally but was prevented by a hundred rebellious officers who refused to let him leave the Ministry.[28]

By mid-morning all Caracas knew of the impending coup. The students at the Central University, acting on false reports that tanks were bearing down on the campus, formed into militia units and prepared to defend the regime against military insubordination. The Patriotic Junta swung into action, and professional guilds held hurried meetings to round up support for the government. By 1:00 P.M. the Junta President, greatly encouraged by the determined stand of his colleagues and by Pérez Morales' visit, returned to his office in Miraflores.[29]

At 1:00 P.M. radio and television stations announced a symbolic strike, called by the Unified National Labor Committee, to begin the next day at 11:00 A.M. The announcement was followed by televised speeches by the current president of the Patriotic Junta, Antonio Requena, the junta's former president Fabricio Ojeda, and other leaders. Upon leaving the studio Requena, Ojeda, and AD leader Raúl Leoni were politely arrested by a military intelligence officer loyal to Castro León and were brought to the Ministry of Defense to mediate the confrontation between the Minister and the President. The three were totally unsympathetic to Castro León's views, refused to deal with him, and were released.

When Requena left the Ministry of Defense, he immediately called Larrazábal to tell him he was organizing a massive demonstration in El Silencio for that afternoon.[30] Within two hours, crowds jammed O'Leary Plaza in El Silencio. The provisional President and party leaders addressed the throng, all stressing united action against military insurrection.

27. Rangel, *La revolución,* 223–27.
28. *El Nacional,* July 13, 1965. Rangel claims 300 officers supported him in the Ministry of Defense headquarters alone (*La revolución,* 227).
29. Umaña Bernal, *Testimonio,* 267.
30. Interview, May, 1965.

At 7:00 P.M., while military personnel were confined to quarters, tensely awaiting developments, Castro León sat at his desk. At that point Caldera, Villalba, and Eugenio Mendoza were ushered into his office to discuss possible solutions to the crisis. The General agreed to minor concessions, but was still adamant about what he considered the inordinate influence of AD and the PCV in national life. For their part, the three mediators told him they had no authority to make binding agreements; instead, they conveyed to him the overwhelming determination of the *Caraqueños* to resist any change in government brought about by force.[31]

At 8:00 P.M. the three intermediaries entered the Palacio Blanco, where government officials and political party representatives had assembled. Acting as spokesman for the mediators, Villalba told the anxious *políticos* that they had just returned from the Ministry of Defense, where some 300 officers pledged to Castro León were resolved to take any action necessary to gain their ends. If no peaceful solution could be found, they would resort to arms. Villalba felt that the government lacked the resources to combat the conspiracy and should therefore negotiate.

The veteran URD leader's recommendation sounded virtually like treason to the stubborn politicians in the audience. According to one eyewitness, Foreign Minister René De Sola, who threatened to resign (along with four other Cabinet members) if the Junta negotiated with the *golpistas,* responded vehemently. What were 300 officers if the government had the support of the Navy, some Army units, and millions of Venezuelans prepared to defend democracy? His idealistic plea was enthusiastically endorsed by Gonzalo Barrios (AD) and Gustavo Machado (PCV). In the face of the absolute determination of the government, parties, business, labor, and students to resist the military's demands even if resistance brought civil war, Villalba and Caldera shifted to a tougher position and volunteered to relay this unanimous feeling to Castro León.

The officers in the Ministry of Defense were not lacking in determination either. They urged the gloomy Castro León to remain steadfast and to use all the means of force at his disposal if necessary. The Minister of Defense now vacillated. Civil war and the massacre of civilians were both

31. Umaña Bernal, *Testimonio,* 270.

abhorrent to him. But the *golpistas* played one last card: Maracay. If Maracay, with its powerful complex of Army and Air Force battalions defected, the government could do nothing but capitulate. And Maracay, as in 1945, proved to be crucial. The crack paratroop corps remained loyal and the junior Army officers threatened to arrest their commander if he moved against the government. At midnight Castro León received final confirmation that Maracay was with the government. The last hope of the rebellious military was crushed. At about 2 A.M., July 23, Castro León drove to the Palacio Blanco, where he wrote out his resignation.[32]

Meanwhile, when the meeting in the Palacio Blanco adjourned at 12:30 A.M., Larrazábal conceded that Castro León was still in rebellion. Upon that report and ignorant of the trend of events at the Ministry of Defense, the Patriotic Junta and other civilian groups increased their activity. Students continued to construct defenses and mount barricades. Labor leaders created a special commission to organize a strike that was to continue until the Minister of Defense tendered his resignation. They did not have long to wait. In the early morning hours, a radio bulletin announced that General Castro León had resigned. The Minister of Defense revealed little of his reasons for retracting. However, there is general agreement that his decision was forced on him by the resolute stand taken by Larrazábal, the Junta, and other high officers. He had also been made aware of the extent of popular hostility to a coup. Moreover, his own irresoluteness proved fatal; it removed the necessary elements of surprise and confusion and gave the Junta time to take defensive measures and negotiate from a position of strength.

At 3:15 A.M. Admiral Larrazábal, flanked by the Junta and by members of the military command, officially announced the resignation of the Minister of Defense. As a face-saving gesture for the Minister's benefit, he said that Castro León's action was "one more proof of his patriotism and sense of civic responsibility."[33] He stated quite accurately that the people and the armed forces had united behind the government to prevent a return to the type of regime they had just overthrown. The armed forces were aware, he added, that "a democratic regime constitutes the best guar-

32. Rangel, *La revolución,* 225, 227–29.
33. *El Nacional,* July 24, 1958.

Castro Leon's Revolt

antee of its uninterrupted perfection and of its technical development," whereas a "dictatorial system would reduce [the military] again to the sad role of apparent accomplices of base interest and covetous passions."[34] He failed to mention, however, that several hundred officers had sided with Castro León against the Junta.

That ceremony marked the end of Castro León's revolt. Nevertheless, the nationwide strike was held as scheduled the next day as a warning to all would-be *golpistas*. On the afternoon of July 24 General Castro León left in a military plane bound for Miami. With him went seven other implicated officers, all lieutenant colonels and majors.[35] Castro León was immediately replaced by Gen. Josué López Henríquez, who, like his predecessor, was a Tachiran and an Air Force officer.

The dismissal of Castro León terminated the gravest crisis faced by the Larrazábal Junta. But undercurrents of unrest persisted. A month after the Castro León episode, Chief of Joint Staff Col. José María Pérez Morales was abruptly dismissed from his post and sent to Washington as military attaché. Although official sources denied that the shift was motivated by political considerations, observers believed that Pérez Morales was in strong disagreement with the Junta and the Minister of Defense on important political questions.[36]

The policy of reassigning and cashiering potentially troublesome officers continued, but more unrest surfaced on September 7, when military rebels briefly seized the Ministry of Defense, the police barracks, and a Caracas radio station. The rebellion broke out at a delicate moment: Larrazábal, who was touring the Oriente, was not expected to return until later in the day. The most critical moment occurred when the rebels trained the guns of several tanks in their command on the Palacio Blanco, to which government officials had hurried to begin defensive operations. The tank commander demanded that the palace gates be opened and that its

34. *El Nacional,* July 24, 1958.

35. Two years later General Castro León led an ill-fated military movement against the Betancourt regime. Unlike his great-uncle Cipriano's revolution, however, the movement, which began on the Colombian border, never got farther than Táchira. The rebel leader was captured, and he died a prisoner in the San Carlos barracks, July 12, 1965, still awaiting final disposition of his case.

36. *El Nacional,* August 26, 1958.

defenders surrender. That demand met flat rejection by Col. Pedro José Quevedo, who had taken charge of military operations against the rebels. The demand was repeated twice, with the addition that a "new junta" be recognized. The ultimatum met no response. Junta member Quevedo, along with Minister of Defense López Henríquez, threatened to use tanks and artillery against the police barracks unless the rebels retired. The threat worked, and within a short time the rebels surrendered, the tanks withdrew from the front of the palace, and Colonel Quevedo went on the air to inform the nation that order had been restored. The whole affair, which erupted about 3:00 A.M., was over by 6:00 A.M.[37]

A huge crowd gathered in front of the palace, where Colonel Quevedo, Minister of Interior Relations Numa Quevedo, and Federal District Governor Julio Diez assured them that the brief uprising had ended. This assurance apparently was not enough; the mob wanted guarantees that the plotters would be punished. Unfortunately, for reasons never fully established, a group attempted to storm the military police barracks. In the confusion that followed, 20 persons were killed and about 400 wounded;[38] the casualties included civilians, military personnel, and police. Acts of violence occurred sporadically in other parts of the country during that and the following day.

At a press conference four days later, the Junta President deplored the disorder that prevailed in the wake of the September 7 uprising: "It would please me if many civilian groups had the same conviction which the Armed Institution has today about democracy."[39] As it was, within the next week a score of civilians were arrested in connection with the insurrection, most of them former functionaries of the dictatorship.

In mid-November intelligence officials uncovered another conspiracy. On November 14 Larrazábal stepped down from the provisional presidency to run for President on the URD ticket. Replacing him was Edgar Sanabria, one of the civilian Junta members. Navy Captain Miguel Rodríguez Olivares was sworn in as the new Junta member to keep the balance between civilians and military and between the service

37. Quevedo, *El gobierno provisorio,* 200–202.
38. Philip B. Taylor, Jr., *The Venezuelan Golpe de Estado of 1958: The Fall of Marcos Pérez Jiménez,* 61.
39. Quevedo, *El gobierno provisorio,* 205.

branches. That evening a secret meeting was dispersed in the neighborhood of Dr. Sanabria's residence. At the rendezvous were both civilians and officers, all allegedly engaged in subversive activity. The reported leader was Col. Héctor D'Lima Polanco, chief of the Technical Office of the Ministry of Defense. Implicated with him were a captain and four lieutenants.[40] They were taken into custody, and with their arrest the entire conspiracy collapsed.

Although rumors of conspiracies and invasions continued, the short but hard-fought election campaign proceeded in an atmosphere remarkably free from subversive activity. By proving time and again its ability to defend itself, the Junta discouraged whatever would-be conspirators remained. For the duration of the provisional government both military and civil–military subversion were on the wane.

In the presidential race with Larrazábal were AD's Rómulo Betancourt and COPEI's Rafael Caldera. The latter two campaigned throughout the country while Larrazábal concentrated mainly on the Caracas and coastal areas. The result of the December 7 election revealed Betancourt to be the winner with 49 per cent of the vote; Larrazábal placed a strong second (35 per cent); and Caldera ran a poor third (16 per cent).[41] The Admiral swept the Caracas area, and his defeat by non-*Caraqueños,* coupled with the traditional hostility to AD in Caracas (where Betancourt finished in last place), provoked two days of rioting in the city. Larrazábal, however, urged his supporters to accept the results with a democratic spirit. Order was soon restored, and the nation was free to prepare for a new constitutional term beginning on February 13, 1959. On that day Rómulo Betancourt was inaugurated President of the Republic, the first freely elected civilian President in eleven years.

*   *   *   *   *

The record of the 1958–1959 provisional government strongly suggests that Junta members were sincerely committed to returning Venezuela to democratic civilian rule.

---

40. *El Nacional,* November 16, 1958.
41. Boris Bunimov-Parra, *Introducción a la sociología electoral venezolana,* Cuadro Anexo VI.

Because of this commitment, Venezuela's interim rulers confronted two basic political problems: first, to keep the military in the barracks long enough to permit the civilian politicians to restore constitutional government on a firm basis, and second, to prevent powerful civilian groups from provoking the military into insubordination to further their own partisan ends. While undergoing many anxious moments and countless threats, Venezuelan leaders grappled successfully with those problems.

The military acquiesced in the shift to civilian rule for a number of reasons and from a variety of motives. Some of the more important factors are listed here. First, Venezuela through most of 1958 was governed by a military provisional president, an officer who had signed the constitutive act of the 1948 military government. The ruling Junta, which had a ratio of three officers to two civilians under Larrazábal, retained the same ratio under Sanabria. Thus, the supreme ruling body, armed with sweeping powers, was in the control of military elements who had steady contact with barracks sentiment. Second, Navy and Air Force personnel tended to be satisfied both because of the popular acclaim accorded them for their leading role in the January 23 insurrection and because of their representation on the Junta for the first time. Third, Larrazábal made sure that the military institution was well taken care of from a material standpoint. Fourth, the Junta's military reorganization program deliberately provided for decentralization of authority in the institution, thereby making it more difficult for a Pérez Jiménez-type figure to re-emerge from an all-powerful staff position. Coupled with the overhaul of the General Staff was the generally successful policy of dismissing and reassigning politically troublesome officers. Fifth, junior officers, especially those involved in the January 23 movement, were more professional in their political attitudes than those of previous generations (they had not been participants in the 1945–1948 civil–military tensions) and willingly cooperated with civilians to encourage the military to restrict itself to its constitutionally sanctioned functions. Sixth, the provisional government did little in the socioeconomic field to alarm the military institution. In the face of the increased strength and prestige of the Communists and other left-wing elements, the government in its policies and appointments revealed its predilection for moderate reform within a basically capitalistic system. Finally, the military was divided and confused after the startling events of January, 1958; many officers felt that the institution had been burned by its ruling experience and should as rapidly as possible turn the government over to civilians in order to polish its tarnished image.

Civilians also gave their support to the interim regime. They did this, first, because they realized that their only chance for resumption of free political life was to maintain a show of unity. This outward unity would be sufficient evidence to the military that civilians could cooperate in a reform regime or, at least, would fight among themselves rather than conspire with military elements against the opposition. In other words, they had learned the long-range lesson of 1948. Second, the brutal and corrupt despotism of the Pérez Jiménez–Vallenilla Lanz–Estrada triumvirate had left so many scars on the body politic that elements ranging from the Junta to the Patriotic Junta, labor, students, and partisan groups fought with conviction for civilian supremacy, and they succeeded in conveying to the military their unswerving faith in the merits of civilian rule.

CHAPTER VIII

THE MILITARY'S ROLE REDEFINED

At the beginning of 1959 the political role of the Venezuelan military appeared to be entering a new phase. With important exceptions, both civilian and soldier were weary of military dictatorship. There was broad support for a return to civilian rule and for a more restricted role for the military. Most officers in the armed forces seemed ready to accept the shift to civilian leadership. More importantly, those who could not adjust were unable to engender sufficient military or popular backing to overthrow the provisional regime.

The transition from military to civilian rule, however, was hindered by the persistent tradition of military supremacy in Venezuela. Bolívar was thoroughly vindicated in his prediction that his fatherland would be the barracks of South America. It indeed became a barracks after his death, in the sense that military strongmen—caudillos—dominated national politics throughout the century after independence.

The process of shifting from caudillism to modern Latin-style militarism began in 1899 with the seizure of power by the *Andinos.* The political role of the Army under Castro, and particularly Gómez, was that of a gendarmery. Lyle N. McAlister accurately describes Venezuela under Gómez as a "gendarmist state," in which one military strongman uses a mercenary army to make himself national ruler, imposes order, tames the army, and uses it to maintain himself in power.[1]

The López Contreras–Medina decade represented a transitional phase away from the gendarmist state toward a more professional, institutionalized, and yet contradictory role for the military. This stage in the evolution of the national army illustrates the dilemma faced by the modernizing military. On the one hand, Academy-trained officers were adopting professional attitudes that stressed the performance of only those functions specifically prescribed in the Constitution.

---

1. Lyle N. McAlister, "Civil–Military Relations in Latin America," *Journal of Inter-American Studies,* 3 (July 1961), 344.

But while young officers became increasingly proud of their professionalism and nonpolitical stance, they were becoming increasingly impatient with politicians whom they regarded as blocks to the necessary modernization of the armed forces in particular and the political system in general. This frustration bred the notion that it was their right, even their duty, to bring to power new forces that would be more responsive to the needs of the Army and the people. To the rejoinder that political activity was a violation of military professionalism came the reply that the "extraordinary circumstances" and their publicly stated determination to hand over the government to democratic civilian reformers justified their action. Their movement was further justified by historical precedent: the military traditionally had been the guardian of the law and the rights of the people. The point here is not that this statement was objectively true, but that the military believed it to be true.

Meanwhile, both López Contreras and Medina, although Andean generals like Castro and Gómez, ruled as civilians. López Contreras relied more heavily on the Army, in the absence of other organized political groups, but he did attempt to differentiate more clearly between military and civilian spheres by removing military officers from normally civilian posts. Medina carried on López Contreras' policy of circumscribing the political role of the military and, in fact, grew less and less reliant on the military. He was the first twentieth-century Venezuelan president to build organized civilian political bases, such as the PDV and the alliance with the PCV.[2] These moves were seen as threats by officers of all ranks. To them, the armed forces appeared to be losing political power vis-à-vis other political interest groups. Pressure had already begun to mount from junior officers under López Contreras, but he was able to keep it under control. Medina, however, did not perceive the depth of the generational rift nor did he understand that his well-intentioned removal of the military from politics would be counterproductive; it was, in fact, exactly so. Both senior and junior officers talked revolution with civilian groups; the junior officers acted first.

During the AD *trienio* the military remained nominally

2. López Contreras' earlier Agrupaciones Cívicas Bolivarianas was hardly an effective or broad-based political movement.

loyal to civilian leadership, but civil–military conflict was sharp throughout the period. The role of the military, well defined and restricted by the Constitution of 1947, was not so well defined in the minds of the officers. They did not understand all the implications for professionalism of their revolutionary pronouncements and, heralded as the makers and defenders of the "revolution," they were reluctant to surrender status or power. Their self-image was that of "regulators";[3] theirs was a rectifying institution, a body that could step disinterestedly into a political crisis, clean up the mess, and then walk away. The military demands made on Gallegos in 1948 indicate that the institution felt it could and should intrude into politics when the situation warranted, despite the Constitution's definition of the armed forces as a "non-political institution, essentially professional, obedient, and not deliberative."[4]

The 1948–1958 period represents the furthest extension of militarism in Venezuela. Pérez Jiménez, unlike López Contreras and Medina, ruled in the name of the armed forces for the sake of the armed forces. He ruled as a military man, complete with uniform. Contrary to Medina, he made no effort to build up civilian support. His system broke down when he could no longer retain the loyalty of the forces that sustained it, and the military was among those forces. In January 1958 some military elements again saw themselves as rectifiers who should correct an intolerable situation, by force, if necessary. Between the fall of Pérez Jiménez and the inauguration of Rómulo Betancourt, the military, although bitterly divided, generally supported the concept of civilian supremacy as stated in the Constitution.

During the 1928–1958 period the Venezuelan military intervened directly in politics when there were simultaneous crises in the military institution and in society—or, to use the terminology of Martin Needler, when there was both an "external stimulus" and an "internal disposition" impelling the officers to intervene.[5] In 1945 military dissatisfaction coin-

3. Lyle N. McAlister, "Changing Concepts of the Role of the Military in Latin America," *The Annals of the American Academy of Political and Social Science,* 360 (July 1965), 91.

4. The Venezuelan Constitution of 1947, Article 93, in Russell H. Fitzgibbon, *The Constitutions of the Americas,* 779.

5. Martin C. Needler, "The Latin American Military: Predatory Reactionaries or Modernizing Patriots?" *Journal of Inter-American Studies,* 11 (April 1969), 240.

cided with the general political crisis in which all Venezuela was divided into three inflexibly antagonistic camps. In 1948 the military's fears over AD intentions and their disillusionment with the party's performance were reinforced by the general ambience of turmoil, aroused political passions, and virulent attacks on the AD government by influential opposition elements. The insurrection of January 23, 1958, provides yet another example of military discontent coinciding with civilian restiveness to produce a successful *coup d'état*. In 1928, although there was considerable antipathy to the dictatorship in both civilian and military circles, it was not of crisis proportions, and active opposition was limited to a relative handful of novices. In 1958 Castro León misread the public attitude. There was considerable civilian disharmony and widespread animosity toward the regime, but civilians were in general united on the principle of civilian political supremacy and they were supported by a large segment of the armed forces.

In the country's history of unrest, military movements tended to be successful when they confronted a ruler who was both intransigent in his attitude and weak in his own defense. This pattern was apparent in 1945 when Medina refused to initiate the constitutional reforms that could well have saved his regime and then, when faced with revolt, could not or would not defend it. In 1948 Gallegos could have saved himself or at least have gained time by acceding to certain military demands. He stubbornly refused, but when it was necessary to defend his government, he was incapable of doing so and was easily displaced. Ten years later Pérez Jiménez, after having obstinately resisted pressure to reform his regime, proved unequal to the task of defending it and finally fled the country. On the contrary, military movements tended to be unsuccessful when they confronted official determination and resolute action. Such a failure occurred in 1928, when the authorities took swift and effective measures against the April insurrectionists; on January 1, 1958, when Pérez Jiménez temporarily proved his toughness; and in July, 1958, when Larrazábal and his collaborators showed extraordinary firmness in the face of military insubordination.

Unity was also crucial to the success of any military venture into politics. This factor was clearly present in 1948 and 1952. The importance of unity can be seen in the later movement when, despite civilian opposition to a blatant power grab by the military, the officers prevailed because they maintained a united front. In July, 1958, on the other hand, the projected *golpe* of Castro León failed, in part, because the officer corps was sharply divided. In 1945 and in January, 1958, the military institution was also divided, but in those actions weak defense by the regime, strong civilian support for the insurgents, and the aggressiveness of the most dynamic elements in the armed forces compensated for the lack of unity.

One factor underlies Venezuela's political upheavals: "military" movements can in most instances be better described as "civilian–military" movements. Venezuela, here, follows the Latin American pattern noted by numerous observers. According to Jacques Lambert, for instance, "the military are constantly being asked to intervene in politics."[6] A student of *coups d'état,* Martin Needler, writes that "a military coup is not made by the military alone."[7] Similar statements by Venezuelans have already been cited elsewhere in this work. In most of the revolts examined here, civilians played a significant role. In 1928 and 1958 reformist civilian groups approached young officers about the possibility of joining forces to overthrow the dictator of the moment. In 1945 it was the military who approached a civilian group, but the result was the same: the forging of a civil–military coalition. In 1948 the military moved unilaterally, but not after intense pressure from civilians to oust AD. In July, 1958, Castro León's *golpistas* had the support, either active or passive, of influential civilian elements who opposed the Larrazábal regime. Throughout 1958, in fact, civilians were arrested along with military personnel for allegedly conspiring against the provisional government. The one possible exception to this general rule occurred in 1952 with the nullification of the election and seizure of power by the armed forces. This military intervention represents the low point of civilian influence on and participation in political decisions. Even in this instance, the military consulted Vallenilla Lanz and other civilian advisers on possible courses of action, and many civilians undoubtedly indicated their preference for a continuation of military rule rather than a return to a situa-

6. Jacques Lambert, *Latin America: Social Structures and Political Institutions,* 237.

7. Martin C. Needler, *Political Development in Latin America: Instability, Violence, and Evolutionary Change,* 63.

tion that approximated the tumultuous *trienio*.

The effect of political propaganda on the officers' decision to intervene should not be underestimated. In 1945 the *Lopecistas* and *Adecos* attacked Medina viciously in the press. In 1948 partisan elements used the press to voice their adamant opposition to AD. In 1958, although communications media were tightly controlled by the regime, underground propaganda, such as the manifesto included in Appendix C, incited the military to topple the dictatorship.

All so-called military regimes from Gómez to Pérez Jiménez had the eager collaboration of civilians at every level of government. An obvious illustration is the importance in the Pérez Jiménez regime of Vallenilla and Estrada as key administrators and confidants of the dictator. That the public was fully aware of their influence is revealed in numerous clandestine documents that focused their propaganda on the infamous "triumvirate" of Pérez Jiménez, Vallenilla, and Estrada. In such documents the latter two are directly attacked, while Pérez Jiménez' military collaborators are seldom if ever mentioned by name. The generals may have been thieves, but they were not sadists.

What motivated Venezuelan officers to intervene directly in politics between 1928 and 1958? This basic question does not have a clear-cut answer; few questions that concern group motivation have. Obviously, a variety of motives, influences, and impulses impelled officers to move against the prevailing government. Even on the assumption that one can list such factors, a secondary problem remains: how much weight should be assigned each motivating element? The assigning of weights at this stage of research is extremely risky. Too many factors and too many individuals interacted over too long a span of time to make precise judgments. In general, though, and allowing for individual differences and idiosyncracies, the activist officers revolted for a combination of personal and professional reasons.

Turning first to consideration of personal factors, it is clear that democratic idealism played a role in certain movements, especially in 1928 and 1958, when junior officers moved against corrupt despots. A large dosage of youthful idealism also contributed to the making of the 1945 revolt. Descending to a lower plane, bread-and-butter issues were invariably wrapped up in the political movements of these years. Personal grievances—against poor living conditions, inadequate remuneration, slow ascent up the career ladder, intolerable superiors—were operative at every critical juncture. They can be documented most clearly in the defeated insurrection of 1928, the successful revolt of 1945, and the 1958 ouster of Pérez Jiménez. Personal ambitions, of course, played an important part in the various movements. The most notoriously ambitious officer was Marcos Pérez Jiménez, whose hunger for power was demonstrated by his takeover of the government in 1952, his device in 1957 to use a plebiscite, and his reluctance to relinquish power until forced to do so by a full-scale uprising. It is possible that other officers, perhaps Delgado Chalbaud, had equal or even grander ambitions, but Pérez Jiménez was the most successful at attaining his.

A number of professional reasons provided fuel for military rebellion, although it should be kept in mind that professional and personal motives frequently overlapped. Students of the Latin American military have pointed out that officers frequently intervene when they conclude that a particular regime is a threat to the power, independence, integrity, or survival of their institution. In Venezuela this professional jealousy, or "corporate self-interest," was evident in 1945, when both senior and junior officers became apprehensive over President Medina's alleged neglect of the armed forces and his creation of a civilian political base as a potential counterpoise to the military. Similar suspicions swept the barracks in 1948, when officers became alarmed that their institution was losing influence relative to an increasingly powerful party, AD, which was backed by nationwide peasant and labor affiliates. The military felt further threatened by alleged organization of party militias, which they feared would be deployed against regular armed forces in the event of a civil conflict. Ten years later, one motive for the junior officers' opposition to the dictatorship was the threat to the military's privileges posed by the octopuslike security apparatus run by civilians. The young officers also felt that the brutality and scandalous public morality of the regime's leadership stigmatized the whole military institution. The professional integrity of their institution was at stake.

Closely related to institutional jealousy was the officers' sensitivity to outside meddling in military affairs. There was a general consensus within the officer corps that nonmilitary meddling with the armed forces was more threatening to military professionalism than military interference in civilian affairs. This attitude was clear in the 1948 coup, where the *adequización* of the military and partisan attempts at dividing the military became major justifications for intervention. In 1958 outside meddling took a different form—SN harassment of military professionals—but the reaction was similar. It should be noted here that in the minds of most officers corporate self-interest and self-sacrificing patriotism were virtually synonymous. In another context Lieuwen refers to "the corporate self-interest of the armed forces [being] equated with the true national interest,"[8] and Needler suggests that "even though military intervention in politics occurs in 'patriotic' response to the requirements of the functioning of the political system, it nevertheless does reflect military self-interest."[9] In the Venezuelan political tradition, certainly, it was relatively easy for soldiers to confuse in their minds patriotic idealism and institutional self-interest.

The militarist mentality, in the Latin American use of the term, undoubtedly played a part in the 1948 and 1952 movements, the attempt to impose an all-military junta after the fall of Pérez Jiménez, and the July, 1958, movement of General Castro León. These affairs were in part inspired by the officers' belief that the military had a ruling function, that military men were more self-sacrificing, dedicated, nationalistic, and efficient than civilian politicians, and that military and defense interests should never be reviewed or restricted by mere partisan politicians. Contempt for and suspicion of civilian politicians partly characterized all the political movements by the military. In addition, military concern over civilian management of the national economy had some bearing on the revolt of 1945, when wartime shortages and inflation caused economic hardships; 1948, when AD's program of socioeconomic reform provoked widespread opposition; and 1958, when the military became aware that the oil boom had peaked and that the business community had lost faith in the regime. Military concern with economic policy needs much closer study than this account provides. Further research on this problem, although

8. Edwin Lieuwen, *Generals vs. Presidents: Neomilitarism in Latin America,* 107.
9. Needler, "The Latin American Military," 239.

difficult, should be extremely rewarding. For example, there is at least some evidence that, contrary to standard accounts, AD's economic policy during the *trienio* was not too radical for the supposedly more conservative military, but it was too poorly administered and not sufficiently nationalistic for certain officers.

Finally, a powerful force within the institution itself that impelled young officers to action was the natural antagonism between generations. Generational cleavages, endemic to any institution, were magnified by the superior training given to successive generations of cadets and junior officers. Their sense of superiority led to elitism among the junior officers, a feeling that they were better equipped to run the military establishment and perhaps the entire government than their incompetent elders. This attitude was present in 1928 and 1958 but was most vividly revealed in the thinking of the men who revolted against Medina.

The most difficult questions to answer are those that try to assess the nature and extent of foreign influences on the political behavior of Venezuelan officers. Outside influences on the military have not been a concern of this study, partly because, after extensive reading and with knowledge gathered in talks with officer participants, I believe that endogenous influences were considerably the more important, and partly because of the difficulty in documenting direct links between exogenous forces and domestic actions. The Peruvian experience of many young officers undoubtedly affected the 1945 military generation and led to such innovations as the secret military lodge. One could also argue that, since the 1948 coup came shortly after the Peruvian coup against a civilian regime, the Venezuelan military command, with close ties to the Peruvian military, might have been encouraged by that success to initiate a similar movement in Venezuela. The January 1958 insurrection, in turn, has been placed by Lieuwen and others in a cycle of antimilitarist movements that included the ouster of Juan Perón in Argentina (1955), Paul Magloire in Haiti (1956), Gustavo Rojas Pinilla in Colombia (1957), and Fulgencio Batista in Cuba (1959).[10] That the fall of Rojas Pinilla, for instance, provided some encouragement to the Venezuelan opposition forces is undoubtedly true, but so far there is little evidence that any of these coups had a

10. Lieuwen, *Generals vs. Presidents,* 4.

profound effect on others. Connections of this sort were precluded by the nationalistic inclinations and the insular outlook of the countries involved, as well as by the distinctive set of political circumstances operative in each country.

Military objectives, like motives, were mixed and varied with each movement and within the various factions that comprised each rebel group. On four occasions, for example, military elements intervened in order to depose military presidents: in 1928, 1945, and in January and July, 1958. But even in these crises the objectives varied. In 1928 and in January of 1958, junior officers moved to oust ruthless strongmen and to impose a more democratic regime. In 1945 the stated objective was to bring to power a civilian reform regime and, this aim accomplished, to retreat to the barracks. This was the case as well in January, 1958, but with important exceptions. While junior officers endeavored to remove their institution from politics, military commanders sought to sacrifice Pérez Jiménez in order to retain control of the government for themselves, as evidenced by their formation of the short-lived military junta. The leaders of the 1948 coup gave assurances of a prompt return to constitutional government, and they perhaps were sincere, but on that occasion they did not hold to their promises. Their overriding objective was simply to get rid of the *Adecos;* they would worry about the consequences later. In 1952 the main goal was to preserve military power in the face of victory by a party the military knew had the support of the hated *Adecos.* The goal of the Castro León clique in July, 1958, was to restore outright military rule to halt the alleged gross inefficiency of the regime and the political power concentrated in the hands of AD and the PCV—two very dangerous groups, from the military standpoint. In general, in all the movements studied, the rebel leaders paid more attention to a short-term goal—the removal of the incumbent regime—than to the long-range effects such intervention would have on national political development.

From Gómez' time to the present, both the civilian and military sectors of Venezuelan society have been confronting the stresses of rapid modernization. The post-World War I petroleum revolution set in train a series of changes that had corresponding effects on life inside and outside the barracks. But the process of development was far from smooth and only partially fulfilled. The increasing national wealth went into relatively few hands and was, in the main, used unproductively. The arbitrary, inefficient, and corrupt manner in which the mounting government revenues were used provoked increasing discontent in both the civilian and military sectors. A premature revolt brought together disgruntled middle-class civilians and military men in 1928, but the time was not yet ripe for revolution. In 1945, however, a similar coalition was formed by young, predominantly middle-class politicians and junior officers who concluded that the country could not be modernized and democratized under the timid and lackadaisical civilian and military leadership then in power; there had been far more talk than action on "sowing the petroleum"—using oil revenues to develop a diversified economy. The 1945 revolt provided impetus to modernization, to be sure, but it also led to stresses on the system that many Venezuelans were psychologically unable to accept. The changes that were taking place were not peaceful, gradual, and harmless, nor could they be. Consequently, those elements who declared their support of orderly progress intervened to rectify the situation. Since the military, in their self-image, embodied orderly progress, they carried out the mission urged on them by civilians.

But the military could not completely control a developing society. The "tendency of army officers to underestimate the difficulties of changing the civilian society,"[11] noted by Lucian Pye, held true in Venezuela. The modernization process had already unleashed powerful forces. Tens of thousands of Venezuelans were committed to political parties. Laborers and *campesinos* had been organized. The burgeoning middle sectors, by-products of the petroleum revolution, were politically restless. *Campesinos* were crowding into the cities. All the tensions of an industrializing, incipiently capitalist society in the throes of development were present. But the military institution, by its very nature, was not a flexible instrument for modernization. The military's concept of governing was limited to maintaining order at all costs while pressing forward with a rather narrowly conceived type of material development centered around a huge public works budget. The military's obsession with public works stemmed

11. Lucian W. Pye, "Armies in the Process of Political Modernization," in John J. Johnson, ed., *The Role of the Military in Underdeveloped Countries,* 81.

in part from political ineptitude. The institution could not assume all the functions of the state, and its leaders lacked the training, capacity, and will to build mass support. They felt that millions of tons of concrete poured onto highways and into structures were adequate substitutes for representative government. Their house stood so long as the economy flourished, but when the economy leveled off at the same time that the consequences of serious political mistakes were catching up with the regime, civilian and military elements combined to pull it down.

The months after the ouster of the dictatorship were difficult. Political frenzy, constant demonstrations, the resurgence of AD and the PCV, the flight of capital, the hastily improvised social welfare policy that was necessitated by rapid urbanization and widespread unemployment, all caused certain soldiers and civilians to seek to impose order on the engulfing chaos. This motivation is implicit in the succession of attempted coups throughout 1958—especially that of Castro León—and subsequently by military uprisings against the Betancourt administration.

Since 1959 the Venezuelan armed forces, despite many inducements to rebel, have backed three popularly elected civilian administrations. The military command and the majority of officers have resisted the course of direct intervention at a time when one or more successful military coups have occurred in at least ten Latin American countries.[12] What accounts for this recent trend toward political aloofness and responsible professionalism?

The answer is that the political role of the military has been undergoing a process of redefinition. Most officers have concluded that their functions as set out by the 1961 Constitution are the only legitimate professional ones. But acceptance of the more restricted political role is a product of several factors. First, inasmuch as the largely negative experience of 1948–1958 was damaging to the institution, officers feared that a new military take-over would bring down on their institution the wrath of an aroused citizenry that was

12. Nevertheless a number of unsuccessful rebellions, from the right and left, that erupted in the 1960s involved military elements. The two most serious were the leftist-inspired revolts at Carúpano (May 1962) and Puerto Cabello (June 1962). The Puerto Cabello affair represents the last serious attempt by the military to overturn duly constituted authority by force.

weary of authoritarianism. Second, the increasingly professional training in the military schools, which stresses the advantages of responsible, civilian-directed democracy, has apparently been bearing fruit. Third, the military policy of the post-1959 administrations has been far from hostile to military interests. Presidents Betancourt, Leoni, and Caldera have striven to maintain good relations with the military command and to maintain military morale at high levels. They have sponsored moderate, generally well-conceived reform and development programs, expanded defense budgets, granted generous salaries and fringe benefits, expressed extravagant praise of the valorous deeds and noble traditions of the national army, and focused the energies of the armed forces on such constructive enterprises as military civic action programs and such vital defense missions as antiguerrilla campaigns. In addition, particularly during the height of the Castroite–Communist guerrilla and terrorist offensive (1962–1966), Presidents Betancourt and Leoni convinced the military command—if indeed it needed convincing—that a military take-over in order to re-establish order would be playing directly into the hands of their archenemies. Communist strategy sought to provoke a military coup that, in turn, would rouse the people into a popular insurrection, control of which would then be captured by the Communists, who would proceed to destroy the military institution.[13] Fourth, the military still bears an indirect yet powerful influence on politics, through which it enjoys considerable budgetary autonomy, a minimum of extrainstitutional scrutiny, and a subtle veto power over any extreme measures. Finally, the governments in power since 1959 have, according to many observers, performed sufficiently well to keep at a minimum the percentage of the politically active citizenry who might look to the military for quick remedies.

Although one is on treacherous ground when hazarding predictions about how the Venezuelan military will interact with civilian leaders in the next decades, a few forecasts of possible courses of action, based on recent trends, are possible. First, for those who pin their hopes on military separation from politics as the best hope for building a stable democracy, there are some encouraging signs. There is evi-

13. See Robert J. Alexander, *The Communist Party of Venezuela*, 83–84, and Lieuwen, *Generals vs. Presidents*, 88.

dence that Venezuelan officers are genuinely proud of their noninterference in the three general elections held since 1958, despite pressure to intervene in all three. The victor in 1958, Betancourt, had long been suspected in certain quarters of the armed forces of harboring antimilitary attitudes. In 1963 the military was under pressure to intervene as a result of the terrorist offensive designed to prevent the national election from taking place. In 1968 there was considerable speculation that the military could not be relied on to guarantee the peaceful transfer of power from one political party to another, an event without precedent in Venezuelan history. All three elections took place with a minimum of violence and were marked by close cooperation between military and civilian authorities. One assumes, then, that each election or political crisis that passes without military interference increases the chances that a nonpolitical military will become a tradition in Venezuela. Concomitantly, the less enthusiasm the military displays for intervention, the less will politicians look to the barracks as a kind of *deus ex machina* to solve political problems they cannot solve by democratic means. With regard to the relationship between Venezuela's social and economic prospects and military politics, one concludes that, because Venezuela has made an impressive start on exploiting its vast material resources, has made a beginning on rational development planning, and has a higher level of social democracy than most of its neighbors, there will be less pressure on the Venezuelan military to defend oligarchic interests on the one hand, or to defend the masses from the oligarchs on the other, than on military institutions in countries with more desperate social problems.

Nevertheless, for those observers who look for the Venezuelan armed forces to evolve in the direction of their counterparts in such countries as Mexico, Costa Rica, or Uruguay, some dark clouds loom on the political horizon. One sign that the political system is, to a degree at least, malfunctioning is the remarkable performance of former Gen. Marcos Pérez Jiménez' Cruzada Cívica Nacionalista (CCN) —Nationalist Civic Crusade, in the 1968 election, in which the party of the former strongman overnight became numerically the fourth largest political group in the nation and its leader won a senate seat in a sweeping personal victory. Although the CCN's surprising showing was more probably an example of the persistence of personalism in Latin American politics and a protest vote against a party that had been entrenched in power for ten years than it was a sudden resurgence of militarist tendencies, it does indicate that somewhere along the line the "democratic" parties have not been keeping pace with popular expectations. The CCN's victory also indicates that democratic liberals have possibly exaggerated the durability of the hostility to the *dictadura militar* and to Pérez Jiménez himself. In either case it appears that the Andean general could well be an important and unpredictable force in Venezuelan politics, direct or indirect, for some years to come. Another kind of political threat could come with the recrudescence of terrorist and guerrilla activity that, if escalated to a sufficient intensity, could provoke the military into intervention to restore order. Politicians, on the other hand, can lessen the dangers of military intervention by being responsive to mass demands and by resisting the temptation to play politics with the military.

An economic crisis could also spell trouble for Venezuela's present democratic system, if it should be critical or prolonged, or if it should coincide with a political crisis. The most serious long-range problem that could bring the military to the political stage would be the ultimate failure of civilian leaders to "sow the petroleum." The inability of the authorities and the private sector to effect a successful change-over from the oil-dominated economy of today to a diversified semi-industrialized economy of tomorrow would be sure to have profound political consequences, including loud reverberations in the barracks.

The future appears uncertain. Even Edwin Lieuwen, who has identified himself with the position that Latin American militarism, at least in the long run, is on the wane, writes that "the military will probably intervene again in [among other countries] Venezuela as new political crises, socially and economically conditioned, confront the civilian authorities there."[14] Venezuela is in a group of countries in which "it is likely that political power will continue to oscillate between the civilians and military men."[15] To many concerned Latin Americans and Latin Americanists, however, the

14. Edwin Lieuwen, *Survey of the Alliance for Progress: The Latin American Military*, 15.

15. Lieuwen, *Survey*, 15. Frank Bonilla also believes it is "premature" to claim the definitive establishment of a "stable and nonpolitical role" for the armed forces (*The Failure of Elites*, 286).

civil-versus-military question has become secondary to the central problem of how to provide for the minimal material needs of rapidly expanding populations in an era when the gap between rich and poor is widening and when cries for profound structural revolution are becoming ever more strident. Venezuela has by no means come close to solving this problem. The responsibility to provide the creative and self-sacrificing leadership needed to move forward simultaneously on all fronts rests with both civilian and military authorities. They must share in the fight for rapid economic development, more equitable distribution of the country's wealth, and the erection of a political system that is sensitive to grass-root needs while preserving basic Western liberties. Failure to meet this challenge will almost certainly lead to some form of authoritarianism, left or right, military or civilian.

DOCUMENTS RELATING TO THE MOVEMENT OF OCTOBER 18, 1945

1. *The Charter of the Patriotic Military Union*[1]

We the undersigned, Officers of the Army, imbued with the need in which the country stands of renovating its institutions and governmental methods by introducing into them norms and men that, with a sense of true patriotism and political honesty, should effect national progress, and lead the Nation into taking the advance post to which it is entitled because of its glorious past; convinced that the time has come to end forever the incompetence, graft, and bad faith that characterize the actions of our governments, and convinced of the sense of historical responsibility that the times demand of the youth of the world; making profession of democratic faith and declaring emphatically that we do not defend personal or class interests and that we support the formation of a government based on the universal and direct suffrage of the Venezuelan citizenry, a reform of the Constitution which would also be the expression of the general will, and the creation of a truly professional army; free of all elements that, through senescence or incompetence, are a cause of developmental lag, and endowed with the material and other moral, technical, and economic means necessary to its development; declaring that we are at last ready to further all such political and economic measures as will contribute to our country's progress, we pledge ourselves, under oath, by our personal honor and the honor of Venezuela, to work for the aims expressed above, establishing a secret organization, submitting with discipline to the principles of the organization, maintaining the most rigorous secrecy, and contributing without faltering to the success of the sacred mission this commitment lays upon us.

2. *Model Oath for Initiates into the Patriotic Military Union*[2]

I, ———, an Officer in the Venezuelan Army, conscious of my duty toward my country and toward the military institution of which I am a part, attendant to the dictates of my conscience, and of my own free will, swear under oath to work loyally and disinterestedly for the moral welfare and dignity of the Nation by becoming a member of the Patriotic Military Union. My life and the welfare

1. My translation of materials reproduced in Ana Mercedes Pérez, *La verdad inédita: historia de la revolución de octubre,* 94.
2. Translated from Pérez, *La verdad,* 95.

of my family are the pledge of my loyalty to the movement. I swear, furthermore, to obey with discipline the orders and watchwords emanating from the Executive Committee. By my most worthy fatherland: [Signed].

Witnesses: [Signed].

3. Charter of the Revolutionary Junta of Government, October 19, 1945[3]

On this day, October 19, 1945, at 8:00 P.M., the following citizens met in the Presidential Office of the Miraflores Palace in Caracas: Major Julio César Vargas, Major Carlos Delgado Chalbaud, Major Celestino Velazco, Captain Mario R. Vargas, Lieutenant Horacio López Conde, Ensign Luis J. Ramírez, Rómulo Betancourt, Doctor Raúl Leoni, Doctor Gonzalo Barrios, Doctor Luis B. Prieto F., Doctor Leonardo Ruiz Pineda, Luis Troconis-Guerrero, Doctor Eligio Anzola Anzola, and Doctor Edmundo Fernández; the abovementioned military and naval officers represented the Military Committee which executed the revolution; the seven mentioned next represented the Acción Democrática Party, which cooperated in the revolution; and the last mentioned [attended] as prime collaborator in the movement and as an agent of liaison between the People's Army and the People's Party; the purpose of the meeting was to form the Revolutionary Junta of Government of the United States of Venezuela.

After examining the political situation created in the Republic as a consequence of the revolution, and hearing the reports submitted by Major Julio César Vargas in the name of the Military Committee, and by Rómulo Betancourt in the name of Acción Democrática, it was resolved:

1. To form a Revolutionary Junta of Government of seven members in whom the executive power of the Nation shall be vested.

2. That the aforementioned Junta exercise the executive power for as long as it shall be necessary before calling a general election and an election for President of the Republic by universal, direct, and secret suffrage; to carry out these elections; and to take steps to reform the National Constitution in accordance with the will of the people.

3. That the Revolutionary Junta of Government be formed by the following citizens; Rómulo Betancourt, President; Doctor Luis B. Prieto F.; Major Carlos Delgado Chalbaud; Doctor Raúl Leoni; Doctor Gonzlao Barrios; Captain Mario R. Vargas; and Doctor Edmundo Fernández.

3. Translated from Pérez, La verdad, 267–68.

Therefore, at the present meeting, the Revolutionary Junta of Government of the United States of Venezuela is declared to be constituted, and it shall take office immediately as the executive power of the Republic.

And its members unanimously resolve to maintain the administrative continuity in the country on the model to be carried into effect following a new Council meeting.

In witness whereof we subscribe our names:

[Names omitted.]

DOCUMENTS RELATING TO THE MILITARY MOVEMENT OF NOVEMBER 24, 1948

1. *First Communiqué of the Venezuelan Armed Forces, November 24, 1948*[1]

The National Armed Forces, confronted with the incapacity of the National Government to resolve the crisis now existing in the country; confronted with interference with the national life by extremist groups, which manifested itself on the morning of this day by the decision to call a general strike of incalculable consequences; and confronted with the incitation of the masses to commit acts of vandalism and disturb public order, have taken charge of the situation in order to guard the security and safety of the whole Nation and to seek the final establishment of social peace in Venezuela.

The National Armed Forces trust that the people of Venezuela, by adopting an attitude of moderation under the full responsibility of their democratic conscience, will back the patriotic and firm resolution of the National Armed Forces.

The next communiqué from the Military Command will inform the Nation clearly of the development of the events that have led to this grave and necessary resolution.

Caracas: November 24, 1948

2. *Constituting Act of the Provisional Government*[2]

In accordance with the fact that the National Armed Forces have taken control of the situation in the Republic, and in accordance with the manifesto broadcast on this day to the people of Venezuela, the undersigned, meeting in the Government Hall of Miraflores Palace, establish with the present Charter a Military Junta of Government, composed of Lieutenant Colonels Carlos Delgado Chalbaud, Marcos Pérez Jiménez and Luis Felipe Llovera Páez, the first of whom shall act as President.

All requisite resolutions, acts, decrees and other provisions shall require an absolute majority of votes. . . . In all constitutional questions, the National Constitution adopted July 20, 1936, as amended May 5, 1945, shall apply. However, provisions of a pro-

1. My translation of materials published by the Government of Venezuela, Oficina Nacional de Información y Publicaciones, *Documentos oficiales relativos al movimiento militar del 24 de noviembre de 1948*, 11.
2. Translated from Venezuela, Oficina Nacional de Información, *Documentos oficiales*, 15–16.

gressive nature in the National Constitution promulgated July 5, 1947, which the National Armed Forces have promised to respect in the above-mentioned manifesto, shall be adhered to, and such measures as may be suggested or decreed by the national interest shall be taken, including measures dealing with the reorganization of the branches of public power. The law and statutes of the Republic shall be operative, except in cases in which they should conflict with the provisions of this Charter and the aims that have brought into being this Provisional Government. . . .

Done, signed and sealed at Miraflores Palace, Caracas, on the twenty-fourth day of November in the year one thousand nine hundred and forty-eight and of Independence the one hundred thirty-ninth, and of Federation the ninetieth.

[Signatures omitted.]

3. *Decree of Dissolution of the Acción Democrática Party*[3]

The Military Junta of Government of the United States of Venezuela:

As empowered by the Charter of the Provisional Government, at a Council of Ministers meeting,

Considering: That the Charter of the Provisional Government accords it, as an exception to the constitutional regime and the laws of the land, the faculty of dictating such measures as are deemed advisable in the national interest;

Considering: That on the premises occupied by the Acción Democrática Party, by educational institutions and public offices, as well as in the private residences of some Party members, arms and military matériel have been found which were intended for the purpose of sabotage and for other destructive purposes, that they have been retained [in the Party's possession] since October, 1945, and have been augmented by means of contraband and the undue use of materials requested by public officials under pretense of equipping Public Defense and Security Forces;

Considering: That said Party has clandestinely incited the people, workers' unions and rural leagues the Party believed to have under its control, to a general strike of a political nature and to other acts detrimental to public order, and has instructed both its membership and foreign elements in the execution of the above-mentioned acts;

Considering: That said Party has attempted to change the essence of the National Armed Forces, trying to make them an instrument of their designs;

Considering: That the Acción Democrática Party has ceased to be a political organization in order to become a faction aspiring to

3. Translated from Venezuela, Oficina Nacional de Información, *Documentos oficiales,* 29–30.

maintain itself in power by force and by means of diverse actions leading to social disintegration;

Considering: That the facts detailed above constitute a falsification of the true and legitimate ends proper to political parties in a democratic regime, and have given Acción Democrática the character of a State within a State, and have transformed the Party into an armed militant faction within the Nation; and that the continued existence of such conditions, besides constituting a permanent threat to the public peace, would render it impossible to restore political equilibrium in the national community as well as impede the free and equitable interplay of democratic institutions;

Considering: That it is the ineluctable duty of the Provisional Government, in accordance with one of the fundamental political aims which originated the Provisional Government, to promote the re-establishment of institutional normalcy in the country and to eliminate irregularities born of political opportunism, of the falsification of the legitimate function of political parties within a democratic regime, and of the undue use of partisanship in government functions:

Decrees:

Article 1. The Acción Democrática Party is hereby dissolved throughout the Republic, its premises closed, and its organs and means of publicity and propaganda suppressed.

Article 2. The Minister of Interior Relations and the heads of the governments in the several States and Federal Territories shall have custody of the property of the dissolved Party and of its publicity and propaganda organs.

Article 3. The Minister of Interior Relations shall be in charge of the execution of the present decree.

Done, signed, sealed and countersigned at Miraflores Palace, on the seventh day of December in the year one thousand nine hundred and forty-eight, and one hundred thirty-ninth of Independence, of Federation the ninetieth.

[Signatures omitted.]

DOCUMENTS RELATING TO THE FALL OF GENERAL MARCOS PÉREZ JIMÉNEZ

1. *Excerpt from the Pastoral Letter of Monsignor Rafael Arias Blanco, Archbishop of Caracas, May 1, 1957*[1]

Social Reality in Venezuela

Our country is rapidly increasing its riches. According to an economic study made by the United Nations, per capita production in Venezuela has reached the index of $540 (five hundred and forty dollars), which ranks Venezuela first among her sister nations and places her above such nations as Germany, Holland, Australia, and Italy. However, no one would dare assert that this wealth is distributed so as to reach all Venezuelans, since the immense majority of our people are living under subhuman conditions. Unemployment plunges many Venezuelans into discouragement, in some cases impelling them to desperation; the major part of our workers must be content with extremely low salaries, while capital invested in industry, which those same workers help increase, sometimes multiplies with unprecedented rapidity; there is still great need, in spite of the commendable efforts of both government and private enterprise, for schools, especially for vocational schools, to ensure that working-class children will have the opportunity to acquire the education and skills to which they have absolute right so that they may lead a more human life than that which their parents have had to endure; there is a need for loan financing for the benefit of working families, so that the working-class family may achieve a better standard of living; there are some inevitable deficiencies in the operation of institutes and special organizations created for the betterment and security of the worker and his family; the Labor Law and other legal instruments for the defense of the laboring class are frequently flouted; women often have to work under unfair conditions; these are the unhappy facts that prevent the mass of the Venezuelan population from sharing in the prosperity of our country in accordance with the will of God. As His Eminence Cardinal Caggiano, Papal Legate to the Second Bolivarian Eucharistic Congress, said at the special session held in his honor by the Federal District Municipal Council: "the wealth of Venezuela is such that all of its people could share in it, free from want and poverty, because destitution need not be where sufficient wealth exists."

1. My translation of extracts of the Archbishop's pastoral letter, from José Umaña Bernal, *Testimonio de la revolución en Venezuela,* 87–88.

2. The Third Manifesto of the Patriotic Junta, January, 1958[2]

The constant outrages committed by the Pérez Jiménez clique against the Constitution, citizens' rights, and national dignity have created a situation of violence in the country. Responsible for this situation are those who, fearing the loss of economic and political privilege, wish to remain indefinitely in power, shamelessly usurping the most elementary principle of popular sovereignty, and trampling upon the hallowed provisions of our Constitution.

The Patriotic Junta, an organization which has disclaimed partisanship from the very moment of its inception, has called for a peaceful solution to the succession question, as is proper among civilized peoples. Later, in open letters addressed to the National Congress and to the Armed Forces, the Junta confirmed its position, petitioning the former for passage of an all-inclusive electoral bill that would permit the free discussion of political ideas—this being the palpable desire of the majority of the people; the Junta wrote to the Armed Forces that the Constitution of the Republic had been violated and trampled upon by the triumvirate formed by Pérez Jiménez, Vallenilla Lanz, and Pedro Estrada, upon their recommendation of a plebiscite, which skirted Articles 103 and 104 of the Constitution. The Junta also called upon the Armed Forces to put an end to the outrages committed by the governing triumvirate, asking that institutional and democratic life be restored in the nation by the Armed Forces.

However, in spite of civic resistance and the repudiation of the electoral farce proposed by the regime, the plebiscite took place under abnormal political conditions, since the jails were filled with political prisoners, the press was gagged, and Venezuelan exiles filled foreign lands, and public employees were being blackmailed; but these conditions did not deter the people from expressing once more its admirable will to oppose the regime. This farce of a plebiscite had been organized and executed with the sole participation of the ruling clique and the complicity of unscrupulous individuals; the results of the plebiscite were falsified, because those few citizens who did vote, voted against the methods employed by the dictatorship.

But, on January 1, the Armed Forces, through the National Junta of Liberation, responded to the popular outcry for the defense of the Constitution which had been outraged and derided. As the National Junta of Liberation itself expressed in the bulletins which were transmitted over Radio Maracay and other stations, the situation created by Pérez Jiménez, Vallenilla Lanz and Pedro Estrada is now

2. Translated from Umaña Bernal, *Testimonio,* 138–39 (portions omitted).

intolerable for both the people and the Army. Thus, the Liberation Movement has won the good will and support of Venezuelan citizens who have decided to unite in their efforts until they see annihilated the government of the Seguridad Nacional. All Venezuelan citizens, civilians and military alike, are now more than ever united against the usurpation of public power, persecution, torture, murder, and embezzlement of public funds committed by those who wish only to maintain their privileged position and who ignore the country's sufferings.

The Patriotic Junta believes that the National Liberation Movement, seemingly defeated by the tyranny, has revealed to the country the strongest rift within the Army since 1945. The most distinguished elements in the Army have rebelled against the continuous violations of the Nation's Constitution, laws, and statutes. Officers who, like General Hugo Fuentes and Colonel J. M. Castro León, have had long military careers, and numerous other members of the Armed Forces, have been jailed and persecuted by the governing triumvirate. All of this brought about the disappearance from the Venezuelan scene of the so-called government by the Armed Forces, and placed it in the hands of Pedro Estrada, Vallenilla and Pérez Jiménez, whose seat of government was at Plaza Morelos [headquarters of the Seguridad Nacional]. The Army is profoundly divided, and only a small group obeys the orders of the Seguridad Nacional and the Ministry of Interior Relations. Therefore, the staggering, weak government of Pérez Jiménez is facing its most difficult dilemma since its inception. At one of the crossroads stand the people, noble and courageous; at the other stand the young officers, honest and uncontaminated, who on the first of January began to indicate their repudiation of the methods of the government in power.

The balance of the situation, therefore, is favorable from all points of view, and it is to be hoped that it will not be long before the total annihilation of the dictatorship is achieved through the concerted efforts of all Venezuelans, and room is made for a government that will restore to the people the free exercise of its sovereignty, and respect for the Constitution and for law.

In consideration of the above, the Patriotic Junta calls upon all sections of the citizenry—upon civilians, the military, students, priests, industrialists, businessmen, workers, and journalists to remain united and work together until final victory is achieved.

GLOSSARY

abrazo: embrace

ACB: Agrupaciones Cívicas Bolivarianas (Bolivarian Civic Groups)

AD: Acción Democrática (Democratic Action)

Adeco: a member of the AD party

adequización: politicalization of the military in favor of AD

Agrupaciones Pro-Candidatura Presidencial de López Contreras: Groups for the Presidential Candidacy of López Contreras

Andinismo: Andeanism; efforts to advance the political interests of the Andean states

Andino: Andean; a native of the Andean region

Aprismo: a Peruvian political movement founded by Víctor Raúl Haya de la Torre

bachillerato: the rough equivalent of a secondary school diploma in the United States

BND: Bloque Nacional Democrático (National Democratic Bloc)

Bolívar (pl. *bolívares*): the Venezuelan unit of currency; traditional free rate: one bolívar = U.S. $0.30

burocracia armada: armed bureaucracy

campesino: countryman; peasant; any lower-class rural inhabitant

Caraqueño: a native or resident of Caracas

Castrista: a supporter of Gen. Cipriano Castro

caudillo: chief; commander; leader

CCN: Cruzada Cívica Nacionalista (Nationalist Civic Crusade)

cesarismo democrático: democratic caesarism; Latin American-style benevolent despotism

civilismo: attitude of respect toward civilian government

civilista: partisan of civilian government

CNT: Confederación Nacional de Trabajadores (National Workers' Confederation)

continuismo andino: Andean continuism

continuismo militar: military continuism

COPEI: Comité de Organización Política Electoral Independiente (Committee for Independent Political and Electoral Organization)

Copeyano: a member of COPEI

CTV: Confederación de Trabajadores de Venezuela (Workers' Confederation of Venezuela)

cuartelazo: barracks uprising

dictadura militar: military dictatorship

Estado Mayor Conjunto: Joint Staff

Estado Mayor General: General Staff

FEI: Frente Electoral Independiente (Independent Electoral Front)

FEV: Federación de Estudiantes de Venezuela (Venezuelan Student Federation)

golpe de estado (golpe): coup d'état

golpista: participant in or advocate of a *coup d'état*

Gomecismo: the political system associated with Gen. Juan Vicente Gómez

Gomecista: a supporter of Gen. Juan Vicente Gómez

gorilas: gorillas; officers who advocate military control of government

Gran Consejo Militar: Grand Military Council

guerrillero: guerrilla fighter; warrior

hacendado: large landholder

hacienda: large estate

hegemonía andina: Andean hegemony

Jefe: chief; military commander

junta: provisional council of government

Junta de Gobierno: Junta of Government

Junta Militar: Military Junta

Junta Patriótica: Patriotic Junta

juventud militar: military youth

Libro Rojo: Red Book

llanero: a native of the Llanos

Llanos: the extensive flatland area drained by the Orinoco River, comprising all or portions of the states of Apure, Barinas, Portuguesa, Cojedes, Guárico, Anzoátegui, and Monagas

logia militar: military lodge

Lopecismo: the political system associated with General Eleazar López Contreras

Lopecista: a supporter of General Eleazar López Contreras

mantuanos: the creole oligarchy

Medinismo: the political system associated with General Isaías Medina Angarita

Medinista: a supporter of General Isaías Medina Angarita

Movimiento Pro-Adhesión: Movement for Adherence

Número Uno: Number One

Oriente: the eastern region of Venezuela

ORVE: Organización Venezolana (Venezuelan Organization)

Paecista: a supporter of Gen. José Antonio Páez

Palacio Blanco: White Palace, the Executive Office Building

PCV: Partido Comunista de Venezuela (Communist Party of Venezuela)

PDN: Partido Democrático Nacional (National Democratic Party)

PDV: Partido Democrático Venezolano (Venezuelan Democratic Party)

PRP: Partido Republicano Progresista (Progressive Republican Party)

Pedevista: a member of the PDV

Perezjimenista: a supporter of Gen. Marcos Pérez Jiménez

Peronismo: the political system associated with Argentine Gen. Juan Domingo Perón

políticos: politicians

pronunciamiento: revolutionary pronouncement

ranchos: the name given to the hillside slums ringing Caracas and other Venezuelan cities; also the individual housing units

SN: Seguridad Nacional (National Security Police)

tachirense: a native of Táchira State

técnico: technical expert; engineer

trienio: triennium; the three-year period of AD rule, 1945–1948

UNR: Unión Nacional Republicana (Republican National Union)

UPM: Unión Patriótica Militar (Patriotic Military Union)

URD: Unión Republicana Democrática (Democratic Republican Union)

Urredista: a member of URD

BIBLIOGRAPHY

I. UNPUBLISHED MATERIALS

Requena, Antonio. Speech in Recognition of the Dissolution of the Patriotic Junta, January 23, 1959. Mimeographed copy in possession of author.

U.S., Department of State, Political and Military Records Relating to Internal Affairs of Venezuela, Decimal Files, 1910–1945. National Archives and Department of State, Washington, D.C.

———, United States Embassy, Caracas, Venezuela. Confidential Political Report, August, 1957. Report read to author.

II. GOVERNMENT PUBLICATIONS

Betancourt, Rómulo. *Tres años de gobierno democrático: 1959–1962.* Caracas, Imprenta Nacional, 1962. 3 vols.

United States, Department of State. *Foreign Relations of the United States: Diplomatic Papers, 1945. IX. The American Republics.* Washington, D.C., U.S. Government Printing Office, 1969.

Venezuela, Consejo de Bienestar Rural. *Problemas económicos y sociales de los Andes venezolanos.* Caracas, 1955–1956 (?). 2 vols.

———, Ministerio de la Defensa Nacional. *Memorias y cuentas del Ministerio de la Defensa Nacional.* Caracas, 1946–1959.

———, Ministerio de Guerra y Marina. *Memorias del Ministerio de Guerra y Marina.* Caracas, 1920–1945.

———, Ministerio de Relaciones Exteriores. *La visita al Perú del Presidente de Venezuela.* Caracas, Ministerio de Relaciones Exteriores, 1955.

———, Ministerio de Relaciones Interiores. *Sentencias del Jurado de Responsabilidad Civil y Administrativa.* Caracas, Imprenta Nacional, 1946. 3 vols.

———, Oficina Nacional de Información y Publicaciones. *Discursos y documentos oficiales con motivo del fallecimiento del Coronel Carlos Delgado Chalbaud.* Caracas, Oficina Nacional de Información y Publicaciones, 1950.

———. *Documentos oficiales relativos al movimiento militar del 24 de noviembre de 1948.* Caracas, Oficina Nacional de Información y Publicaciones, 1949.

———. *Síntesis de las actividades administrativas de los gobiernos regionales: 1950–1951.* Caracas, Oficina Nacional de Información y Publicaciones, 1951.

———. *Síntesis de las labores realizadas por la Junta de Gobierno de los Estados Unidos de Venezuela durante un año de gestión administrativa: 24 de noviembre de 1950–24 de noviembre de 1951.* Caracas, Oficina Nacional de Información y Publicaciones, 1951 or 1952.

————, Presidencia de la República. *150 años de vida republicana: 1811–1961.* Caracas, Ediciones de la Presidencia de la República, 1963. 2 vols.

————. *Documentos que hicieron historia: siglo y medio de vida republicana, 1810–1961.* Caracas, Presidencia de la República, 1962. 2 vols.

————. *Las Fuerzas Armadas de Venezuela en el siglo XIX: textos para su estudio.* Caracas, Presidencia de la República, 1963–1971. 12 vols.

————, Publicaciones de la Secretaría General de la Presidencia de la República. *Victoria democrática en Venezuela: editoriales de la prensa mundial.* Caracas, Presidencia de la República, 1964.

————, Publicaciones del Gobierno Revolucionario de Venezuela. *La revolución venezolana ante la opinión de América.* Caracas, Imprenta Nacional, 1946.

Venezuela, República de. *Cinco discursos del General Marcos Perez Jiménez, Presidente de la República, pronunciados durante el año 1955 y obras realizadas por el gobierno en 1955.* Caracas, Imprenta Nacional, 1955.

————. *Constitución de la República de Venezuela y disposiciones transitorias: 1961.* Caracas, Distribuidora Escobar, n.d.

————. *Obras dadas al servicio durante el primer año de gobierno del Coronel Marcos Pérez Jiménez.* Caracas, Imprenta Nacional, 1953.

————. *Obras dadas al servicio durante el segundo año de gobierno del Coronel Marcos Pérez Jiménez.* Caracas, Imprenta Nacional, 1954.

————. *Venezuela bajo el nuevo ideal nacional: realizaciones durante el segundo año de gobierno del General Marcos Pérez Jiménez.* Caracas, Imprenta Nacional, 1955.

————. *Venezuela bajo el nuevo ideal nacional: realizaciones durante el tercer año de gobierno del General Marcos Pérez Jiménez.* Caracas, Imprenta Nacional, 1956.

III. BOOKS AND PAMPHLETS

Abreu, José Vicente. *Se llamaba S.N.* 2d ed. Caracas, José Agustín Catalá, Editor, 1964.

Acción Democrática, Comité Ejecutivo Nacional. *Acción Democrática ante la farsa electoral.* Caracas, n.p., 1952.

————. *Acción Democrática: doctrina y programa.* Caracas,

Publicación de la Secretaria Nacional de Propaganda, 1962.
_____. *Venezuela bajo el signo del terror: 1948-1952.* 2d ed. Santiago de Chile, Publicaciones Valmore Rodríguez, 1956.
Aguilar, Arturo. *Tierra sin justicia: historia y política contemporáneas.* Caracas, Tipografía Vargas, S.A., 1958.
Aguirre Rojas, Alberto. *La Guardia Nacional de Venezuela.* Caracas, Tipografía La Nación, 1952.
Alba, Víctor. *El militarismo.* Mexico City, Universidad Nacional Autónoma de México, 1960.
Alcubilla, Antonio, and others. *La milicia como tema de nuestro tiempo.* Madrid, Ediciones Cultura Hispánica, 1955.
Alexander, Robert J. *The Communist Party of Venezuela.* Stanford, Calif., Hoover Institution Press, 1969.
_____. *The Venezuelan Democratic Revolution: A Profile of the Regime of Rómulo Betancourt.* New Brunswick, N.J., Rutgers University Press, 1964.
_____. *Prophets of the Revolution: Profiles of Latin American Leaders.* New York, The Macmillan Company, 1962.
Almond, Gabriel, and James S. Coleman. *The Politics of Developing Areas.* Princeton, N.J., Princeton University Press, 1960.
Andrade, Ignacio. *¿Por qué triunfó la Revolución Restauradora?* Caracas, Ediciones Garrido, 1955.
Arcaya, Pedro Manuel. *The Gómez Regime in Venezuela and Its Background.* Washington, D.C., The Sun Printing Co., 1936.
Arellano Moreno, Antonio. *Guía de historia de Venezuela: 1492-1945.* Caracas and Madrid, Ediciones Edime, 1955.
_____. *Mirador de historia política de Venezuela.* Caracas, Imprenta Nacional, 1967.
Así se fraguó la insurrección: documentos clandestinos, 1956-1958. Caracas, Ediciones de la Revista Cruz del Sur, 1958.
Baralt, Rafael María. *Resumen de la historia de Venezuela.* Maracaibo, Edición Universidad de Zulia, 1960.
Barrios, Gonzalo. *Los días y la política.* Caracas, Editorial Arte, 1963.
Bernstein, Harry. *Venezuela and Colombia.* Englewood Cliffs, N.J., Prentice-Hall, Inc., 1964.
Betancourt, Rómulo. *Pensamiento y Acción.* Mexico City, Impresor Beatriz de Silva, 1951.
_____. *Posición y doctrina.* Caracas, Editorial Cordillera, 1959.
_____. *Trayectoria democrática de una revolución.* Caracas, Imprenta Nacional, 1948.
_____. *Venezuela: política y petróleo.* 2d ed. Caracas, Editorial Senderos, 1967.
_____. *Venezuela rinde cuentas.* San José, Costa Rica, Combate, 1962.
Betancourt Sosa, Francisco. *Pueblo en rebeldía: relato histórico de*

la sublevación militar del 7 de abril de 1928. Caracas, Ediciones Garrido, 1959.

Blanco Peñalver, Pedro Luis. *López Contreras ante la historia.* Caracas, C. A. Tipografía Garrido, 1957.

Bonilla, Frank. *The Failure of Elites.* Vol. II, *The Politics of Change in Venezuela.* Cambridge, Mass., The M.I.T. Press, 1970.

————, and J. A. Silva Michelena, eds. *A Strategy for Research on Social Policy.* Cambridge, Mass., The M.I.T. Press, 1967.

Bonsal, Stephen. *The American Mediterranean.* New York, Moffat, Yard & Co., 1912.

Brandt, Carlos. *Bajo la tiranía de Cipriano Castro.* Caracas, Tipografía Vargas, S.A., 1952.

Briceño, Olga. *Cocks and Bulls in Caracas.* Boston, Houghton Mifflin Company, 1945.

Briceño, Santiago. *Cartas sobre el Táchira.* Caracas, Biblioteca de Autores y Temas Tachirenses, n.d.

Briceño Perozo, Mario. *Los infidentes del Táchira: contribución a la independencia.* Caracas, Biblioteca de Autores y Temas Tachirenses, 1961.

Bunimov-Parra, Boris. *Introducción a la sociología electoral venezolana.* Caracas, Editorial Arte, 1968.

Bureau of the American Republics. *Venezuela.* Washington, D.C., U.S. Government Printing Office, 1892.

El candidato venezolano. N.p., n.d. [On the 1941 election.]

Cárdenas, Horacio. *Bibliografía tachirense.* Caracas, Biblioteca de Autores y Temas Tachirenses, 1964.

Cárdenas, Rodolfo José. *El combate político.* 2d ed. Caracas, Editorial Doña Barbara, 1966.

————. *La insurrección popular en Venezuela.* Caracas, Ediciones Catatumbo, 1961.

Cardozo, Arturo. *Proceso de historia de los Andes.* Caracas, Biblioteca de Autores y Temas Tachirenses, 1965.

Cardozo, Evaristo. *Pérez Jiménez ante la historia.* Caracas, n.p., 1968.

Carrera Damas, Germán. *Historia de la historiografía venezolana: textos para su estudio.* Caracas, Universidad Central de Venezuela, 1961.

Carrizales, Luisa Amelia, and others. *Defensa del General Jesús María Castro León.* Maracay, Tipografía Violeta, 1963.

Claudio, Iván. *Breve historia de URD.* Caracas, n.p., 1968.

Clements (John A.) Associates. *Report on Venezuela.* New York, John A. Clements Associates, 1958 or 1959.

Colmenares Díaz, Luis. *La espada y el incesario: la iglesia bajo Pérez Jiménez.* Caracas, n.p., 1961.

Corredor, Rubén. *Las fuerzas armadas insurgen, deliberan y sirven en Iberoamérica.* Madrid, n.p., 1963.

Cova García, Luis. *Fundamento jurídico del nuevo ideal nacional.* Caracas, Jaime Villegas Editor, 1955.

Daalder, H., and others. *Política militar.* Buenos Aires, Jorge Alvarez Editor, 1963.

Dávila, Vicente. *Destrucción de Pregonero.* Caracas, Tipografía Americana, 1936.

Díaz Sánchez, Ramón. *Evolución de la historiografía en Venezuela.* Caracas, n.p., 1956.

_____. *Guzmán: elipse de una ambición de poder.* 3d ed. Caracas, Ediciones "Hortus," 1953.

_____. *Transición: política y realidad en Venezuela.* Caracas, Ediciones La Torre, 1937.

Diez, Julio. *Historia y política.* 2d ed. Caracas, Pensamiento Vivo, C.A., 1963.

_____. *Lo que yo vi.* Caracas, n.p., 1965.

Egaña, Manuel R. *Tres décadas de producción petrolera.* Caracas, Tipografía Americana, 1947.

Fernández, Pablo Emilio. *Gómez el Rehabilitador.* Caracas, Jaime Villegas Editor, 1956.

Figueroa S., Marco. *Por los archivos del Táchira.* Caracas, Biblioteca de Autores y Temas Tachirenses, 1961.

_____. *El Táchira de ayer y de hoy.* Caracas, Impresores Unidos, 1941.

Finer, Samuel Edward. *The Man on Horseback: The Role of the Military in Politics.* New York, Frederick A. Praeger, Publishers, 1962.

Fitzgerald, Gerald E. *The Constitutions of Latin America.* Chicago, Henry Regnery Company, 1968.

Fitzgibbon, Russell H. *The Constitutions of the Americas.* Chicago, University of Chicago Press, 1948.

Ford, Guy S., ed. *Dictatorship in the Modern World.* Minneapolis, University of Minnesota Press, 1939.

Foreign Area Studies Division, Special Operations Research Office, The American University. *U.S. Army Area Handbook for Venezuela.* Washington, D.C., U.S. Government Printing Office, 1964.

Gabaldón Márquez, Joaquín. *Archivos de una inquietud venezolana.* Caracas, Ediciones Edime, 1955.

Gallegos, Gerardo. *En el puño de Juan Vicente Gómez.* 2d ed. Mexico City, Editorial Diana, S.A., 1956.

Gallegos Ortiz, Rafael. *La historia política de Venezuela: de Cipriano Castro a Pérez Jiménez.* Caracas, Imprenta Universitaria, 1960.

García Gil, Pedro. *Cuarenta y cinco años de uniforme: memorias— 1901 a 1945.* Caracas, n.p., 1947 (?).

García Naranjo, Nemesio. *Venezuela and Its Ruler.* New York, Carranza & Co., 1927.

García Villasmil, Martín. *Escuelas para formación de oficiales del ejército: origen y evolución de la Escuela Militar.* Caracas, Ministerio de la Defensa, 1964.

————. *¿Qué es la Escuela Militar?* Caracas, Escuela Militar, 1963.

Gerbasi, José. *¿Qué publicó la prensa venezolana durante la dictadura?* Caracas, Imprenta Universitaria, 1959.

Gil Fortoul, José. *Historia constitucional de Venezuela.* 4th ed. Caracas, Ministerio de Educación, 1954. 3 vols.

Gilmore, Robert L. *Caudillism and Militarism in Venezuela: 1810–1910.* Athens, Ohio University Press, 1964.

Gómez, Juan Vicente. *El General J. V. Gómez: Documentos para la historia de su gobierno.* Caracas, Litografía del Comercio, 1925.

González Valbuena, Ricardo. *El Táchira histórico: apuntaciones.* Caracas, Tipografía La Nación, 1943.

Guerrero, Emilio Constantino. *El Táchira físico, político e ilustrado.* Caracas, Editorial "Cecilio Acosta," 1943.

Hahner, June E. *Civilian-Military Relations in Brazil: 1889–1898.* Columbia, University of South Carolina Press, 1969.

Hamill, Hugh M., Jr. *Dictatorship in Spanish America.* New York, Alfred A. Knopf, Inc., 1966.

Howard, Michael, ed. *Soldiers and Governments: Nine Studies in Civil-Military Relations.* London, Eyre & Spottiswoode, 1957.

Huntington, Samuel P., ed. *Changing Patterns of Military Politics.* New York, The Free Press of Glencoe, Inc., 1962.

————. *The Soldier and the State: The Theory and Politics of Civil-Military Relations.* Cambridge, Mass., Belknap Press of Harvard University Press, 1959.

Imaz, José Luis de. *Los que mandan.* Buenos Aires, Editorial Universitaria de Buenos Aires, 1964.

Institute for the Comparative Study of Political Systems. *Venezuela Election Factbook: Election, December 1963.* Washington, D.C., Institute for the Comparative Study of Political Systems, 1963.

Inter-American Statistical Yearbook. New York, 1940 and 1942.

Jankus, Alfred P., and Neil M. Malloy. *Venezuela: Land of Opportunity.* New York, Pageant Press, 1956.

Janowitz, Morris. *The Military in the Development of New Nations: An Essay in Comparative Analysis.* Chicago, University of Chicago Press, 1964.

————. *The Professional Soldier: A Social and Political Portrait.* Glencoe, Ill., The Free Press, 1960.

————. *Sociology and the Military Establishment.* New York, Russell Sage Foundation, 1959.

Johnson, John J. *The Military and Society in Latin America.* Stanford, Calif., Stanford University Press, 1964.

————, ed. *The Role of the Military in Underdeveloped Countries.*

Princeton, N.J., Princeton University Press, 1962.

Lambert, Jacques. *Latin America: Social Structures and Political Institutions.* Berkeley, University of California Press, 1969.

Landaeta, Federico. *Cuando reinaron las sombras.* Madrid, n.p., 1955.

_____. *Mi general: breve biografía del General Marcos Pérez Jiménez.* La Coruña, Spain, n.p., 1957.

_____. *Nueve lustros y cuatro generales: 1899–1944.* Caracas, Impresores Unidos, 1944.

La Riva, Edecio. *Los fusiles de la paz.* Caracas, n.p., 1968.

Lavin, John. *A Halo for Gómez.* New York, Pageant Press, 1954.

Lieuwen, Edwin. *Petroleum in Venezuela: A History.* Berkeley, University of California Press, 1954.

_____. *Venezuela.* New York, Oxford University Press, Inc., 1961.

_____. *Arms and Politics in Latin America.* Rev. ed. New York, Frederick A. Praeger, Publisher, 1961.

_____. *Generals vs. Presidents: Neomilitarism in Latin America.* New York, Frederick A. Praeger, Publishers, 1964.

_____. *Mexican Militarism: The Political Rise and Fall of the Revolutionary Army, 1910–1940.* Albuquerque, University of New Mexico Press, 1968.

_____. *Survey of the Alliance for Progress: The Latin American Military.* (A Study Prepared at the Request of the Subcommittee on American Republics Affairs of the Committee on Foreign Relations, U.S. Senate.) Washington, D.C., U.S. Government Printing Office, 1967.

_____. *The United States and the Challenge to Security in Latin America.* Columbus, Ohio State University Press, 1966.

Lipset, Seymour Martin. *Political Man: The Social Bases of Politics.* Garden City, N.Y., Doubleday & Company, Inc., 1963.

_____, and Aldo Solari. *Elites in Latin America.* New York, Oxford University Press, Inc., 1967.

Liscano, Juan. *La violencia en Venezuela.* Caracas, Publicaciones del Círculo de Estudio "Revolución Nacional," 1963.

López Contreras, Eleazar. *Gobierno y administración: 1936–1941.* Caracas, Editorial Arte, 1966.

_____. *Páginas para la historia militar de Venezuela.* Caracas, Tipografía Americana, 1944.

_____. *El pensamiento de Bolívar Libertador.* Caracas, Biblioteca de Autores y Temas Tachirenses, 1963.

_____. *Proceso político-social: 1928–1936.* 2d ed. Caracas, Editorial Ancora, 1955.

_____. *El triunfo de la verdad: documentos para la historia venezolana.* Mexico City, Edición Genio Latino, 1949.

Lugo, Francisco Aniceto. *Pérez Jiménez: fuerza creadora.* 2d ed. Caracas, Editorial Ragón, C.A., 1954.

Luttwak, Edward. *Coup d'Etat: A Practical Handbook.* Greenwich, Conn., Fawcett Publications, Inc., 1969.

Luzardo, Rodolfo. *Notas historico-económicas: 1928-1963.* Caracas, Editorial Sucre, 1963.

———. *Río Grande.* Caracas, Editorial Sucre, 1965.

MacDonald, Austin F. *Latin American Politics and Government.* 2d ed. New York, Crowell, 1954.

Magallanes, Manuel Vicente. *Partidos políticos venezolanos.* Caracas, Tipografía Vargas, S.A., 1959.

Mancera Galletti, Angel. *Civilismo y militarismo.* Caracas, n.p., 1960.

Marsland, William D., and Amy L. Marsland. *Venezuela Through Its History.* New York, Thomas Y. Crowell Company, 1954.

Martz, John D. *Acción Democrática: Evolution of a Modern Political Party in Venezuela.* Princeton, N.J., Princeton University Press, 1966.

———. *The Venezuelan Elections of December 1, 1963: An Analysis.* Washington, D.C., Institute for the Comparative Study of Political Systems, 1964.

Medina Angarita, Isaías. *Cuatro años de democracia.* Caracas, Pensamiento Vivo C. A. Editores, 1963.

Mercier Vega, Luis. *Roads to Power in Latin America.* New York, Frederick A. Praeger, Publishers, 1969.

Mijares, Augusto. *La interpretación pesimista de la sociología hispanoamericana.* 2d ed. Madrid, Afrodisio Aguado, S.A., 1952.

Mister X [Germán Borregales]. *Rómulo Betancourt: estadista y diplomático.* 2d ed. Caracas, Tipografía "El Compas," 1948.

Morón, Guillermo. *A History of Venezuela.* London, George Allen & Unwin, Ltd., 1964.

Mosca, Gaetano. *The Ruling Class.* New York, McGraw-Hill, Inc., 1939.

Naranjo Ostty, Rafael. *Breve exégesis sobre el caso del General (r) Marcos Pérez Jiménez, ex-presidente de la República de Venezuela.* Caracas, n.p., 1964.

———. *La verdad de un juicio trascendental.* Caracas, Ediciones Garrido, 1968.

Needler, Martin C. *Latin American Politics in Perspective.* Princeton, N.J., D. Van Nostrand Company, Inc., 1968.

———. *Political Development in Latin America: Instability, Violence, and Evolutionary Change.* New York, Random House, Inc., 1968.

Newton, Jorge. *Radiografía de Venezuela.* Caracas, Editorial "Atlas," 1957.

North, Liisa. *Civil-Military Relations in Argentina, Chile and Peru.* Berkeley, University of California, Institute of International Studies, 1966.

Nunn, Frederick M. *Chilean Politics, 1920–1931: The Honorable Mission of the Armed Forces.* Albuquerque, University of New Mexico Press, 1970.

O'Connor, Harvey. *World Crisis in Oil.* New York, Monthly Review Press, 1962.

Pacanins A., Guillermo. *Siete años en la gobernación del Distrito Federal.* Caracas, n.p., 1965.

Pacheco, Luis Eduardo. *Orígenes del Presidente Gómez.* Caracas, n.p., 1968.

Páez, José Antonio. *Autobiografía.* New York, H. R. Elliot, 1946.

Paredes, Antonio. *Como llegó Cipriano Castro al poder.* 2d ed. Caracas, Ediciones Garrido, 1954.

Parra, Darío. *Venezuela: "democracia" vs. "dictadura."* Madrid, n.p., 1961.

Penzini Hernández, Juan. *Democracia habemos . . . !* Caracas, Coop. Artes Gráficas, 1939.

Pérez, Ana Mercedes. *Síntesis histórica de un hombre y un pueblo.* Caracas, n.p., 1954.

————. *La verdad inédita: historia de la revolución de octubre.* 2d ed. Buenos Aires, Editorial Colombo, 1953.

Pérez Jiménez, Marcos. *Así progresa un pueblo: diez años en la vida de Venezuela.* Caracas, Imprenta Nacional, 1956.

————. *Frente a la infamia.* 2d ed. Caracas, Ediciones Garrido, 1968.

————. *Pensamiento político del Presidente de Venezuela.* Caracas, Imprenta Nacional, 1954.

Picón-Salas, Mariano. *Los días de Cipriano Castro.* Caracas, Ediciones Garrido, 1953.

————. *1941: cinco discursos sobre pasado y presente de la nación venezolana.* Caracas, Editorial La Torre, 1940.

————, and others. *Venezuela independiente: 1810–1960.* Caracas, Fundación Eugenio Mendoza, 1962.

Pocaterra, José Rafael. *Gómez: The Shame of America.* Paris, A. Delpeuch, 1929.

Potash, Robert A. *The Army and Politics in Argentina: 1928–1945.* Stanford, Calif., Stanford University Press, 1969.

Pulido Méndez, Manuel A. *Régulo Olivares y su época.* Caracas, Biblioteca de Autores y Temas Tachirenses, 1962.

Quevedo, Numa. *El gobierno provisorio: 1958.* Caracas, Pensamiento Vivo C.A.—Libreria Historia, 1963.

Quintero, Rodolfo. *Sindicalismo y cambio social en Venezuela.* Caracas, Universidad Central de Venezuela, 1966.

R. H. [Laureano Vallenilla Lanz, *hijo*]. *Editoriales de "El Heraldo" por R. H.* Caracas, Ediciones de El Heraldo, n.d.

Ramirez Mac-Gregor, Carlos. *Una época: acontecimientos nacionales e internacionales (1949–1953) vistos por un periodista.*

Caracas-Madrid, Ediciones Edime, 1955.

Rangel, Domingo Alberto. *Los andinos en el poder: balance de una hegemonía, 1899–1945.* Caracas, n.p., 1964.

―――. *La revolución de las fantasías.* Caracas, Ediciones Ofidi, 1966.

Rivas Rivas, José, ed. *Historia gráfica de Venezuela.* Caracas, Pensamiento Vivo, 1962–1963. 4 vols.

Rojas, Pedro José. *Betancourt, violador de los derechos humanos.* N.p., 1961.

Rosales, Rafael María. *Bajo el alegre cielo.* Caracas, Biblioteca de Autores y Temas Tachirenses, 1961.

―――. *El Táchira en la emancipación.* Caracas, Biblioteca de Autores y Temas Tachirenses, 1964.

Rosas Marcano, Jesús. *La prensa nacional y las elecciones generales de 1958.* Caracas, Instituto Venezolano de Investigaciones de Prensa, 1961.

Rourke, Thomas. *Gómez: Tyrant of the Andes.* New York, William Morrow & Co., Inc., 1941.

Royal Institute of International Affairs. *Venezuela: A Brief Political and Economic Survey.* New York, Oxford University Press, Inc., 1958.

Ruiz Pineda, Leonardo. *Ventanas al mundo.* Caracas, Biblioteca de Autores y Temas Tachirenses, 1961.

Sánchez Pacheco, Ciro. *Los "Andinos"* [novela]. Caracas, Ediciones Garrido, 1968.

Santana, Arturo. *Manual del soldado.* Caracas, Imprenta Nacional, 1916.

Serxner, Stanley J. *Acción Democrática of Venezuela: Its Origins and Development.* Gainesville, University of Florida Press, 1959.

Silva Michelena, José A. *The Illusion of Democracy in Dependent Nations.* Vol. III, *The Politics of Change in Venezuela.* Cambridge, Mass., The M.I.T. Press, 1971.

Siso, Carlos. *La formación del pueblo venezolano: estudios sociológicos.* Madrid, Editorial García Enciso, 1953. 2 vols.

Siso Martínez, José María. *Historia de Venezuela.* 6th ed. Mexico City, Editorial Yocoima, 1962.

Suárez, Santiago Gerardo. *El régimen de López Contreras.* Caracas, Editorial Arte, 1965.

―――. *Temas militares.* Caracas, n.p., 1970.

Sumario de Occidente: publicación del centro cultural del Estado Táchira, I. Caracas, September, 1945. [Only volume published.]

Swomley, John M., Jr. *The Military Establishment.* Boston, Beacon Press, 1964.

Szulc, Tad. *Twilight of the Tyrants.* New York, Henry Holt and

Company, 1959.

Tamayo Suárez, Oscar. *De frente a la realidad venezolana.* Limoges, n.p., 1963.

Tarnói, Ladislao T. *El nuevo ideal nacional de Venezuela: vida y obra de Marcos Pérez Jiménez.* Madrid, Ediciones Verdad, 1954.

Taylor, Philip B., Jr. *The Venezuelan Golpe de Estado of 1958: The Fall of Marcos Pérez Jiménez.* Washington, D.C., Institute for the Comparative Study of Political Systems, 1968.

Umaña Bernal, José. *Testimonio de la revolución en Venezuela.* Caracas, Tipografía Vargas, S.A., 1958.

Universidad Central de Venezuela, Instituto de Filosofía. *Documentos para la historia colonial de los Andes venezolanos: siglos XVI al XVIII.* Caracas, Universidad Central de Venezuela, 1957.

Urbina, Rafael Simón. *Victoria, dolor y tragedia: relación cronológica y autobiográfica de Rafael Simón Urbina.* N.p., n.d. [c. 1936.]

Uslar Pietri, Arturo. *Materiales para la construcción de Venezuela.* Caracas, Ediciones Orinoco, 1959.

———. *Las vacas gordas y las vacas flacas.* Caracas, Ediciones del Concejo Municipal del Distrito Federal, 1968.

Vagts, Alfred. *A History of Militarism.* Rev. ed. New York, Meridian Books, Inc., 1959.

Vallenilla Lanz, Laureano. *Cesarismo democrático: estudio sobre las bases sociologicas de la constitución efectiva de Venezuela.* Caracas, Edición de "El Cojo," 1919.

Vallenilla Lanz, Laureano, *hijo. Allá en Caracas.* Caracas, Tipografía Garrido, 1948.

———. *Escrito de memoria.* Caracas, Ediciones Garrido, 1967.

———. *Razones de proscrito.* Caracas, Ediciones Garrido, 1967.

Veliz, Claudio. *The Politics of Conformity in Latin America.* New York, Oxford University Press, 1967.

Vila, Marco-Aurelio. *Geografía del Táchira.* Caracas, Corporación Venezolana de Fomento, 1957.

Villafañe, José Gregorio. *Apuntes estadísticos del Táchira.* Caracas, Biblioteca de Autores y Temas Tachirenses, 1960.

Villanueva, Víctor. *El militarismo en el Perú.* Lima, Empresa Gráfica T. Scheuch, 1962.

Wilgus, Alva Curtis, ed. *The Caribbean: Its Political Problems.* Gainesville, University of Florida Press, 1956.

———. *The Caribbean: Venezuelan Development—A Case History.* Gainesville, University of Florida Press, 1963.

Wise, George S. *Caudillo: A Portrait of Antonio Guzmán Blanco.* New York, Columbia University Press, 1951.

Ybarra, Thomas Russell. *Young Man of Caracas.* Garden City, N.Y., Garden City Publishing Co., Inc., 1942.

IV. ARTICLES

Alba, Víctor. "Armas, poder, y libertad." *Combate,* 1, Nos. 1–6 (July–August 1958 to May–June 1959).
————. "El ascenso del militarismo tecnocrático." *Panoramas,* 6 (November–December 1965), 5–39.
Arciniegas, Germán. "Venezuela's Novelist-President." *United Nations World,* 2 (April 1948), 60–61.
Arnade, Kurt C. "The Technique of the Coup d'Etat in Latin America." *United Nations World,* 4 (February 1950), 21–25.
Barrenechea, Mauro. "Militarismo y sindicalismo: un caso aleccionador." *SIC, Revista Venezolana de Orientación,* No. 32 (February 1969), 68–71.
Betancourt, Rómulo. "¿Adonde va Venezuela?" *Cuadernos Americanos,* 90 (November–December 1956), 7–37.
————. "El caso de Venezuela y el destino de la democracia en América." *Cuadernos Americanos,* 8 (July–August 1949), 27–66.
Burggraaff, Winfield J. "Las Fuerzas Armadas de Venezuela en transición: el período de López Contreras." *Boletín Histórico,* 17 (May 1968), 184–201.
————. "The Military Origins of Venezuela's 1945 Revolution." *Caribbean Studies,* 11 (October 1971), 35–54.
————. "Venezuelan Regionalism and the Rise of Táchira." *The Americas,* 25 (October 1968), 160–73.
Castro León, Jesús María. "Memorias de Castro León." *Elite* (August 7, 1965), 34.
Chapman, Charles E. "The Age of the Caudillos: A Chapter in Hispanic American History." *Hispanic American Historical Review,* 12 (August 1932), 281–300.
Cusack, Thomasine. "A Reappraisal of the Economic Record of Venezuela, 1939–1959." *Journal of Inter-American Studies,* 3 (October 1961), 477–96.
Dealy, Glen. "Prolegomena on the Spanish American Political Tradition." *Hispanic American Historical Review,* 48 (February 1968), 37–58.
Díaz Ugueto, M. "Deliberancia e institución." *Fuerzas Armadas de Venezuela,* Nos. 184–186 (October–December 1961), 2–7.
"Euforia en Miraflores." *Elite* (February 1, 1958), 36.
Fitzgibbon, Russell H. "What Price Latin American Armies?" *Virginia Quarterly Review,* 36 (Autumn 1960), 517–32.

Freeman, Felton D. "The Army As a Social Structure." *Social Forces*, 27 (October 1948), 78–83.

Gámez, Luis Eloy. "El golpe de 24 de noviembre." *Elite* (November 23, 1968), 22–27.

García Villasmil, Martín. "Usos legítimos del poder: los militares como fuerza positiva en el desarrollo democrático." *Siempre Firmes*, Nos. 98–99 (July–October 1964), 13–29.

Garrido, Luis T. "Cinco fechas inolvidables de año." *Venezuela Gráfica* (January 2, 1959), 6.

Goldwert, Marvin. "The Rise of Modern Militarism in Argentina." *Hispanic American Historical Review*, 48 (May 1968), 189–205.

Gómez, Ramón Florencio. "Las Fuerzas Armadas: columna vertebral de sistema democrático." *Política*, 6 (April 1967), 21–31.

Griffin, Charles C. "Regionalism's Role in Venezuelan Politics." *Inter-American Quarterly*, 3 (October 1941), 21–35.

Guillen, Pedro. "Militarismo y golpes de estado en América Latina." *Cuadernos Americanos*, 140 (May–June 1965), 7–19.

Hadley, Paul E. "Latin America: Retreat from Violence." *Western Political Quarterly*, 11 (June 1958), 385–87.

Holmes, Olive. "Army Challenge in Latin America." *Foreign Policy Reports*, 25 (December 1949), 166–75.

"El hombre de 1958." *Venezuela Gráfica* (January 2, 1959), 3.

Kantor, Harry. "The Development of Acción Democrática de Venezuela." *Journal of Inter-American Studies*, 1 (April 1959), 237–55.

Kling, Merle. "Towards a Theory of Power and Political Instability in Latin America." *Western Political Quarterly*, 9 (March 1956), 21–35.

Lander, Luis. "La doctrina venezolana de Acción Democrática." *Cuadernos Americanos*, 52 (July–August 1950), 20–39.

Laswell, Harold D. "The Garrison State." *American Journal of Sociology*, 46 (January 1941), 455–68.

Leal, Roque. "La pava persigue a los generales." *Venezuela Gráfica* (October 3, 1958), 6.

Lieuwen, Edwin. "The Changing Role of the Military in Latin America." *Journal of Inter-American Studies*, 3 (October 1961), 559–70.

———. "The Military: A Revolutionary Force." *The Annals of the American Accademy of Political and Social Science*, 334 (March 1961), 30–40.

———. "Neo-Militarism in Latin America: The Kennedy Administration's Inadequate Response." *Inter-American Economic Affairs*, 16 (Spring 1963), 11–19.

———. "Political Forces in Venezuela." *The World Today*, 16 (August 1960), 345–55.

Liscano, Juan. "Sobre 'el señor presidente' y otros temas de la dictadura." *Cuadernos Americanos*, 17 (March–April 1958), 63–75.

"Los que el año se llevó . . . y los que trajo." *Venezuela Gráfica* (January 2, 1959), 8.

Lott, Leo B. "Executive Power in Venezuela." *American Political Science Review*, 1 (June 1956), 422–41.

———. "The 1952 Venezuelan Elections: A Lesson for 1957." *Western Political Quarterly*, 10 (September 1957), 541–58.

McAlister, Lyle N. "Changing Concepts of the Role of the Military in Latin America." *The Annals of the American Academy of Political and Social Science*, 360 (July 1965), 85–98.

———. "Civil–Military Relations in Latin America." *Journal of Inter-American Studies*, 3 (July, 1961), 341–58.

———. "Recent Research and Writings on the Role of the Military in Latin America." *Latin American Research Review*, 2 (Fall 1966), 5–36.

Martínez, Enrique Codo. "The Military Problems in Latin America." *Military Review*, 44 (August 1964), 11–19.

Martz, John D. "The Growth and Democratization of the Venezuelan Labor Movement." *Inter-American Economic Affairs*, 15 (Autumn 1963), 3–18.

———. "Venezuela's 'Generation of '28': The Genesis of Political Democracy." *Journal of Inter-American Studies*, 6 (January 1964), 17–32.

Mendoza, Elvira. "Las fuerzas navales dieron el golpe mortal." *Elite* (February 1, 1958), 50.

"La mentira del 18 de octubre." *Elite* (June 19, 1965), 36.

Mörner, Magnus. "Caudillos y militares en la evolución hispanoamericana." *Journal of Inter-American Studies*, 2 (July 1960), 295–310.

"La muerte de Castro León." *Elite* (July 17, 1965), 30.

Nava, Julian. "The Illustrious American: The Development of Nationalism in Venezuela Under Antonio Guzmán Blanco." *Hispanic American Historical Review*, 45 (November 1965), 527–43.

Needler, Martin C. "The Latin American Military: Predatory Reactionaries or Modernizing Patriots?" *Journal of Inter-American Studies*, 11 (April 1969), 237–44.

———. "Political Development and Military Intervention in Latin America." *American Political Science Review*, 60 (September 1966), 616–26.

Ochoa Briceño, Santiago. "Evolución del ejército venezolano." *Sumario de Occidente*, 1 (September 1945), 111–20.

Oropeza Ciliberto, J. A. "Así mataron a Rafael Simón Urbina." *Elite* (June 19, 1965), 14.

Ortega, Paco. "Táchira: café amargo." *Elite* (July 17, 1965), 18.

Pierson, William W. "Foreign Influence on Venezuelan Political Thought, 1830–1930." *Hispanic American Historical Review,* 15 (February 1935), 3–42.

Pinzón, Rafael. "Tres revoluciones en Venezuela." *Sumario de Occidente,* 1 (September 1945), 171–231.

Rangel, Domingo Alberto. "Una interpretación de las dictaduras latinoamericanas." *Cuadernos Americanos,* 77 (September–October 1954), 33–42.

Reynolds, Keld J. "The Lautaro Lodges." *The Americas,* 24 (July 1967), 18–32.

Rippy, J. Fred. "Latin America's Postwar Golpes de Estado." *Inter-American Economic Affairs,* 19 (Winter 1965), 73–80.

———. "Venezuelan Vicissitudes, 1945–1956." *Inter-American Economic Affairs,* 11 (Winter 1957), 73–82.

Rojas, Dámaso. "La verdad del fracaso del golpe de San Cristóbal." *Elite* (July 24, 1965), 44.

Romero, César Enrique. "¿Crisis del gobierno civil en América Latina?" *Revista de Estudios Políticos,* 122 (March–April 1962), 227–32.

Salera, Virgil. "Venezuela's Sow-the-Oil Policy." *Inter-American Economic Affairs,* 8 (Spring 1955), 3–22.

Silva Herzog, Jesús. "Las juntas militares de gobierno." *Cuadernos Americanos,* 8 (July–August 1949), 7–13.

Spindler, G. Dearborn. "The Military: A Systematic Analysis." *Social Forces,* 27 (October 1948), 83–88.

Stokes, William S. "Violence As a Power Factor in Latin-American Politics." *Western Political Quarterly,* 5 (September 1952), 445–68.

———. "Violence: The South American Way." *United Nations World,* 5 (December 1951), 51–54.

Taylor, Philip B., Jr. "Hemispheric Defense in World War II." *Current History,* 56 (June 1969), 333–39.

Tugwell, Franklin. "The Christian Democrats of Venezuela." *Journal of Inter-American Studies,* 7 (April 1965), 245–68.

Ugalde, Martín de. "¿Quién mató a Delgado Chalbaud?" *Elite* (February 8, 1958), 48.

Valeri, José. "Rasgos biográficos del General Cipriano Castro." *Boletín del Archivo Histórico de Miraflores,* 1 (July–August 1959), 73–80.

"22 días bastaron para ser libres." *Elite* (January 25, 1958), 6.

Watters, Mary. "The Present Status of the Church in Venezuela." *Hispanic American Historical Review,* 13 (February 1933), 23–45.

Wyckoff, Theodore. "The Role of the Military in Contemporary Latin American Politics." *Western Political Quarterly,* 12 (September 1960), 745–63.

V. NEWSPAPERS AND PERIODICALS

A. CARACAS
Ahora, 1944–1945
La Esfera, 1935–1965
Gaceta Oficial, 1936–1941
El Gráfico, 1948
El Heraldo, 1935–1948, 1953–1958
El Nacional, 1945–1968
El País, 1945–1948
Revista de las Fuerzas Armadas, 1946–1958
El Tiempo, 1944–1945
El Universal, 1935–1959

B. SAN CRISTÓBAL, TÁCHIRA
El Centinela, 1941–1948
Hoy, 1939–1943
El Liberal, 1940–1943
El Nacionalista, 1940
Táchira, 1940–1941

C. UNITED STATES
Hispanic American Report, 1948–1958
New York Times, 1908–1958

INDEX